Continental Realism and Its Discontents

EDITED BY MARIE-EVE MORIN

EDINBURGH
University Press

Edinburgh University Press is one of the leading university presses in the UK. We publish academic books and journals in our selected subject areas across the humanities and social sciences, combining cutting-edge scholarship with high editorial and production values to produce academic works of lasting importance. For more information visit our website: edinburghuniversitypress.com

© editorial matter and organisation Marie-Eve Morin, 2017
© the chapters their several authors, 2017

Edinburgh University Press Ltd
The Tun – Holyrood Road
12(2f) Jackson's Entry
Edinburgh EH8 8PJ

Typeset in 11/13 Adobe Garamond by
Servis Filmsetting Ltd, Stockport, Cheshire

A CIP record for this book is available from the British Library

ISBN 978 1 4744 4410 1 (pbk.)
ISBN 978 1 4744 2114 0 (hardback)
ISBN 978 1 4744 2115 7 (webready PDF)
ISBN 978 1 4744 2116 4 (epub)

The right of Marie-Eve Morin to be identified as the editor of this work has been asserted in accordance with the Copyright, Designs and Patents Act 1988, and the Copyright and Related Rights Regulations 2003 (SI No. 2498).

Contents

Acknowledgements   v

Introduction: Continental Realism – Picking Up the Pieces   1
Vladimir Dukić and Marie-Eve Morin

Part I: Responses and Interventions

1 Empirical Realism and the Great Outdoors: A Critique of Meillassoux   21
 G. Anthony Bruno

2 The Ecstatic Realism of the Late Schelling   38
 Sean J. McGrath

3 Before Infinitude: A Levinasian Response to Meillassoux's Speculative Realism   59
 Lee Braver

Part II: Convergences and Correctives

4 Kantian Realisms: The Noumenal, Causation and Grounding   83
 Alison Assiter

5 Pessimism, or The Importance of Indifference, Time and Suffering in Realist Ontologies   100
 Rick Elmore

6 Being (with) Objects   116
 Anna Mudde

Part III: Challenges and Prospects

7 Merleau-Ponty and the Challenge of Realism, or How (Not) to
   Go beyond Phenomenology   137
   Marie-Eve Morin

8 The Radical Contingency of Temporality, Correlation and
   Philosophy: Merleau-Ponty's Indirect Ontology contra
   Meillassoux's Hyper-Anthropocentric Idealism   155
   David Morris

9 The Realist Challenge: Thinking the Reality of Language after
   Deconstruction   175
   Peter Gratton

Notes on Contributors   188
Index   191

Acknowledgements

I would like to thank the participants of the workshop 'Taking Up the Speculative Realist Challenge', which took place at the University of Alberta on 10–11 April 2015: Lee Braver, G. Anthony Bruno, Rick Elmore, Peter Gratton, Sean McGrath, David Morris and Ted Toadvine. The richness of the conversation over these two days convinced me of the need for publishing a volume that carefully engaged with the recent turn to realism and speculation in continental philosophy. I would also like to thank Anna Mudde and Alison Assiter, whose contributions helped result in a more complete volume. I am thankful to the graduate students at the University of Alberta for their incisive questions and thoughtful commentary over the course of the workshop: Vladimir Dukić, Luke McNulty, Charles Rodger, Yasemin Sari, Paul Showler and Jay Worthy. I am especially grateful to Vladimir Dukić, whose assistance with editing the volume resulted in numerous, substantive improvements. My thanks also go to Carol Macdonald at Edinburgh University Press for her enthusiasm for the project as well as to Peter Gratton and Sean McGrath for hosting this volume in their *New Perspectives in Ontology* series. Special thanks also to the copyediting and production team at Edinburgh University Press for their careful work on the typescript, and to Dr Eloy LaBrada for reading the proofs and preparing the index. Both the workshop and the production of this volume were supported by a research grant from the Social Sciences and Humanities Research Council of Canada.

New Perspectives in Ontology
Series Editors: Peter Gratton and Sean J. McGrath, Memorial University of Newfoundland, Canada

Publishes the best new work on the nature of being

After the fundamental modesty of much post-Heideggerian Continental philosophy, the time is now for a renaissance in ontology after the rise of the new realisms and new materialisms. This new series aims to be an interdisciplinary forum for this work, challenging old divisions while borrowing from the ontological frameworks of post-humanism, ecological studies, critical animal studies, and other post-constructivist areas of endeavour. While often working within the Continental tradition, the books in this series will move beyond the stale hermeneutics and phenomenologies of the past, with authors boldly reopening the oldest questions of existence through a contemporary lens.

Editorial Advisory Board
Thomas J. J. Altizer, State University of New York at Stony Brook
Maurizio Farraris, University of Turin
Paul Franks, Yale University
Iain Hamilton Grant, University of the West of England
Garth Green, McGill University
Adrian Johnston, University of New Mexico
Catherine Malabou, Kingston University
Jeff Malpas, University of Tasmania
Marie-Eve Morin, University of Alberta
Jeffrey Reid, University of Ottawa
Susan Ruddick, University of Toronto
Michael Schulz, University of Bonn
Hasana Sharp, McGill University
Alison Stone, Lancaster University
Peter Trawny, University of Wuppertal
Uwe Voigt, University of Augsburg
Jason Wirth, Seattle University
Günter Zöller, University of Munich

Books available
The Political Theology of Schelling by Saitya Brata Das
Continental Realism and Its Discontents edited by Marie-Eve Morin
The Contingency of Necessity: Reason and God as Matters of Fact by Tyler Tritten
The Late Schelling and the End of Christianity by Sean J. McGrath

Visit the series web page at: www.edinburghuniversitypress.com/series/epnpio

Introduction: Continental Realism – Picking Up the Pieces

Vladimir Dukić and Marie-Eve Morin

The return of the real

The speculative realist movement sprung out of a one-day workshop held at Goldsmiths' College, University of London in April 2007, a little more than a year after the publication of Quentin Meillassoux's book *Après la finitude*.[1] The workshop brought together four thinkers – Ray Brassier, Graham Harman, Iain Hamilton Grant and Quentin Meillassoux – with the explicit aim of discussing diverse approaches to realism in the continental tradition.[2] The impetus for the original event was, as Brassier describes it, 'to revive questions about realism, materialism, science, representation, and objectivity, that were dismissed as otiose by each of the main pillars of continental orthodoxy: phenomenology, critical theory, and deconstruction'.[3] 'Speculative realism' thus became, at least for a while, the name of a movement towards a revival of realist and materialist metaphysics as an attempt to counter what they saw as the dominance of a certain legacy of transcendental idealism in continental philosophy, reflected above all in its focus on the subject, its critical limitation of knowledge to the phenomenal world, and its rejection of speculative metaphysics.

Following the 2007 workshop, it quickly became apparent that, aside from calling for a revival of metaphysics, the various projects grouped under the banner of speculative realism had little in common. It became apparent, for instance, that Brassier's nihilist ontology shares little with object-oriented ontologies of Harman or the nature-philosophy of Grant, something that can also be said of Meillassoux's brand of speculative materialism. As the editors of *The Speculative Turn* admit, despite being 'so far the best organized movement of the next generation', by the time they were putting together their collected volume, 'the group ha[d] already begun to break into various fragments'.[4] To complicate matters further, in addition to four original participants of the 2007 workshop, these fragments increasingly came to include not only other proponents of object-oriented and flat ontologies such as Levi Bryant, Tristan Garcia, Bruno Latour and Timothy Morton, but also such realist metaphysicians as Maurizio Ferraris and Markus Gabriel, as well as transcendental philosophers of nature such as Adrian Johnson.

Given the disparate and often wholly incompatible projects brought together under this banner – Jon Roffe calls speculative realism a 'Frankenstein's monster' and a 'hydra-headed beast'[5] – it is perhaps unsurprising that a coherent speculative realist programme failed to materialise. Indeed, even the label 'speculative realism', as well as the question of the movement's very existence, continue to divide speculative realists. Of the four original participants of the workshop at Goldsmiths' College, Harman has been the fiercest defender of the 'speculative realist' label, despite his preference for the moniker 'object-oriented philosophy' to refer to his own approach.[6] In his book on Meillassoux, Harman affirms again that speculative realism 'has been so far the most visible of the new movements in continental philosophy in the twenty-first century'.[7] In his view, speculative realism has passed the test of existence since it is

> now the topic of a thriving book series at a major university press, and the subject of at least one forthcoming monograph. It is embedded in the editorial policy of several philosophy journals. It has become a *terme d'art* in architecture, archaeology, geography, the visual arts, and even history. It has crossed national boundaries with ease, and is surely the central theme of discussion in the growing continental philosophy blogosphere. Speculative Realism is the topic of several postdoctoral fellowships offered in the United States this year. It has been the subject of semester-long classes at universities as well as graduate theses in Paris.[8]

By contrast, Brassier has been openly critical about the existence of a 'real' speculative realist movement in philosophy. For all the talk of speculative realism, Brassier points out, there has never been a coherent speculative realist programme whose proponents share a set of common philosophical commitments. In an interview in *Kronos*, he said:

> The 'speculative realist movement' exists only in the imaginations of a group of bloggers promoting an agenda for which I have no sympathy whatsoever: actor-network theory spiced with pan-psychist metaphysics and morsels of process philosophy. I don't believe the internet is an appropriate medium for serious philosophical debate; nor do I believe it is acceptable to try to concoct a philosophical movement online by using blogs to exploit the misguided enthusiasm of impressionable graduate students. I agree with

Deleuze's remark that ultimately the most basic task of philosophy is to impede stupidity, so I see little philosophical merit in a 'movement' whose most signal achievement thus far is to have generated an online orgy of stupidity.[9]

Even though blogging and open-access publishing have meant that debates and controversies surrounding speculative realism have achieved greater exposure and have taken place much more rapidly than what one is used to in academic settings, the internet presence of speculative realism is not in itself responsible for the contention surrounding the existence of such a movement. Rather, as was already clear in the mind of the organisers of the first workshop in 2007, it is the great diversity of theories that get lumped together under this name that makes it difficult to explain just what exactly the positive philosophy of the speculative realists would look like. This inability to converge on a positive philosophical programme has also made it difficult to precisely distinguish speculative realists from other proponents of a revival of metaphysics in contemporary continental philosophy – for instance, from the proponents of new materialism and neo-vitalism such as Jane Bennet, Elizabeth Grosz, Manuel DeLanda and Steven Shapiro, as well as from other philosophers working in the continental tradition today, including Alain Badiou, Slavoj Žižek and many others.

Despite their lack of a common, positive philosophical programme, it would be misleading to claim that nothing unites speculative materialists, transcendental nihilists and object-oriented philosophers, as well as various other proponents of the recent turn to realism and speculation in continental philosophy. What continues to unite these philosophers is the very thing that prompted the 2007 workshop at Goldsmiths' College: their opposition to a common enemy in the guise of phenomenology, hermeneutics, deconstruction and all manner of post-Kantian and post-metaphysical thought that has historically defined the landscape of continental philosophy. Almost without exception, speculative realists maintain that 'things went grossly awry when Kant, having been roused from his dogmatic slumbers by the challenge of Humean scepticism, responded by announcing his "Copernican revolution" in epistemology'.[10] Likewise, they view the linguistic turn, with its constructivism and relativism, as a direct successor of this Kantian revolution. They are thus against any philosophical approach that emphasises subjective access to things, the finitude of human cognitive capacities and the limitations of reason in its speculative use, as well as against a kind of 'mannered portentousness'[11] that they see as running rampant in continental circles today.

Perhaps the clearest philosophical statement of this opposition can be found in *After Finitude*, where Meillassoux applies the term 'correlationism' to any philosophy that denies human access to the 'Absolute' – that is, the real as independent of human thought and interest. In that work, Meillassoux understands 'correlation' as 'the idea according to which we only ever have access to the correlation between thinking and being, and never to either term considered apart from the other', defining 'correlationism' in general as 'any current of thought which maintains the unsurpassable character of the correlation so defined'.[12] Refining this admittedly broad definition – applying, as it does, to Kant and nearly every major philosopher in his wake – Meillassoux introduces a further distinction between 'weak' and 'strong' correlationism. The proponents of the former stance, attributed primarily to 'subjective idealism' of the Kantian variety, indeed admit that there is something independent of human knowledge – the noumenon, Kant's 'thing in itself' – and this something may even provide the conditions for all knowledge and thought. According to Meillassoux, weak correlationists simply deny our ability *to know* that independent something with any degree of certainty, compelling us to constrain our thinking only to what can be known – to Kant's world of phenomena. Meillassoux contrasts this form of correlationism with 'strong correlationism', the view that anything that would be 'outside' of the correlational structure is not only *unknowable* but entirely *unthinkable*, even in principle. In turn, some proponents of strong correlationism (for example, some Heideggerian phenomenologists as well as analytic philosophers of language like Wittgenstein) hold that, since it is unthinkable, anything that would be outside of this correlation cannot be an object of philosophical investigation and should not concern us in the least. Other proponents of strong correlationism may even go so far as to assert that there is nothing outside of this correlation of thought and being, which is also to say that nothing could exist that would be inaccessible to thought. Whatever the case may be, Meillassoux argues, for strong correlationism, 'to be' is simply 'to be a correlate' – it is to be a term in this correlational structure.[13]

In order to appreciate the force and novelty of Meillassoux's critical gesture – and that of speculative realism in general – it is important to notice the ways in which this critique of correlationism repeats, while also differing from, the historical critiques of idealism in philosophy. In the first place, correlationism should not be equated with idealism, even though idealist philosophies generally fall under the rubric of correlationism. For example, whereas weak correlationists of the subjective idealist variety typically privilege one side of the correlation (the side of the thinking subject, ego, consciousness and the like), strong correlationists assert the primacy of the correlation itself, a gesture Meillassoux calls the correlationist 'two-step':

> Generally speaking, the modern philosopher's 'two-step' consists in this belief in the primacy of the relation over the related terms; a belief in the constitutive power of reciprocal relation. The 'co-' (of co-givenness, of co-relation, of the co-originary, of co-presence, etc.) is the grammatical particle that dominates modern philosophy, its veritable 'chemical formula'. Thus, one could say that up until Kant, one of the principal problems of philosophy was to think substance, while ever since Kant, it has consisted in trying to think the correlation.[14]

Meillassoux also points out that some versions of strong correlationism assume an explicitly anti-idealist stance. For instance, he argues that in order to escape 'speculative idealism', which attempts to deduce the necessity of the Absolute, Heideggerian phenomenology asserts the fundamental contingency of facticity itself.[15] Nevertheless, all correlationist philosophies share something in common with idealism in so far as they assume an explicitly anti-realist stance. Since they maintain the unsurpassable nature of the correlation between thinking and being, correlationists reject any notion of the 'real' that would not be already reduced to the terms of the correlation or to the terms of its givenness to human beings. Or stated in terms of access: correlationists cannot legitimately say anything about objects independently of their mode of access to them. As Harman argues, 'everything is reduced to a question of human access to the world, and non-human relations are abandoned to the natural sciences'.[16] Since correlationists cannot step out of their mode of access, they lack the means of 'distinguish[ing] between those properties which are supposed to belong to the object, and those properties belonging to the subjective access to the object'.[17] Recalling Hegel, Meillassoux notes that, for correlationism, 'thought cannot get *outside itself* in order to compare the world as it is "in itself" to the world as it is "for us", and thereby distinguish what is a function of our relation to the world from what belongs to the world alone'.[18]

The ultimate aim of speculative realism, then, is to shake philosophy out of this 'post-critical slumber'. It is to break philosophy free from its obsession with finitude and the limits of thought and renew the philosophical concern for the Absolute, for what is *not* in any way for us. However, rather than overturning correlationism, or even Kant's critical turn in philosophy, speculative realism professes to go 'beyond' correlationism, towards 'post-critical' and 'post-correlationist' thought. In their introduction to *The Speculative Turn*, Bryant et al. write:

> The speculative turn, however, is not an outright rejection of these critical advances; instead, it comes from a recognition of their inherent limitations. Speculation in this sense aims at something 'beyond' the critical and linguistic turns. As such, it recuperates the pre-critical sense of 'speculation' as a

concern with the Absolute, while also taking into account the undeniable progress that is due to the labour of critique.[19]

For his part, Meillassoux goes as far as to claim that the arguments in favour of correlationism are powerful and appear to be indefeasible. For this reason, his strategy in *After Finitude* consists in proceeding from a certain form of strong correlationism with the aim of showing how, when pushed to its limits, it gives way to a thought of the uncorrelated: what he calls the principle of 'factiality', or the necessity of contingency.[20] 'It is through facticity, and through facticity alone' he writes, 'that we are able to make our way towards the absolute.'[21]

The need for speculation

If it is so urgent to undermine the wide, unquestioned acceptance of correlationist premises in continental circles and go 'beyond' correlationism, it is not – or not merely – because the latter is a misguided philosophical position. Rather, it is the unwillingness and the inability of correlationists to confront the challenges of our time that calls for speculative thought. From the speculative realist perspective, by constraining themselves to questions of access, subjectivity and human finitude, correlationists have turned towards themselves at the expense of the 'real world' while simultaneously condemning philosophical attempts to think the latter. According to the editors of *The Speculative Turn*, '[i]n the face of the looming ecological catastrophe, and the increasing infiltration of technology into the everyday world (including our own bodies), [correlationism] actively limits the capacities of philosophy in our time'.[22] More precisely, this unwillingness and inability of correlationists to confront the events of our time is a direct consequence of three features of correlationist thought: its investable anthropocentrism (and anthropomorphism), its aversion from the sciences, and its tolerance of fideism and the return of religious fundamentalisms.

Correlationism is anthropocentric because it reduces everything that exists to its being encountered by (or given to) human beings. Correlationism thus radically distinguishes the human being as the site of meaning or truth; all other beings are reduced to merely objects at human disposal. This is human exceptionalism in the extreme: things are not worthy of concern in themselves since, unlike human beings, they are unable to enter into meaningful relations with their environment. In so far that things are worthy of human concern at all, they are such only to the extent that they are appropriated into the circuit of human thinking or manipulation. Such anthropocentrism is apparent in philosophy's focus not only on human cognition but on human languages, cultures and institutions as most worthy of understanding, whereas artefacts and natural things are worthy of philosophical concern only in relation to human cognitions, languages, cultures and institutions. The study of these things 'in themselves' is thus left to the empirical sciences, all the while such scientific endeavour is denigrated as 'naive' and 'non-philosophical'.

The speculative realists want to undo the privilege of the human as the centre of the world and the agent of meaningful encounters. At the same time, however, they cannot merely attribute human predicates – whatever it is that makes human beings 'special': thought, agency, feelings – to other living beings or even to matter itself. This would still be 'man making the world in his own image'. What is needed is a mode of thinking that does not privilege the human, either by holding that humans possess a special capacity for meaningful encounters that other entities lack or by saying that 'all things think, feel, or experience *like us*'. To be sure, the relation of the various strands of speculative realism to anthropocentrism and anthropomorphism is complex, and there is no direct link between the rejection of anthropocentrism and that of anthropomorphism. Indeed, as Shaviro points out, the former can be accomplished by embracing a kind of 'cautious anthropomorphism':

> The point is that a certain cautious anthropomorphism is necessary in order to avoid anthropocentrism. I attribute feelings to stones precisely in order to get away from the pernicious dualism that would insist that human beings alone (or at most, human beings together with some animals) have feelings, while everything else does not.[23]

At the same time, this attribution of a capacity for thought or feeling to everything that exists (animals, plants, minerals, artefacts and so on) must come with a dislocation of our concept of thinking and feeling from its conscious and intentional mode in human beings. Such a dislocating is essential to 'cautious anthropomorphism' and prevents us from smuggling anthropocentrism back into our philosophy, something Shaviro thinks Meillassoux is guilty of doing.[24]

Another charge levelled against the dominance of correlationism in contemporary continental philosophy concerns the latter's purported aversion towards the sciences, though it might be more accurate to call it an aversion towards scientism, that is, toward a certain philosophical interpretation of the sciences as providing access to a real that is otherwise veiled. For correlationism, science is simply another mode of access, and a founded one at that. It can claim no privilege to 'get us out' of the correlation to the truth of the object 'as it is without us'. According to the speculative realists, this dismissal of scientism, or of a realist interpretation of scientific claims, leads the correlationist into all sorts of rhetorical contortions when she tries to interpret, for example, scientific claims about the creation of the universe. This is the point of Meillassoux's discussion of the arche-fossil and of the problem of ancestrality in *After Finitude*.[25] Rather than assert the power of science (and especially of mathematics) to discourse of what is 'without us', the correlationist says that it only discourses about how things that are not given are given to us. As a result, correlationists are unable to take scientific claims at their intended meaning – because they do not take 'the real' about which these claims are made seriously – and can assert, against what science has proven to be false, things like: 'The earth does not move' or 'The existence of a Nature cannot be the condition for the existence of consciousness' or 'Nature is not the ground of thought'.[26]

At the same time as they dismiss the power of science to give us access to the real, correlationists radically limit the claim of reason to access the Absolute. In thus relinquishing their claim to the Absolute, correlationists open the space for 'fideism', something that is of particular concern to Meillassoux. Whereas Kant still thinks that the logical prerequisites of thought (such as the law of non-contradiction) apply to the noumenon, even though we cannot apply the forms of intuition and the categories of the understanding to it, the strong correlationist typically asserts the contingency of the correlation itself. The structures of thought need not be the way they are even though it is impossible for us to imagine them being otherwise, so that the limit of thought cannot be said to be the limit of being, and this despite the strict correlation between thought and being. To give an example: that I cannot think without making use of the law of non-contradiction does not prove anything about its being necessary. The 'absolutely Other' is possible – or, better, not-impossible a priori – but it is completely opaque. In fact, this possibility of an absolute Other is not really a possibility but rather the impossibility of proving its impossibility.[27] This, Meillassoux claims, robs us of any tools to rationally counter the claims of religious dogmatists: the strong correlationist's affirmation of the facticity of the correlation 'entails a specific and rather remarkable consequence: it becomes rationally illegitimate to disqualify *irrational* discourses about the absolute on the pretext of their irrationality'.[28] As long as the religious dogmatist makes no claim to knowledge or to reason, she can assert whatever she wants about the Absolute. Thus, according to Meillassoux:

> Scepticism with regard to the metaphysical absolute thereby legitimates *de jure* every variety whatsoever of belief in an absolute, the best as well as the

worst. The destruction of the metaphysical rationalization of Christian theology has resulted in a generalized becoming-religious of thought, viz., in a fideism of any belief whatsoever.[29]

In other words, by restricting the scope of reason to say anything about the Absolute, correlationists surrender the ability to challenge irrational and even fundamentalist forms of religion, effectively giving them free rein regarding the Absolute, all the while maintaining a respectful distance. To counteract the religious or irrational investment of the Absolute, speculative realists claim, we need a positive discourse of the Absolute rather than a critical discourse of the limits of our thinking.

In order to effectuate a post-critical turn towards realism in metaphysics and counter the pernicious consequences of correlationist thought – fideism, anthropocentrism and its anti-scientific bias – and do justice to the real as independent of human beings, speculative realists argue for a renewal of 'speculation' in philosophy. As pointed out previously, the notion of speculation 'recuperates the pre-critical sense of "speculation" as a concern with the Absolute', while also aiming to be post-critical.[30] However, when we attempt to specify what, precisely, speculation entails for each of the thinkers in this movement, we are faced with further fragmentation.

For Meillassoux, the term 'speculative' names, following Kant, the use of reason that gains access to the Absolute.[31] Whereas in Kant's critical philosophy the speculative use of reason cannot grant us knowledge of the Absolute, it is precisely this power of speculation that asserts itself in his speculative metaphysics. At the same time, Meillassoux claims that his speculative brand of philosophy is not dogmatic and not metaphysical because the Absolute it thinks is not some absolutely necessary entity, but what he calls 'the principle of unreason', that is, the necessity of contingency. On the other hand, taking its lead from Schelling's speculative physics, Grant's philosophy of nature is 'speculative' in the sense that this term acquires in the post-Kantian tradition of German idealism. However, when one turns to object-oriented ontologies, it is unclear whether the term 'speculative' retains its German idealist meaning, or whether it is not merely used in its everyday sense. Moreover, Harman's embrace of speculation for 'hint[ing] at starry landscapes haunted by poets and mad scientists'[32] will do little to allay the worries that speculation is simply another way of making claims without having to justify them, a concern raised by Brassier: 'the term "speculative" is reduced to its ordinary adjectival sense, meaning "conjectural, fanciful, unsubstantiated by evidence or fact". Prefixed to an ill-defined "realism", it becomes the alibi for a doctrine that wishes to spare itself the trouble of justification.'[33]

Brassier's sentiment is not entirely baseless. When attempting to explain what speculation is for the four original 'Goldsmiths speculative realists', Sparrow writes that 'speculation, they maintain, is theoretically capable of disengaging objects from subjects in nonarbitrary ways, some of which approximate science fiction but none of which are, in the last analysis, fictitious'.[34] Yet he never really specifies what distinguishes non-arbitrary from arbitrary ways of disengaging objects from subjects. To make matters worse, he admits that Harman's 'weird realism' is not about providing justifications for its descriptions and aiming at the truth. He writes candidly:

> Harman is not interested in providing an account of reality that precisely matches how the world 'really is' when humans are not around to experience it, as if realism is just about being 'able to state correct propositions about the real world'. . . . Hence the importance he places on metaphor and allusion *as precise metaphysical devices*, and why speculative realism often comes so close to speculative or science fiction, or why poetry might have something important to tell us about ontology. While it may be possible to give bad descriptions or accounts of things — precisely because things sincerely are what they are and nothing other than what they are — Harman's brand of speculative realism is less interested in accuracy than it is committed to drawing out every possible dimension of the real, no matter how far-fetched, absurd, terrifying, obvious, or paradoxical. And he aims to do so without arbitrariness, frivolity, or rhetorical sleight-of-hand, just like any good realist.[35]

But yet again, we are not told what makes a metaphor precise, what leads to a good description rather than a bad one, and neither are we provided with a method that would allow us to draw out the various dimensions of the real 'without arbitrariness'.

It is not only the meaning of the term 'speculative' that has been put into question, but also the possibility of apposing it to 'realism'. First, though speculative realism is often associated with Meillassoux, he does not use the phrase in *After Finitude*, choosing instead to refer to 'speculative materialism'.[36] It is Brassier, in his *Nihil Unbound*, who uses the term 'speculative realism' to argue, with the help of François Laruelle's non-philosophy, against what he sees as Meillassoux's idealism of intuition.[37] Christopher Norris also shares a similar sentiment. He finds in Meillassoux's *After Finitude* a tension between the scientific, objectivist realism of the first part, and the 'speculative bent' of the second part, which 'leans so far in a "radical" (self-consciously heterodox) direction as to lose touch with any workable variety of scientific realism'.[38] Some have also argued that Harman's object-oriented philosophy, despite its purported focus on objects, is a consolidation rather than a critique of correlationism and that he remains 'trapped in the same transparent cage as Kant and his successors'.[39] Indeed, this is the central claim in Peter Wolfendale booklength thorough reconstruction of and critical engagement with Harman's philosophy.

Leaving aside whether there is a coherent movement called 'speculative realism' or not, and whether 'speculative realism' is the right name for it or not, we must at least admit that there is a new voice on the continental philosophical scene. This voice is provocative, at times accusatory, and even dismissive of the authors and texts that are considered canonical in the continental tradition. This raises the question of how to engage with such a new voice: should we ignore it? Should we attempt to engage in a dialogue? Should we defend the tradition against the attacks of the new realists? Many in continental circles have chosen the first option and look at the speculative realist movement from afar, as a new trend that for sure generates lots of excitement, but will likely die off soon and is not worth getting into. Others have chosen to defend their favourite philosophers against the charges of correlationism. In a recent article, Dan Zahavi chooses the third option and defends phenomenology, and specifically Husserl's, against the charges raised by the speculative realists.[40] This article is exemplary because it makes many, if not all, of the argumentative moves available to a so-called 'correlationist' in response to the speculative realists' accusations. Zahavi admits that phenomenology is a form of correlationism, also admits that Husserl is a transcendental idealist, but then emphasises the fact that, of course, such idealism is not incompatible with scientific realism (and he does so by turning to Putnam to show that such a position is not an idiosyncrasy of continental philosophy); he points out that scientific realism is not the only option when it comes to realism and that it itself comes under attack not only in phenomenology but also within more traditional philosophy of science; he reminds us that, if one is attacking phenomenology from a scientific or metaphysical realist perspective, then this has already been done by analytic philosophy. Finally, he claims that, if what we are looking for is an affirmation of the reality of everyday objects (of the natural world), speculative realism 'fails miserably', or, in other words, phenomenology is methodologically better equipped to account for the real world in its familiarity as well as strangeness. The exercise can be repeated for Kant, Heidegger, Derrida and many others.

But the interesting question is: does the encounter with speculative realism change anything? If we let our own thinking be challenged by it, do we then have to read the canonical texts differently? Do we see a new thread in our favourite philosophers? Are we compelled to push them to answer new questions? Are we led to change the way in which we present the views of our favourite philosophers? Do we leave them behind at some point?

About this volume

The idea for this volume originated in a workshop around the 'speculative realist challenge', held at the University of Alberta in April 2015, the goal of which was to address these questions. Invited were people who specialised in different strands of what we could call 'mainstream' continental philosophy – Kant, German idealism, phenomenology, deconstruction – but who also had been challenged or provoked by the speculative turn. The focus of our discussion was Meillassoux's speculative materialism and, to a lesser degree, Harman's object-oriented ontology. The goal was not merely to criticise speculative realism and object-oriented ontology, nor was it merely to defend our favourite philosophers against the charges of correlationism. All the participants also wanted to 'take up' the speculative realist challenge, that is, to let themselves be challenged by the provocation of being pointed at for not being able to account for the 'real'. Many participants challenged the diagnosis of correlationism, or else they accepted the label but challenged the supposed consequences of correlationism. In the background of these discussions was the desire to engage in a constructive dialogue with the new thinkers of the speculative realist movement, a dialogue we hope to make public by publishing this volume.

Continental Realism and Its Discontents opens with a section titled 'Responses and interventions'. The three authors in this section turn to Kant, Schelling and Levinas respectively to challenge Meillassoux's diagnosis of correlationism and show how, rightly understood, these three figures are already 'realist' thinkers of the 'great outdoors'. Opening this section is G. Anthony Bruno's 'Empirical realism and the great outdoors: a critique of Meillassoux', which examines some underlying assumptions in Meillassoux's interpretation of Kant. Through a close textual analysis of Kant's writings, Bruno argues that Meillassoux mistakenly interprets Kant through a Cartesian lens while also misunderstanding Kant's arguments for the necessity of causality. Furthermore, according to Bruno, Meillassoux misconstrues the Kantian revolution as subjective, rather than perspectival. When properly understood, Bruno contends, Kant's 'empirical realism' yields nothing less than 'the great outdoors'.

In the next chapter, Sean McGrath argues that, from his early Nature philosophy to his late, positive philosophy, what remains constant in Schelling's writings is a commitment to an 'ecstatic' realism, which ultimately paves the way for the post-idealist realisms of Nietzsche, Kierkegaard and the late nineteenth- and early twentieth-century positivists of France, England and Germany. According to McGrath, Schelling's project of positive philosophy proceeds not from the immediate experience of the real, but from the positing of being without any prior potency determining it. However, although his negative or correlationist act of positing is a starting point for positive philosophy, the latter is by no means trapped by it. For Schelling, McGrath argues, correlationism is a presupposition of positive philosophy because its failure to reveal existence is positive philosophy's clue to the uncorrelated or unprethinkable origin of being.

Finally, Lee Braver takes up Meillassoux's critique of correlationism, focusing in particular on the latter's 'problem of ancestrality', by turning to Levinas's radical appropriation of Huserlian phenomenology. Braver distinguishes between two kinds of correlation: the correlation of simple awareness of some experience and the stronger, more restrictive kind of correlation that consists in reducing what can be experienced to the conditions of knowledge or understanding. Although Levinas accepts the first kind of correlation, he also radicalises phenomenology by locating within experience that which exceeds all bounds of intelligibility or knowledge: the encounter with the face of the Other. As Braver points out, although the face of the Other is correlated with thought, it always also exceeds our ability to understand or think it.

The authors in the next section, 'Convergences and correctives', look to the philosophical tradition not so much to provide a critique of speculative realism, but rather to complement the speculative realist project and provide corrective to its actual trajectory. In 'Kantian Realisms: The Noumenal, Causation and Grounding', Alison Assiter turns to Kant's own 'empirical realism' in order to respond to some long-standing realist critiques of Kant. In particular, through a careful examination of Kant's notion of 'spontaneous causation', she provides a defence of Kant's attempt to ground the phenomenal in the noumenal. Furthermore, by juxtaposing the arguments for Kant's 'transcendental idealism' against the 'transcendental realism' of Roy Bhaskar, she suggests that it is possible to push Kant in a more realist direction than is generally accepted. At the same time, Kant reminds the realist that any characterisation of the real's nature will necessarily remain speculative and may generate paradoxes.

In 'Pessimism, or The importance of indifference, time and violence in realist ontologies', Rick Elmore traces significant parallels between the philosophical tradition of pessimism and recent turns to realism. Turning to the works of Dienstag, Thacker, Ligotti and others, Elmore argues that pessimism is best understood as an anti-correlationist realism that is ontologically committed to a world indifferent to, and independent from, human life. For pessimists, this conception of the world ultimately accounts for the unhappy and suffering-laden character of human life. Moreover, Elmore argues that, by connecting a realist ontology to questions of suffering, violence and time, pessimism exposes and resists the dangerously ideological character of optimistic or anti-realist metaphysics.

Anna Mudde's chapter focuses on object-oriented philosophy and provides a new rejoinder to Harman's object-oriented ontology by drawing on the writings of feminist phenomenologists on the topic of objectification. Mudde argues that, given Harman's attempt to understand the ways in which our contact with worldly things is always partial and limited, a 'caricature' of their withdrawn reality, it is crucial to consider what it is like to be a thing – respected, withdrawn, distorted or caricatured. According to Mudde, such considerations attune us to the dangerous presuppositions about the ways in which objects withdraw and are withdrawn, and she suggests that those who learn 'first and best' how to live as objectified often know what it is to withdraw from the perceptions and conceptualisations of another, exceeding their distortions and caricatures.

The volume closes with three chapters grouped under the heading 'Challenges and prospects'. These chapters take up Meillassoux's realist challenge while at the same time addressing questions opened by the recent realist turn in continental philosophy, and by Meillassoux's speculative materialism more specifically. Turning to Merleau-Ponty, Derrida and Nancy, the authors in this section raise the issue of the relation between inside and outside, of the contingency of philosophy itself, and of the reality of the sign, all questions that new realisms must address. In 'Merleau-Ponty and the challenge of realism, or How (not) to go beyond phenomenology', Marie-Eve Morin argues that phenomenology harbours much needed resources to think 'the outside' as it is demanded by our time. She finds in Merleau-Ponty's later philosophy an attempt to think a kind of radical outside akin to Meillassoux's 'hyperchaos' or Harman's 'inner life of objects'. Yet, Meillassoux and Harman can only maintain the integrity and exteriority of their outside by severing it from the world of human experience. Merleau-Ponty, on the other hand, uses the notions of depth and latency to complicate the relation between inside and outside, allowing us to think as well as experience an outside that is wild, strange and inhuman.

In the next chapter, David Morris also draws on Merleau-Ponty but focuses on his attempt to think the conditions of phenomenology as a way of responding to Meillassoux's critique of correlationism. According to Morris, Merleau-Ponty locates such conditions in the radical contingency of 'wild being', which paradoxically appears as non-appearing, as resistance to manifestation. Morris argues that, although both Meillassoux and Merleau-Ponty agree on the necessity of contingency, Meillassoux deduces such necessity by presupposing thought and philosophy whereas Merleau-Ponty locates it in something older than thinking, in a 'radical contingency' of wild being, thus finding philosophy itself to be radically contingent.

Closing this volume is Peter Gratton's 'The realist challenge: thinking the reality of language after deconstruction'. Taking up the topic of language and signification, Gratton defends deconstruction against a charge of 'linguistic idealism', which, he argues, rests on a misunderstanding of language. Such misunderstanding, termed 'naïve linguisticism' by Gratton, holds either that we cannot speak of an extra-linguistic reality or, what amounts to the same, that language is merely a representation of such a reality. Turning to Jacques Derrida's *Of Grammatology*, Gratton argues that Derrida's rejection of any transcendental signified allows us to think the reality of the sign without reducing it to a mere representation of the real. Gratton further argues that such a thinking is accomplished by Jean-Luc Nancy's logic of 'exscription' whereby the sign and the thing do not maintain relations of exteriority to each other, but are exscribed in each other as the same thing.

In sum, this volume aims to show that, rather than leading us to dismiss continental thinkers outright, the charges raised by the new realists can lead us to take on the continental tradition anew with an eye to the resources it provides to think the 'great outdoors'.

Notes

1. Quentin Meillassoux, *Après la finitude. Essai sur la nécessité de la contingence* (Paris: Seuil, 2003), trans. Ray Brassier as *After Finitude: An Essay on the Necessity of Contingency* (London: Continuum, 2008).
2. An edited transcript of the event was published in the journal *Collapse*. See Ray Brassier, Iain Hamilton Grant, Graham Harman and Quentin Meillassoux, 'Speculative Realism', *Collapse III* (2007), p. 307.
3. Ray Brassier, 'Postscript', in Peter Wolfendale, *Object-Oriented Philosophy: The Noumenon's New Clothes* (Falmouth: Urbanomic, 2014), pp. 409–21, here p. 417.
4. Levi Bryant, Nick Srnicek and Graham Harman, 'Towards a speculative philosophy', in Levi Bryant, Nick Srnicek and Graham Harman (eds), *The Speculative Turn: Continental Realism and Materialism* (Melbourne: re.press, 2011), p. 2.
5. Jon Roffe, 'The future of an illusion', *Speculations: A Journal of Speculative Realism* IV (2013), pp. 48–52, here p. 52.
6. Graham Harman, 'On the undermining of objects: Grant, Bruno, and Radical Philosophy', in Bryant et al., *The Speculative Turn: Continental Realism and Materialism* (Melbourne: re.press, 2011), pp. 21–40, here pp. 21–2. In various places, Graham also uses 'object-oriented metaphysics' and 'object-oriented ontology' to refer to his approach.
7. Graham Harman, *Quentin Meillassoux: Philosophy in the Making* (Edinburgh: Edinburgh University Press, 2011), p. 77.
8. Graham Harman, 'The current state of speculative realism', *Speculations: A Journal of Speculative Realism*, IV (2013), pp. 22–7, here p. 22. The one forthcoming monograph mentioned by Harman is Peter Gratton, *Speculative Realism: Problems and Prospects*

(London: Bloomsbury, 2014). Tom Sparrow repeats the same point in *The End of Phenomenology: Metaphysics and the New Realism* (Edinburgh: Edinburgh University Press, 2014), p. xii.
9. Ray Brassier, 'I am a nihilist because I still believe in truth', An interview with Marcin Rychter, *Kronos*, 4 March 2011, <http://www.kronos.org.pl/index.php?23151,896>. For a more nuanced discussion of blogging's impact on the speculative realism movement, see Adam Kostko, 'A very dangerous supplement: speculative realism, academic blogging, and the future of philosophy', *Speculations: A Journal of Speculative Realism*, IV (2013): pp. 35–7. For a list of blogs related to speculative realism, see Bryant et al., 'Towards a speculative philosophy', p. 6 n.16.
10. Norris, 'Speculative realism', p. 38. See also Bryant et al., 'Towards a speculative philosophy', p. 4.
11. Brassier, 'Postscript', p. 414.
12. Meillassoux, *After Finitude*, p. 5.
13. Ibid. p. 28.
14. Ibid. p. 6.
15. Ibid. p. 59.
16. Graham Harman, *Prince of Networks: Bruno Latour and Metaphysics* (Melbourne: re.press, 2009), p. 156.
17. Quentin Meillassoux, 'Time without becoming', Lecture given at Middlesex University, London, 8 May 2008, p. 2.
18. Meillassoux, *After Finitude*, p. 3.
19. Bryant et al. 'Towards a speculative philosophy', p. 3.
20. See Meillassoux, *After Finitude*, ch. 3, esp. pp. 79–80.
21. Ibid. p. 63.
22. Bryant et al. 'Towards a speculative philosophy', p. 3.
23. Steven Shaviro, *The Universe of Things: On Speculative Realism* (Minneapolis: University of Minnesota Press, 2014), p. 61.
24. Ibid. p. 125. It is because thought is limited to its rationalist or intentionalist definition that only humans think and that attributing thought to other entities seems to be an undue projection of our subjective mode of being on to the rest of what exists. Meillassoux reaffirms human exceptionalism by asserting that all there is to thought is what thought is for us. See Quentin Meillassoux, 'Iteration, reiteration, repetition: a speculative analysis of the meaningless sign', Lecture given at the Freie Universität, Berlin, p. 5. Harman, on the other hand, rejects anthropocentrism by asserting a flat ontology (all objects are equally objects; there is no privileged object). However, his approach opens the door to anthropomorphism, for example when he writes about the 'sincerity of objects'. See Graham Harman, *Guerrilla Metaphysics: Phenomenology and the Carpentry of Things* (Chicago: Open Court, 2005), p. 135.
25. Meillassoux, *After Finitude*, pp. 13–18.
26. See, for example, this statement in Brassier's PhD thesis, 'Alien theory: the decline of materialism in the name of matter', available at <http://go.warwick.ac.uk/wrap/4034> (last accessed 5 December 2017): 'Now, 142 years after Darwin, Husserl's idealism is utterly indefensible – unless it be by those who approve of phenomenology's apparently boundless contempt for natural science. The choice with which we are confronted is as clear as it is unavoidable: either Darwin or Husserl. To continue to persist on the course initiated by the latter is to plunge headlong into intellectual disaster and the ruin of philosophy as a credible theoretical enterprise. The future vouchsafed to philosophy by phenomenology is too dismal to contemplate: a terminally infantile, pathologically narcissistic anthropocentrism. The situation is too grave, the stakes too high to allow for equivocation or compromise' (p. 28). Or, again, a couple of pages later: 'It might be apposite to remind ourselves here that as far as the committed phenomenologist is concerned, contrary to what a flimsy scientific dogmatism mired in the natural attitude dares to suggest, the earth does not move (i.e. the 'archi-originary'

earth subtending the 'transcendental' corporeality of phenomenological subjectivity). Divine surprise! Thus, and perhaps appropriately, the phenomenologist is one who believes that the earth shall always be flat. Phenomenological wonders shall never cease' (pp. 38–9 n. 40).
27. Meillassoux, *After Finitude*, p. 42.
28. Ibid. p. 41.
29. Ibid. p. 46.
30. Bryant et al., 'Towards a speculative philosophy', p. 3. See also Brassier, 'Postscript', p. 415.
31. Meillassoux, *After Finitude*, p. 34.
32. Harman, 'Undermining of objects', p. 21.
33. Brassier, 'Postscript', p. 416.
34. Sparrow, *End of Phenomenology*, p. 62.
35. Ibid. p. 163. The quote is from Graham Harman, *Weird Realism: Lovecraft and Philosophy* (Winchester: Zero Books, 2012), p. 16.
36. Meillassoux, 'Time without becoming', p. 6.
37. Ray Brassier, *Nihil Unbound: Enlightenment and Extinction* (London: Palgrave Macmillan, 2007), esp. chs 3 and 5.
38. Christopher Norris, 'Speculative Realism: interim report with just a few caveats', *Speculations: A Journal of Speculative Realism*, IV (2013), pp. 38–47, here p. 42.
39. Peter Wolfendale, *Object-Oriented Philosophy: The Noumenon's New Clothes* (Falmouth: Urbanomic, 2014), p. 201.
40. Dan Zahavi, 'The end of what? Phenomenology vs. speculative realism', *International Journal of Philosophical Studies*, vol. 24, no. 3 (2016): pp. 289–309.

Part I
Responses and Interventions

Chapter 1

Empirical Realism and the Great Outdoors: A Critique of Meillassoux

G. Anthony Bruno

> If finitude is placed at the point of departure for transcendence as clearly as it is by Kant, then it is not necessary, in order to escape an alleged 'subjective idealism', to invoke a 'turn to the Object', a turn which is praised again today all too noisily and with all too little understanding of the problem. In truth, however, the essence of finitude inevitably forces us to the question concerning the conditions for the possibility of a preliminary Being-oriented toward the Object, i.e., concerning the essence of the necessary ontological turning-toward the object in general.
>
> Martin Heidegger, *Kant and the Problem of Metaphysics*

Introduction

Central to the new realist movement in contemporary continental philosophy, Quentin Meillassoux's *After Finitude: An Essay on the Necessity of Contingency*[1] is an unabashed pursuit of knowledge of the Absolute, that is, of reality independent of the structures of human experience. It is informed by the history of philosophy to the extent that it requires that any claim to such knowledge be *post-Kantian*. A post-Kantian claim to absolute knowledge would be non-metaphysical in so far as it would reject the rationalist idea of a necessary entity, following Kant's association of this idea with dogmatism. The dogmatic path is characterised in the *Critique of Pure Reason* by an unreflective use of the principle of sufficient reason (PSR), according to which an entity is only intelligible locally, in its particular context, if its relative explanatory ground is known and globally, in relation to all other entities, if its absolute explanatory ground is known. The dogmatist seeks the latter ground for systematic reasons, locating it in God, the necessary entity whose existence is allegedly proven by the ontological argument. Her unchecked use of the PSR thus leads her to the kind of metaphysical claims to knowledge that Kant subjects to critique. By eschewing such claims, Meillassoux's argument for absolute knowledge aims to be post-Kantian.[2]

And yet, Meillassoux's argument is explicitly *anti-Kantian*. Its conclusion – that no entity, but only contingency itself, is necessary – rests on rejecting the PSR as a temptation to metaphysics.[3] This differs markedly from Kant, for whom critique is meant only to limit the PSR. The principle traditionally necessitates the ontological argument as the source of knowledge of the absolute explanatory ground of the intelligibility of all entities and thus leads to dogmatism. Kant's critique consists in restricting the theoretical use of the PSR to appearances, and does so for the sake of morality. It serves to show that our theoretical concern for why things are as they are, that is, for their sufficient reasons, presupposes our practical concern for how things ought to be.[4] By rejecting the PSR for what he calls 'the principle of unreason',[5] which signifies the chaos of necessary contingency, Meillassoux defends a position whose standpoint, while post-Kantian in so far as it is non-dogmatic, is resolutely anti-Kantian. This point bears emphasising: Meillassoux aims to overcome Kant on the basis of the latter's refutation of dogmatic metaphysics and thus, in pursuing absolute knowledge, aims to do so on Kantian terms.

Meillassoux seeks '*intellectual intuition* of the absolute' and identifies this knowledge with 'our grasp of facticity'.[6] By 'facticity', he means 'the property whereby everything and every world *is* without reason, and is thereby *capable of actually becoming otherwise without reason*'.[7] Meillassoux blames Kant for inaugurating what he calls the 'correlationist' fusion of thinking and being, which, by proscribing independent access to either, replaces '*adequation*' between them with '*intersubjectivity*' as the 'criterion of objectivity'.[8] It is by abandoning the PSR and embracing unreason in the form of necessary contingency that we are said to grasp facticity as the Absolute. In particular, according to Meillassoux, this is the only way of giving a satisfactory account of the meaning of the 'ancestral statements' of science, statements whose referent is 'reality antecedent to the emergence of the human species'.[9]

In order to assess Meillassoux's argument for absolute knowledge, I will examine three charges on which it depends: (1) Kant distorts the meaning of ancestral statements, preventing us from affirming the findings of science; (2) Kant fallaciously infers the necessity of the causal structure of experience, obscuring a proper conception of facticity; (3) Kant's revolution is Ptolemaic, not Copernican, yielding a realism that is incapable of grasping 'the great outdoors'. By Meillassoux's lights, (1) represents correlationism's weakness in the face of science, (2) its naive faith in reason and (3) its uselessness for ordinary life.

I want to resist these charges. (1) interprets Kant through Cartesian lenses. This, I argue, explains Meillassoux's false assumption that for transcendental idealism objects do not exist in the absence of subjects. (2) misreads Kant's defence of causality's necessity: he infers it, not from the stability of experience, but from our inability to experience without it. I suggest that a correct reading reveals a hitherto undeveloped Kantian conception of facticity to which Meillassoux's is at best an unmotivated alternative. (3) casts Kant's revolution as subjective, ignoring his portrayal of it as perspectival. If we view the transcendental turn through this portrayal, I claim, we see that empirical realism grasps nothing less than the great outdoors.

Preliminaries

Before evaluating these charges, I want to clarify Meillassoux's method as well as the focus of my objection.

First, Meillassoux rejects the metaphysical supposition that the Absolute must be an entity, seeking instead a 'form of absolute' that is not a 'being'. By employing what he calls speculative thinking,[10] he aims to show that the Absolute is no entity, but is contingency itself, and thereby to avoid the dogmatic consequences of metaphysics. Speculation without metaphysics has two conditions: (S1) we must know 'a world that is essentially unaffected by whether or not anyone thinks it'; (S2) we must know this world 'without reactivating the principle of reason', with its 'mysteries of real necessity'.[11] Meeting (S1) as a post-Kantian requires proving (1) and (3), for it requires showing that, since Kant undermines statements about reality prior to human existence and thereby subjectivises reality, we need a way of knowing the world as it is absolutely independent of human thought. Meeting (S2) requires proving (2), for it requires showing that, since Kant illegitimately endorses the necessity of causality, we need a conception of the world as it is absolutely independent of thought that nevertheless avoids a misguided faith in reason.

Second, Meillassoux differentiates between 'weak' and 'strong' correlationism, identifying the former with Kant and the latter with various post-Kantians, particularly Heidegger and Wittgenstein. Their difference concerns whether or not 'the thing in itself' is thinkable. I will focus my objection on Meillassoux's critique of weak correlationism for three reasons. First, he devotes the bulk of his critique to Kant. Second, he provides no textual analysis of works by Fichte, Hegel or Schelling and makes only scant reference to Heidegger and Wittgenstein. Third, he claims that strong correlationism is the 'exacerbated consequence' of 'the Kantian catastrophe',[12] implying that his critique of the former depends on the strength of his critique of the latter. As I will argue, his critique consists of a misreading of Kant.

Empirical and transcendental idealism

The charge that Kant distorts the meaning of ancestral statements is the conclusion to 'the argument from the arche-fossil', which I reconstruct as follows. The first premise states a criterion for realism: a position is realist only if it affirms scientific knowledge claims about 'occurrences of matter independent of humanity'. 'Arche-fossil' denotes such occurrences in that 'it does *not* designate an ancient event [...] but] an event *anterior* to terrestrial life and *hence anterior to givenness itself*'.[13] An arche-fossil is thus not a phenomenon, for phenomena are always already given to us in experience. It is rather a thing in itself. Ancestral reality, then, is not empirical, but transcendental.[14] The second premise is that Kant cannot affirm knowledge claims about such a reality. Hence, Kant is not a realist. For Meillassoux, a correlationist such as Kant is bound to this failure because she cannot but qualify, and so undermine, the claim '*x* preceded human existence' with a codicil: ' – *for humans*'.[15]

It is worth considering an implication of this argument. Its first premise suggests a criterion for idealism: a position is idealist only if it denies ancestral statements. One can satisfy this criterion in many ways, such as by denying that ancestral reality is thinkable, denying that an arche-fossil is possible, or asserting that ancestral statements are meaningless. Although these are claims that Berkeley might hold, Meillassoux, recognising that ancestral statements are analogous to statements about the in-itself, attributes them to Kant.[16] But Kant holds none of them. He asserts in the first *Critique* that the in-itself is thinkable on the grounds that its concept is implied by that of an appearance.[17] Although the in-itself is not a real possibility of experience, he observes in several *Reflexionen* that it is nevertheless a logical possibility.[18] And although the in-itself is unknowable, Kant argues in the first *Critique* and in *Prolegomena to Any Future Metaphysics* that thinking it is meaningful for no less than the unity of empirical knowledge.[19] Neither these considerations nor the context of either the *Prolegomena* or the Refutation of Idealism deter Meillassoux from explicitly conflating Berkeleyian and Kantian idealism.[20] Indeed, he sees no difference between empirical and transcendental idealism when he states that an ancestral statement has a realist sense or 'no sense at all',[21] for, as the first premise of his argument states, this sense can only be transcendental.

An illuminating historical precedent for Meillassoux's misreading of Kant occurs in Jacobi's *David Hume on Faith, or Idealism and Realism, a Dialogue*. There, Jacobi criticises the transcendental idealist's claim to objectivity:

> according to the common use of language, we must mean by 'object' a thing that *would be present outside us in a transcendental sense*. . . . But since the whole of transcendental idealism would collapse as a result, and would be left with no application or reason for being, whoever professes it must disavow that presupposition. For it must not even be *probable* to him that there be things present outside us in a transcendental sense, or that they have connections with us *which we would be in a position of perceiving in any way at all*. . . . The transcendental idealist must have the courage, therefore, to assert the strongest idealism that was ever professed, and not be afraid of the objection of speculative egoism, for it is impossible for him to pretend to stay within his system if he tries to repel from himself even just this last objection.[22]

Our common presupposition, according to Jacobi, is that objects are transcendentally real. Contra transcendental idealism, what is '*present outside us*' is independent of us, not simply in terms of its sensible matter, but also formally. This is because the purported a priori forms of human experience – space, time, the categories, the ideas of reason – do not condition the possibility of objects' external presence, but are merely internal to a perceiving mind.[23] It would follow from this presupposition that externality is univocally transcendental, while internality is univocally empirical.

As a criticism of transcendental idealism, this will not do. It imposes a Cartesian picture of a mind barred from objectivity in the absence of divine intervention. This ignores Kant's claim in the Fourth Paralogism to 'distinguish empirically external objects from those that might be called "external" in the transcendental sense, by directly calling them "things that are to be encountered in space"'.[24] Empirical externality is a reality to which we have a legitimate, because sensible, access. If we can distinguish this reality from a reality to which we have no legitimate access, then, according to Kant, we can distinguish empirical from transcendental reality.

Compare Jacobi's gloss of the ordinary standpoint with Meillassoux's view of the scientific perspective. He claims that this perspective, which the scientist 'shares with the "ordinary man"', is one from which we experiment, not in order to demonstrate what is valid for 'all scientists', but instead 'with a view to external references which endow these experiments with meaning'.[25] Meillassoux's claim is that demonstrating the validity of our judgements of experience to individuals who share our perspective is not an indication of what is really, externally present. This would follow if, as the first premise of the argument from the arche-fossil states, what is really present transcends this – or any – perspective. Jacobi and Meillassoux's common assumption is that external reality can only be construed transcendentally. Both infer from this that transcendental realism contrasts with an idealism for which such distinctions as 'empirical' and 'transcendental' are simply useless.[26] Hence, just as Jacobi exhorts the transcendental idealist to cease speaking inconsistently about externality and embrace 'egoism', so Meillassoux presses the Kantian to see the subjective idealist in the mirror:

> the consistent correlationist should stop being modest and dare to assert openly that he is in a position to provide the scientist with an *a priori* demonstration that the latter's ancestral statements are *illusory*. . . . Confronted with the arche-fossil, *every variety of idealism converges and becomes equally extraordinary* – every variety of correlationism is exposed as an extreme idealism.[27]

Like the passage from the *David Hume*, this passage imposes a Cartesian picture on to Kant's position. Specifically, it projects the Cartesian problematic concerning whether statements about a mind-independent world are veridical or illusory. Berkeley plausibly operates within this problematic and concludes that such statements are illusory. By contrast, Kant is driven, not by the question of the truth or falsity of statements about a mind-independent world, but by the question of what makes true and false statements about the world possible in the first place.[28] The Kantian problematic concerns, not whether our judgements are veridical, but how they could even be said to be veridical.[29] Thus, the relevant, but ignored, context for Meillassoux's critique is not the question of whether what appears thus-and-so is thus-and-so in itself, but the question of how anything can so much as appear thus-and-so.

Meillassoux's Cartesian misreading perhaps stems from his own driving concern, namely, how we can grasp the meaning of ancestral statements, that is, how we can know whether such statements designate anything real.[30] This question falls squarely within the Cartesian problematic. But although this suits Meillassoux's intention of providing a 'contemporary' defence of a Cartesian claim to know the arche-fossil *qua* thing in itself,[31] it shows that he fails to critique Kant in light of the appropriate problematic.[32] As Meillassoux himself illustrates, a Cartesian assumes that meaning generally is possible and asks of a particular kind of statement – about the external world, about other minds, about the arche-fossil – whether it is actually meaningful. By contrast, a Kantian assumes that statements generally are actually meaningful and asks what in particular makes this possible. It is crucial for any critique of transcendental idealism to address this founding premise, rather than simply its conclusion.

To close my rebuttal of (1), the charge that Kant distorts the meaning of ancestral statements, I suggest that Meillassoux's misreading accounts for an assumption that runs throughout his critique of Kant:

> scientists are much more likely to side with Cartesianism than with Kantianism: they would have little difficulty in conceding that secondary qualities only exist as aspects of the living creature's relation to its world – but they would be much less willing to concede that (mathematizable) primary qualities only exist so long as we ourselves exist, rather than as properties of things themselves.[33]

He goes on to write that 'we must grasp how thought is able to access *an absolute* . . . whose separateness from thought is such that it presents itself to us as non-relative to us, and hence as capable of existing whether we exist or not'.[34] Ultimately, Meillassoux concludes that his preferred 'Galilean-Copernican revolution has no other meaning than that of the paradoxical unveiling of thought's capacity to think what there is whether thought exists or not'.[35] These passages reveal the assumption that, for transcendental idealism, objects of experience depend on the existence of subjects in just the way that perceptions and memories do and therefore that the empirical is tantamount to the internal.[36] In other words, Meillassoux assumes that transcendental idealism is tantamount to empirical idealism.

Kant would hold this view if, when thinking away the experiential conditions that are enacted by our existence, he were to infer that the phenomenal world cannot or does not exist. When thinking just this in the Transcendental Aesthetic, however, he infers otherwise:

> We can accordingly speak of space, extended being, and so on, only from the human standpoint. If we depart from the subjective condition under which alone we can acquire outer intuition, namely that through which we may be affected by objects, then the representation of space signifies nothing at all.[37]

Kant's inference from our non-existence is not that nature cannot or does not exist. It is rather that nothing whatsoever is signified. Compare this inference with his claim in Chapter III of the Analytic of Principles:

> the doctrine of sensibility is at the same time the doctrine of the noumenon in the negative sense, i.e., of things that the understanding must think without this relation to our kind of intuition, thus not merely as appearances but as things in themselves, but about which, however, it also understands that in this abstraction it cannot consider making any use of its categories, since they have significance only in relation to the unity of intuitions in space and

time, and can even determine this unity *a priori* through general concepts of combination only on account of the mere ideality of space and time. Where this [spatial and] temporal unity cannot be encountered, thus in the case of the noumenon, there the entire use, indeed even all significance of the categories completely ceases; for then we could not have insight even into the possibility of the things that would correspond to the categories.[38]

When thinking beyond the human standpoint, judgements of existence lack all sense.[39] Hence, although a transcendental idealist holds that, without subjects, nothing is cognised, she does not infer from this absence that nothing exists, but only that the very idea of existence becomes meaningless.[40]

This does not mean that a transcendental idealist cannot meaningfully speak of an arche-fossil. Her ancestral statement is meaningful precisely as a fallible judgement about an externally present fact that contributes to our knowledge of an indefinite empirical past.[41] In Meillassoux's words, it consists of '*a retrojection of the past on the basis of the present*'.[42] One begs the question in favour of transcendental realism if one objects that the transcendental idealist thereby sacrifices the determination of the measure of the arche-fossil for the demonstration of this measure's validity for those of a common perspective.[43] These are inseparable on her view.[44] It is this fallacy that ultimately undermines (1). The Cartesian projection on which it rests, I suggest, is what leads Meillassoux to confuse the correlationist link between thinking and being for an ontic relation between beings, one in which objects depend on subjects for their existence.

Necessity and facticity

Meillassoux's critique of Kantian claims about ancestrality is hamstrung by a Cartesian projection of an antithesis between the empirical and the external.[45] This is not the case in his critique of Kant's deduction of the category of causality. He charges, (2) that Kant fallaciously infers causality's necessity from the stability of our experience and thereby fails to grasp the truth of facticity, namely, that contingency alone is necessary. I will show that this charge rests on a misreading, one consequence of which is to neglect a competing, and hitherto unexplored, Kantian conception of facticity.

A preliminary remark is in order. Meillassoux claims that Hume also assumes the necessity in question and that he 'merely doubts our capacity to ground [it] through reasoning'.[46] This is mistaken. Rather, Hume assumes our use of the idea of causation, seeks its justification, and finds none. Thus, he says in the *Enquiry Concerning Human Understanding* that 'we are not entitled to form a general [causal] rule' and that, while causal inference is necessary for our subsistence, it arises from mere 'sentiment'.[47] It is precisely the justificatory threat that this poses to our inferential practice – not an assumption of causal necessity – that, for Kant, calls for a transcendental deduction.

I turn to Meillassoux's charge that Kant fallaciously infers the necessity of causality and of the natural laws that presuppose it. By his lights, Kant argues as follows: (N1) if natural laws were not necessary, they would frequently change without reason; (N2) they do not frequently change without reason; (N3) hence, they are necessary.[48] Meillassoux discerns this argument from the following passage from Section II of the Transcendental Deduction:

> Unity of synthesis in accordance with empirical concepts would be entirely contingent, and, were it not grounded on a transcendental ground of unity, it would be possible for a swarm of appearances to fill up our soul without experience ever being able to arise from it. But in that case all relation of cognition to objects would also disappear, since the appearances would lack connection in accordance with universal and necessary laws, and would thus be intuition without thought, but never cognition, and would therefore be as good as nothing for us.[49]

In this section, Kant argues that experience has a single form, a unity whose ground lies in the categories of the understanding, one of which is causality. The cited passage infers this ground's necessity from the impossibility of unified experience that would result from its absence. Kant does not infer that experience would become fragmented, taking on varying and vanishing forms. Indeed, he does not even mention the frequent alteration of natural laws when considering causality's absence, for the scenario is one in which there would be no standpoint from which to discern anything, much less shifts in the rules by which objects interact.[50] This is sufficient to reject Meillassoux's reconstruction, with its inclusion of (N1) and (N2).

Meillassoux's misreading partly stems from interpreting (N2) as representing the '*fact*' of the causal stability of experience.[51] On this interpretation, Kant's deduction would indeed be 'tautological', for (N2) would contain 'the condition of consciousness' deduced in (N3).[52] However, Kant does not assume the conditions of experience, which would make a transcendental deduction redundant. The Kantian problematic starts rather from our experience of a world and interrogates its conditions of possibility. The only '*fact*' we assume prior to a deduction is that we have some empirical knowledge.

This will not allay Meillassoux. His mantra of 'an absolute without an absolute entity'[53] commits him to the exclusive necessity of contingency, that is, to facticity as signified by the principle of unreason. Deducing the necessity of causality, as Kant does, does not simply oppose this thesis: it assumes reason's ability to vouchsafe the PSR by grounding its validity in the human standpoint. In this, Meillassoux suspects a threat comparable to dogmatism.[54] But we misconstrue the necessity proved by a transcendental deduction if we suppose that it is anything stronger than anthropic,[55] for it is logically possible that causality is not necessary and that, consequently, appearances are 'less than a dream'.[56] Kant's inference to necessity simply shows that the conditions of the possibility of experience lie between logical necessity and empirical contingency, for such conditions are contingent with respect to the principle of non-contradiction – since their absence entails no logical contradiction – yet necessary with respect to our empirical knowledge – since experience is impossible without them.[57]

Although I do not have the space to develop this thought here, and while he does not use the term, I want to suggest that, for Kant, the logical contingency and empirical necessity of the conditions of the possibility of experience converge to express facticity, in so far as they are brute facts of experience that are incapable of derivation from rational principles. These conditions function as the a priori forms of the faculties of cognition: space and time, the categories and the ideas. Notice that it is brute fact that our cognition involves sensibility, that sensibility is spatio-temporal, that space is three-dimensional and chiral, and that time is unidirectional. Notice, also, that the ideas represent the unconditioned condition of cognition for which it is reason's 'peculiar fate'[58] endlessly to strive, a desire the fact of which is as brute as it is a temptation to dogmatism. Notice, finally, that neither does an absolute first principle ground the table of judgements from which the table of categories is derived nor is the deduction of the categories possible without our openness to the justificatory threat that is posed by Humean scepticism, a receptivity whose contingency is exemplified by Kant waking from his dogmatic slumber. For these reasons, at least, the conditions of the possibility of experience are factical.[59]

Meillassoux, of course, has an alternative to this Kantian conception of facticity. But motivating his alternative requires that he meet (S2), according to which we know the Absolute without recourse to a principle of reason. This he cannot do since he fails to prove (2). As a result, Kantian facticity remains a live option.

Ptolemy and Copernicus

We saw that rebutting the distortion charge in (1) leaves transcendental idealism's account of ancestral statements intact. The restricted, empirical realism of this account, however, may appear useless to the ordinary standpoint, particularly if Jacobi is right about the 'common use of language'. If so, then (3), the charge that Kant's revolution is Ptolemaic and therefore insufficiently realist, might arise and, with it, another chance to meet (S1). I will show that, in raising (3), Meillassoux misrepresents transcendental philosophy and so does not show that empirical reality and the great outdoors differ in any meaningful sense.

> Meillassoux defends (3) by reclaiming the term 'Copernican revolution': what we have in mind is not so much the astronomical discovery of the decentering of the terrestrial observer within the solar system, but rather the much more fundamental decentering which presided over the mathematization of nature, viz., *the decentering of thought relative to the world within the process of knowledge.*[60]

According to Meillassoux, the Copernican revolution consists in the restoration of the human standpoint to the secondary position of dependence on a world whose existence is absolutely primary. He credits this revolution to Galileo, for whom the world is an exhaustively mathematisable substance that persists in spite of human thought. It is because such a revolution depicts transcendental reality that, for Meillassoux, it provides the proper means of grasping the great outdoors.

By contrast, Kant ushers what Meillassoux calls a 'Ptolemaic counterrevolution' according to which the subject is 'central to the process of knowledge':

> What was the fundamental question on the basis of which the first *Critique* reconfigured the whole of philosophy? It was the question about the conditions under which modern science is thinkable – *that is to say, the conditions of the Copernican revolution in the literal and genuine sense of the term.* In other words, the philosopher who placed the task of understanding the conditions of possibility for modern science at the heart of his project is also the philosopher who responded to this exigency by abolishing its initial condition.[61]

Meillassoux's conflation of empirical and transcendental idealism is evident in his gloss of the revolution that Kant himself calls 'Copernican', for he insists that transcendental idealism undermines our capacity for scientific knowledge, where this is construed as knowledge of transcendental reality. If this threatens our grasp of the world as such, irrespective of ancestrality, it must appear fanciful from the ordinary standpoint.

However, this disregards why Kant does not call his revolution 'Ptolemaic'. When, in the B Preface to the first *Critique*, he says that objects of cognition must conform to the subject, he does not compare this to a view on which our claims about the world are grounded in an absolute standpoint that determines how the world is by fiat. He rather likens it to a view on which our claims are *perspectival*, namely, Copernicus's view that the observer's standpoint is not absolute, but revolves around fixed celestial bodies.[62] Meillassoux misreads the transcendental turn as yielding an idealism for which the subject is so 'central' that the world's existence is by comparison dubious or false – an idealism that Kant explicitly refutes.[63] In fact, Kant's is an idealism for which the world's knowable properties are determined by conditions that, from the human standpoint, apply to any possible claims about such properties.[64] The convergent logical contingency and empirical necessity of these conditions – what I suggest is their facticity – reflects the peculiarity, not the centrality, of the anthropic perspective.

For Kant, a Copernican revolution in philosophy investigates the conditions that simply having a cognitive perspective places on the claims we can make. Such a revolution departs from the Galilean view by locating our claims along a peculiar orbit in logical space.

Meillassoux's neglect of Kant's Copernican affiliation would seem to explain his confusion about the motivation for and consequences of the transcendental turn. Regarding the turn's motivation, he says that science is the 'impetus' for the transcendental critique of metaphysics and that this critique seeks to prove 'the primacy of scientific knowledge', which obviously it does not do.[65] Were the transcendental turn so motivated, it would refuse both to adopt Humean scepticism and to limit knowledge for the sake of morality. However, it does not. Regarding the turn's consequences, Meillassoux says that transcendental philosophy degrades scientific claims as 'apparent, secondary and derivative' and thereby obscures science's *'eminently speculative character'*.[66] Were the results of the transcendental turn as he describes them, it would be unable to conceive of true as opposed to false appearances and so would be forced to identify empirical reality with illusion. Once again, it does not.

Heidegger acknowledges the importance of this second point in the *Phenomenological Interpretation of Kant's* Critique of Pure Reason:

> Appearance not only presupposes 'the relation to a consciousness that is at least possible' . . . but appearance is also appearance *of* something – as Kant puts it: of the *thing itself*. However, in order to eliminate right away the grossest misunderstanding, we must say that appearances are not mere illusions, nor are they some kind of free-floating emissions from things. Rather appearances are objects themselves, or things. Furthermore, appearances are also not other things next to or prior to the things themselves. Rather appearances are just those things themselves *that* we encounter and discover as extant within the world. However, what remains closed off to us is the thing itself insofar as it is thought as object of an absolute knowledge, i.e., as object of an intuition which does not first need the interaction with the thing . . . an *infinite* intuition which first of all produces . . . things.[67]

Appearances are not to be construed as *mere* appearances, to be contrasted in a Cartesian manner from a knowable reality. Rather, they are appearances *to some perspective*, as Kant intends by the idea of a Copernican revolution. Grasping the non-Ptolemaic character of Kant's revolution requires keeping its Humean premises and non-Berkeleyian conclusions clearly in view. In this way, we avoid the 'improper and irrational complaint', which he dismisses in the Amphiboly,[68] that we cannot know – which is to say, cannot produce – the in itself. We thereby avoid falsely supposing that empirical realism is somehow second-rate and instead see that it is as wide open as the world we know.

Conclusion

In his preface to *After Finitude*, Alain Badiou says it is 'no exaggeration' to claim that Meillassoux escapes Kant's classification of philosophy into dogmatism, scepticism and criticism.[69] This is not at all obvious. As I have argued, Meillassoux misconstrues transcendental idealism in his bid for post-Kantian transcendental realism. He thereby succeeds only in talking past Kant. This raises serious questions. Can he truly claim to be post-Kantian? By not interpreting transcendental idealism on its own terms, is his argument for absolute knowledge a non sequitur? Does his criticism of correlationism simply repeat the complaint dismissed in the Amphiboly? However we choose to respond, it is clear that renewing the pursuit of the Absolute as Meillassoux does is guaranteed to meet with an undeterred critique.

Notes

1. Quentin Meillassoux, *After Finitude: An Essay on the Necessity of Contingency*, trans. Ray Brassier (New York: Continuum, 2008).
2. Ibid. p. 28: 'we must take up once more the injunction to know the absolute, and break with the transcendental tradition that rules out its possibility. Is this to say that we must once again become pre-critical philosophers, or that we must go back to dogmatism? The whole problem is that such a return strikes us as strictly impossible – we cannot go back to being metaphysicians, just as we cannot go back to being dogmatists. On this point, we cannot but be heirs of Kantianism.'
3. Ibid. p. 33: 'although thought may well be able to account for the facts of the world by invoking this or that global law – nevertheless, it must also, according to the principle of reason, account for why these laws are thus and not otherwise, and therefore account for why the world is thus and not otherwise. And even were such a 'reason for the world' to be furnished, it would yet be necessary to account for this reason, and so on ad infinitum. If thought is to avoid an infinite regress while submitting to the principle of reason, it is incumbent upon it to uncover a reason that would prove capable of accounting for everything, including itself – a reason not conditioned by any other reason, and which only the ontological argument is capable of uncovering'.

4. For a lucid account of this presupposition, see Omri Boehm, *Kant's Critique of Spinoza* (Oxford: Oxford University Press, 2014), ch. 4.
5. Meillassoux, *After Finitude*, p. 60.
6. Ibid. p. 82.
7. Ibid. p. 53.
8. Ibid. p. 4. It is not difficult to see that 'the idea according to which we only ever have access to the correlation between thinking and being, and never to either term considered apart from the other' (ibid. p. 5) fails to capture Kant's Copernican revolution, for which a 'critique of pure reason' denotes reason's access to itself because it implies the subjective no less than the objective genitive. Meillassoux overlooks the judiciary function of thinking whereby reason, in its critical mode, poses to itself the question *quid juris* regarding its entitlement to a priori concepts. See Kant, *Critique of Pure Reason*, trans. Paul Guyer and Allen W. Wood (Cambridge: Cambridge University Press, 1998), A739/B767.
9. Meillassoux, *After Finitude*, p. 10.
10. Ibid. p. 34.
11. Ibid. pp. 116, 126, 128.
12. Ibid. p. 124.
13. Ibid. pp. 18, 20.
14. Meillassoux obscures this point somewhat when he says that the referents of ancestral statements 'can be posited as real (albeit in the past) once they are taken to have been validated by empirical science' (ibid. p. 12), for empirical validation presupposes givenness.
15. Ibid. pp. 13–14.
16. Ibid. pp. 15–17. Meillassoux is inconsistent in attributing the first claim; see p. 38.
17. See Kant, *Critique of Pure Reason*, Bxxvii: 'even if we cannot cognize these same objects as things in themselves, we at least must be able to think them as things in themselves. For otherwise there would follow the absurd proposition that there is an appearance without anything that appears.'
18. See Immanuel Kant, *Notes and Fragments*, trans. Curtis Bowman, Paul Guyer and Frederick Rauscher (Cambridge: Cambridge University Press, 2005), Ak. XVIII: 111–12, 232, 349.
19. See Kant, *Critique of Pure Reason*, A326–7/B383–4. See also Immanuel Kant, *Prolegomena to Any Future Metaphysics*, trans. Gary Hatfield, in Henry Allison and Peter Heath (eds), *Theoretical Philosophy after 1781* (Cambridge: Cambridge University of Press, 2002), Ak. IV: 354–5: 'We should, then, think for ourselves an immaterial being, an intelligible world, and a highest of all beings (all noumena), because only in these things, as things in themselves, does reason find completion and satisfaction, which it can never hope to find in the derivation of the appearances from the homogeneous grounds of those appearances.'
20. See Meillassoux, *After Finitude*, pp. 18, 122. Curiously, Žižek ignores this. See Slavoj Žižek, *Less Than Nothing: Hegel and the Shadow of Dialectical Materialism* (London: Verso, 2012), pp. 625–6.
21. Meillassoux, *After Finitude*, p. 17.
22. Friedrich Heinrich Jacobi, 'David Hume on faith, or Idealism and realism: a dialogue', in *Main Philosophical Writings and the Novel Allwill*, trans. George di Giovanni (Montreal: McGill-Queen's University Press), pp. 227–9.
23. See Jacobi, 'David Hume', pp. 216–17: 'what we realists call actual objects or things independent of our representations are for the transcendental idealist only internal beings which exhibit nothing at all of a thing that may perhaps be there outside us, or to which the appearance may refer. Rather, these internal beings are merely subjective determinations of the mind, entirely void of anything truly objective.'
24. Kant, *Critique of Pure Reason*, A373. For an account of Jacobi's misreading, see

Paul Franks, *All or Nothing: Systematicity, Transcendental Arguments and Skepticism in German Idealism* (Cambridge, MA: Harvard University Press, 2005), pp. 156–60.
25. Meillassoux, *After Finitude*, pp. 13, 17.
26. Meillassoux takes the requirement of the existence of the transcendental subject – conceived as the site of the enactment of the a priori conditions of experience – as sufficient to collapse the distinction between the transcendental and the empirical (ibid. pp. 24–5). This ignores the fact that developments in post-Kantian philosophy cast the subject's existence as itself an a priori condition of experience. Thus, neither the existence of a community of subjects, for Fichte, nor the social existence of Dasein, for Heidegger, is to be construed merely empirically.
27. Ibid. pp. 17–18.
28. Thus, Johnston errs when he says 'the one thing that saves Kant from being Berkeley is the thing-in-itself'. Adrian Johnston, 'Hume's revenge: À Dieu, Meillassoux?', in Levi Bryant, Nick Srnicek and Graham Harman (eds), *The Speculative Turn* (Melbourne: re.press, 2011), p. 111. Compare his acquiescent account of Meillassoux's critique of Kant in Adrian Johnston, 'The world before worlds: Quentin Meillassoux's and Alain Badiou's anti-Kantian transcendentalism', *Contemporary French Civilization*, vol. 33, no. 1 (2009), pp. 78, 82.
29. For an analysis of the Cartesian and Kantian problematics, see James Conant, 'Varieties of skepticism', in Denis McManus (ed.), *Wittgenstein and Skepticism* (London: Routledge, 2004).
30. Meillassoux, *After Finitude*, pp. 9–10.
31. See ibid. p. 2.
32. See ibid. p. 18: 'might not the meaning of the arche-fossil be to test the philosopher's faith in correlation, even when confronted with data which seem to point to an abyssal divide between what exists and what appears?'
33. Ibid. p. 13.
34. Ibid. p. 28.
35. Ibid. p. 116.
36. For a similar assumption, see William Blattner, 'Heidegger's Kantian idealism revisited', *Inquiry*, vol. 47, no. 4 (2004), pp. 321–37, here p. 322.
37. Kant, *Critique of Pure Reason*, A26–7/B42–3.
38. Ibid. B308. Compare ibid. A507/B535: 'appearances in general are nothing outside our representations, which is just what we mean by their transcendental ideality'.
39. Compare Martin Heidegger, *Being and Time*, trans. John Macquarrie and Edward Robinson (Oxford: Blackwell, 1962), H. 212: 'When Dasein does not exist, "independence" "is" not either, nor "is" the "in-itself". In such a case this sort of thing can be neither understood nor not understood. In such a case even entities within-the-world can neither be discovered nor lie hidden. *In such a case* it cannot be said that entities are, nor can it be said that they are not.'
40. Kant is therefore not committed to what Gabriel calls 'ontic nonsense'. See Markus Gabriel, *Fields of Sense: A New Realist Ontology* (Edinburgh: Edinburgh University Press), p. 78. Contrast Marcus Gabriel, 'The mythological being of reflection: an essay on Hegel, Schelling and the contingency of necessity', in Markus Gabriel and Slavoj Žižek (eds), *Madness, Mythology and Laughter: Subjectivity in German Idealism* (New York: Continuum, 2009), p. 87.
41. Compare Peter Hallward, 'Anything is possible: a reading of Quentin Meillassoux's *After Finitude*', in *The Speculative Turn*, p. 137: 'from an orthodox Kantian perspective there is little difference in principle between my thinking an event that took place yesterday from an event that took place six billion years ago. It's not clear that Kant should have any more trouble in accepting an ancestral statement about the accretion of the earth than he would in accepting a new scientific demonstration of the existence of previously unperceived "magnetic matter", or the discovery of hitherto undetected men on the moon (to cite two of his own examples)'.

42. Meillassoux, *After Finitude*, p. 16.
43. See ibid. p. 17. Compare Ray Brassier, *Nihil Unbound: Enlightenment and Extinction* (Houndmills, Basingstoke: Palgrave Macmillan, 2007), p. 63: 'if correlationism is true, science's ancestral claims are false; if the latter are true, correlationism is false'.
44. Compare Maurice Merleau-Ponty, *Phenomenology of Perception*, trans. Donald A. Landes (Oxford: Routledge, 2012), p. 495: 'For what exactly is meant by saying that the world existed prior to human consciousnesses? It might be meant that the earth emerged from a primitive nebula where the conditions for life had not been brought together. But each one of these words, just like each equation in physics, presupposes our pre-scientific experience of the world, and this reference to the lived world contributes to constituting the valid signification of the statement. Nothing will ever lead me to understand what a nebula, which could not be seen by anyone, might be. Laplace's nebula is not behind us, at our origin, but rather out in front of us in the cultural world.'
45. Compare the misreading of Kant in Maurizio Ferraris, 'Transcendental realism', *The Monist*, vol. 98, no. 2 (2015), pp. 215–32. Ferraris claims that ontology has sense only if it grounds epistemology and that transcendental idealism, since it grounds ontology on epistemology, must be rejected. This fails to rise to the meta-metaphysical standpoint of Kant's critical turn, for it is from this standpoint that we can see that metaphysics is not on the path to a science and that scepticism and dogmatism distract it from this path. For an analysis of Heidegger's account of Kant's meta-metaphysical standpoint, see Camilla Serck-Hanssen, 'Towards fundamental ontology: Heidegger's phenomenological reading of Kant', *Continental Philosophy Review*, vol. 48, no. 2 (2015), pp. 217–35. See also Heidegger, *Being and Time*, H. 10–11: 'the positive outcome of Kant's *Critique of Pure Reason* lies in what it has contributed towards the working out of what belongs to any Nature whatsoever, not in a "theory" of knowledge. His transcendental logic is an *a priori* logic for the subject-matter of that area of Being called "Nature".'
46. Meillassoux, *After Finitude*, p. 90.
47. David Hume, *An Enquiry Concerning Human Understanding and Other Writings*, ed. Stephen Buckle (Cambridge: Cambridge University Press, 2007), pp. 55, 74–5.
48. Meillassoux, *After Finitude*, p. 94.
49. Kant, *Critique of Pure Reason*, A111.
50. See Hilary Putnam, 'Philosophers and human understanding', in *Realism and Reason: Philosophical Papers, Volume 3*, p. 195: 'Replying to the contention that the future might be wholly lawless, might defeat every "induction" we have made, Kant pointed out that if there is any future at all – any future *for us*, at any rate, any future we can grasp as thinkers and conceptualize to see if our predictions were true or false – then, in fact, many regularities must *not* have been violated. Otherwise why call it a *future?*'
51. Meillassoux, *After Finitude*, p. 84.
52. Ibid. p. 93.
53. Ibid. p. 34.
54. Ibid. p. 128: 'If Hume's problem woke Kant from his dogmatic slumber, we can only hope that the problem of ancestrality succeeds in waking us from our correlationist slumber, by enjoining us to reconcile thought and absolute.'
55. Compare the interpretation of Wittgenstein in Stanley Cavell, *The Claim of Reason: Wittgenstein, Skepticism, Morality and Tragedy* (Oxford: Oxford University Press, 1979), pp. 118–19: '[Wittgenstein's] philosophy provides, one might say, an anthropological, or even anthropomorphic, view of necessity; and that can be disappointing; as if it is not really necessity which he has given an anthropological view of. As though if the a priori has a history it cannot really be the a priori in question. – "But something can be necessary whatever we happen to take as, or believe to be, necessary".'
56. See Kant, *Critique of Pure Reason*, A112.

57. Compare Merleau-Ponty on the world: 'the contingency of the world should be understood neither as a lesser being, a gap in the tissue of necessary being, a threat to rationality, nor as a problem to be resolved as soon as possible through the discovery of some deeper necessity. This is an ontic contingency, or contingency within the world. Ontological contingency or the contingency of the world itself, being radical, is on the contrary what establishes once and for all our idea of truth. The world is the real, of which the necessary and the possible are merely provinces' (Merleau-Ponty, *Phenomenology of Perception*, p. 459).
58. See Kant, *Critique of Pure Reason*, Avii.
59. Meillassoux thinks that, for Kant, the forms of cognition are somehow factical, but his thought is incomplete: he includes space and time, but does not specify why they are factical; he omits the ideas of reason entirely; and he includes the categories, but denies falsely that they are deducible. See Meillassoux, *After Finitude*, p. 38.
60. Ibid. p. 115.
61. Ibid. p. 118.
62. Kant, *Critique of Pure Reason*, Bxvi. See Franks, *All or Nothing*, pp. 159–60.
63. See Kant, *Critique of Pure Reason*, B274.
64. Harman similarly misses this point: '[Meillassoux] rightly adds that despite Kant's famous claim to have performed a "Copernican Revolution" in philosophy, he is actually guilty of the opposite: a "Ptolemaic Counter-Revolution". For whereas Copernicus removed humans from the center of the world by putting the earth in motion, Kant's insistence that reality revolves around the conditions of our knowing it makes a better match with Ptolemy's ancient geocentric astronomy.' Graham Harman, *Quentin Meillassoux: Philosophy in the Making* (Edinburgh: Edinburgh University Press, 2011), p. 10; compare pp. 51–2.
65. Meillassoux, *After Finitude*, p. 120.
66. Ibid. p. 119.
67. Martin Heidegger, *Phenomenological Interpretation of Kant's* Critique of Pure Reason, trans. Parvis Emad and Kenneth Maly (Bloomington: Indiana University Press, 1997), pp. 97–9.
68. See Kant, *Critique of Pure Reason*, A277–8/B333–4: 'If the complaints "That we have no insight into the inner in things" are to mean that we do not understand through pure reason what the things that appear to us might be in themselves, then they are entirely improper and irrational; for they would have us be able to cognize things, thus intuit them, even without senses, consequently they would have it that we have a faculty of cognition entirely distinct from the human not merely in degree but even in intuition and kind.'
69. Alain Badiou, 'Preface', in Quentin Meillassoux, *After Finitude*, p. vii.

Chapter 2

The Ecstatic Realism of the Late Schelling

Sean J. McGrath

It is disconcerting to see the history of modern philosophy repeat itself without advancing, and indeed, in some cases, retreating from positions that were once well known and extensively discussed only a century before. The inexhaustible industry of academic philosophy, with its endless stream of PhDs, conferences, journals and books, depends in part upon ignorance of the history of philosophy: academic philosophers are kept busy working at tasks that have already been accomplished or long abandoned by others as not worthwhile. Ahistorical bravado was a maxim of analytical philosophy in the mid-twentieth century; it appears increasingly to have become one for continental philosophy (ironically, at a time when the analysts are discovering the history of philosophy and energetically exploring it like an unknown continent).

This forgetfulness of history appears to be pre-eminently the case in the speculative realism movement, which has graduate programmes in continental philosophy abuzz with the problem of 'correlationalism', Meillassoux's simplification of what was once known as idealism. Correlationalism makes being dependent upon 'access' in precisely the same way that idealism once made metaphysics dependent upon epistemology. We can only speak about that to which we have epistemic access, so Meillassoux imputes to the correlationalist, and only in the terms by which we access it; we cannot speak of being 'in itself' but only of being in so far as it is 'for us'. Before we sign up for Meillassoux's speculative project, which purports to break free of the circle of correlation by means of mathematics, it might be worth recalling how the problem of idealism was dealt with in the first half of the nineteenth century in Germany. I will not undertake a thorough review here since others have already done so.[1] I will, however, stage a minor intervention in the correlationist debate by discussing the late Schelling's strategy for breaking free of the bonds of idealism. The historical significance of Schelling's late philosophy, which I will call ecstatic realism, and the care and rigour with which he developed it, is missed where the history of German idealism – without question the most vital period of speculative philosophy in the modern age – is unknown.[2] I will therefore foreground my presentation of late Schellingian realism (section II) in a short overview of Schelling's role in the rise and fall of German idealism (section I). I will conclude with a gesture to where I think Schelling fits into the correlationist/anti-correlationist divide. The late Schelling is neither a correlationist nor an anti-correlationist and would reject the terms of the dilemma. Conditioned access does not necessarily preclude unconditioned ontology. It all depends on how it is done.

The end of German idealism

Schelling's positive philosophy, which was first unveiled in Berlin in 1841 (although intimations of it had been presented in lectures in Erlangen in 1821 and in Munich in 1827 and 1832[3]), was his much-anticipated response to the Hegelian legacy. Although Schelling had not published anything since the short 1815 treatise *The Deities of Samothrace*, it was well known that he had been working on a critique of his old friend and schoolmate, Hegel, for many years. Even more intriguingly, Schelling had been developing an alternative to 'the system' that would be as comprehensive as Hegel's without, however, totalising or domesticating the worlds of art, politics and religion under a single rationalist framework. Schelling called this work the philosophy of mythology and revelation, and it appeared to be the outcome of his stillborn *Weltalter* project; it was either what was left of the project itself, upon which Schelling had laboured for over a decade, or it was, in the face of the failure of the *Weltalter*, its more sustainable substitute.

When Schelling assumed the lectern in Berlin in 1841, as Hegel's royally appointed successor, the hall was packed with everyone who was anyone in German intellectual life, including such venerable scholars as Jakob Burckhardt, who stood alongside young revolutionaries that included Engels and Bakunin as well as the new generation of still-unknown thinkers such as Søren Kierkegaard. Everyone, friends and enemies of Hegelianism alike, wanted to know what the old man was going to say. After several decades of overblown idealism, Schelling proclaimed the advent of a new realism in philosophy and culture. For Schelling, idealism engages the essences of things a priori and so has a merely negative relation to existence. It needs to be supplemented and corrected by a positive philosophy the departure point of which is being, not as essence, ideality, or correlate of thinking, but as that which precedes and makes possible thinking. It is not the ideal that is the condition of the possibility of the real for Schelling, it is the real that is the condition of the possibility of the ideal. The announcement was met with enthusiasm from the younger generation. Kierkegaard, for example, enthused that 'the child of thought leapt for joy within me as in Elizabeth, when he [Schelling] mentioned the word "actuality"'.[4] But Schelling quickly disappointed most, including Kierkegaard, as he used the Berlin chair to expound in great detail his final philosophy, the outlines of which had already been well worked through years before, as a reading of the 1831 *Urfassung der Philosophie der Offenbarung*[5] makes clear.

The leitmotif of Schelling's work, from the early nature-philosophy to the late positive philosophy is the irreducibility of the real. In the nature-philosophy, Schelling's realism is cast in terms of a theory of the objective existence of reason, or the *reality* of the ideal; in the positive philosophy, the concern is the irreducibility of the real to the conceptual – a different emphasis to be sure, but one which resolves around a common theme: *pace* Hegel, the real is not the rational and the rational is not the real. Rationality is no doubt *real* and reality is *to some extent* rational; but for Schelling, contra Hegel, being is not reducible to thinking, notion or reason, subjectively, transcendentally or idealistically construed. Instead, thinking is contingent upon being, which is always at bottom unprethinkable, an indivisible remainder to any conceptual process.[6] Nowhere is this transcendental realism more apparent than in Schelling's last work, *The Philosophy of Revelation*,[7] and its two companion pieces, *The Philosophy of Mythology* (the prolegomenon to *The Philosophy of Revelation*)[8] and *The Presentation of the Purely Rational Philosophy*, the prequel to the whole positive philosophy.[9]

To grasp the radicality of Schelling's late realism, it is necessary to first of all recognise that German idealism is idealism in a much more robust sense than was envisioned by early modern philosophers such as Berkeley, or even by Kant himself. Idealism is no longer associated with subjectivism: reason is rather as much *in* the world as it is *in* the mind. With this notion of objective reason, idealism no longer has an outside, is no longer relativised by a sensible other, a thing-in-itself, or even a genuinely transcendent God. A reason without limits can only be the infinite itself and Schelling said as much in one of his first publications.[10] The move towards, first, object idealism and then, as a logical consequence of this, absolute idealism began with Fichte's rejection, on logical, metaphysical and ethical grounds, of Kant's claim that the objects of human cognition are appearances and not things-in-themselves. Although Kant seemed to maintain the realism of objects, at least as a possibility, it was not clear how this was consistent with his epistemology. If a subject only ever knows phenomena, and if phenomena are by definition objects for a subject, the conditions of possibility of which lie entirely in the a priori structure of transcendental subjectivity (space, time, the categories of the understanding and the ideas of reason), what sense could there be to Kant's claim that the matter of cognition, that is, sense data (by distinction from the form of cognition, which is a priori) is a posteriori and mind independent?[11] How could an object, a thing-in-itself, *exist* outside space, time and causality? What is an object other than causally conditioned existence in space and time? As the early Schelling put the problem, 'To the extent to which [the thing-in-itself] is a thing (object) it is not in itself, and if it is not in itself, it is not a thing.'[12]

The Fichtian/early Schellingian theory of unconditioned mind, reason that is limited to neither the subjective nor the objective, not only dissolved the chimera of the thing-in-itself, it solved the dilemma of the relation of Kant's three critiques to one another. The inconclusive finish of Kant's philosophy, with practical philosophy necessarily postulating realities that theoretical philosophy could not know, and theoretical philosophy uncovering an activity of reason prior to theory which makes theory itself possible, inspired an intense search for a general system of philosophy. System meant, as Karl Leonhard Reinhold was the first to point out, that all the parts of a philosophy could be derived from a single principle.[13] This first principle could only be the Absolute, the unconditioned that precedes all conditioned concepts or beings, all that is limited by opposites. If the starting point were not the Absolute, that is, if it stood in relation to something else, it would not be the first principle governing all relations and terms. This assumption made the German idealists sympathetic to Spinoza and his effort to found philosophy in the concept of the infinite or substance. However, the German idealists criticised Spinoza's insufficiently nuanced account of subjectivity: Spinoza's substance only achieves absoluteness by means of reducing subjectivity to an attribute of substance; for Schelling and Hegel, the Absolute must be considered both subject *and* substance if it is to be truly absolute. A genuine absolute must be *adequate* to all dimensions of experience, both physical and moral. If subjectivity is an attribute of substance, freedom is rendered illusory, and necessity reigns over all levels of being.

Fichte argued that reason's other, which he called the 'not-I' (*das nicht Ich*), is generated unconsciously or posited by reason itself. In reason's activity of overcoming the otherness of the not-I, by reducing the object to conceptual knowledge (the work of theoretical philosophy), or by mastering it so as to make nature habitable by rational beings (the work of practical philosophy), reason comes to know itself for what it truly is, not an object but a pure subject that subsists only in its activity. The early Schelling pursued this thesis in his first major works,[14] only to supplement it, to Fichte's dismay, with a philosophy of nature, arguing that the unconscious self-positing subject can also be approached through a systematic study of nature in itself. Nature understood as endlessly productive ground (which Schelling called, after Spinoza, *natura naturans*), by distinction from its objects produced (*natura naturata*), is nothing other than the pure activity identified with subjectivity by Fichte, which generates limits (finite entities) for the sake of overcoming them.[15] Nature annuls the limits thrown in the way of its unlimited drive to manifest itself by sacrificing the individual to the universal, a process that occurs at all levels but most visibly in organic life in which the single organism becomes the means to the species through sexuation. The absolute subject and absolute nature coincide in the early Schelling; they are to be considered as 'indifferent' from one another. Hence, alongside a transcendental philosophy of the subject, like that of Fichte, Schelling advocated a transcendental philosophy of the object of the kind that was being developed in various ways by Romantic scientists under the banner *Naturphilosophie*.

Along with the poet Hölderlin, Hegel had been Schelling's classmate in Tübingen from 1790 to 1793. His first work mediated the dispute between Fichte and Schelling by describing Fichte's work as 'subjective' idealism by distinction from Schelling's 'objective' idealism.[16] Hegel argued that Fichte's absolute subject fails to recognise the absolute identity of the I and the not-I. By contrast, argued Hegel, Schelling established the identity of subject and object by means of his notion of the objectivity of the subject, the subject as a product of nature, and the subjectivity of the object, that is, nature as absolute non-thinged (*unbedingt*) productivity. The truth of the matter could only be found in a position that was neither subjective nor objective but maintained the unity of the subject–object, or the Absolute. Schelling's philosophy thus prepared the way for such an absolute idealism and was celebrated as such by Hegel, much to Schelling's delight.[17]

To his surprise, in 1807, when Hegel published his *Phenomenology of Spirit*, Schelling discovered that Hegel rejected the premise of his new identity-philosophy entirely. Hegel attacked Schelling's early notion of the Absolute – the ineffable origin of thought and action that could only be known through intellectual intuition – as obscurantist, and called for a reinstatement of public and discursive reason.[18] Schelling was devastated by the underhanded critique of his friend and former collaborator. Hegel argued in his own defence that it was not Schelling that he had in mind – but who else could he have been thinking of? According to Hegel,

Schelling's conception of the identity of subject and object elided the distinctions that determine the different forms of consciousness, distinctions that are crucial for the concrete universalisation of reason or Spirit (*Geist*).[19] More importantly, Hegel presumed to include history in his system, which Schelling never did. Schelling's identity-philosophy argued that an a priori system could know nothing of history (it must indeed deny the existence of history) and the ontic plurality that it produces.[20] The presumption to logically systematise history is the fatal flaw in Hegel's philosophy according to Schelling, and it indicates the insurmountable limitations of German idealism. When Hegel includes history in the system, the system breaks and German idealism begins to unravel. In the pivotal 1804 *Philosophy and Religion*, Schelling argued that a philosophy of history, a philosophy of finite being, must assume that the world as we know it is discontinuous with the Absolute and cannot therefore be known a priori.[21] The late Schelling considered Hegel's system a barbarous confusion of what he calls negative philosophy (a priori idealist philosophy) and positive philosophy (a posteriori historical philosophy).[22]

Schelling's late philosophy marks a return to the very inception of German idealism and contests its founding assumption that reason has no *real* limits. According to Fichte, the young Schelling and Hegel, any limits reason encounters – for example, in matter, in sense data, in the mechanical necessities of nature, in the unconscious or even in the transcendent realities of religion – are limits that reason *has set for itself* for the sake of overcoming them. Reason in German idealism is not a static faculty of cognition but a dynamic power that acts in the world and realises itself in its action. Fichte's notion of the self as not a substance but an act of self-realisation was the clue, but this notion was itself nothing more than a precise definition of the structure of reason that Kant had already unveiled in his three critiques. Reason is autonomous and self-sufficient: it produces for itself the objects of knowledge by which it comes to know itself as reason. On the question of the limits of reason, the late Schelling changed his views radically. Although he does not simply reinstate Kant's thing-in-itself, nor does he become a Jacobian fideist: the humiliation of reason before the real, on the one hand, and the divine, on the other, is a central leitmotif of Schelling's later thought. Idealism knows only what Schelling calls 'negative philosophy', the philosophy innate to reason. But if reason is to move beyond idealism and know history, the really real, it will need to pass through the a posteriori. Such a philosophy is 'positive philosophy', and because it thinks the real rather than the virtual, it alone counts for genuine knowledge. For this reason, the late Schelling represents the beginning of the end of German idealism, the first movement towards the post-idealist realism that will be taken up in the philosophies of Nietzsche, Kierkegaard and the late nineteenth- and early twentieth-century positivists of France, England and Germany (for example Comte, Cousin, Russell, Fechner and Wittgenstein).

Schelling's late realism

Schelling's 'positive philosophy' is a posteriori without being reductive. He describes it as a kind of metaphysical empiricism, 'the empiricism of what is *a priori* insofar as it proves that the *prius per posterius* exists as God'.[23]

> The preposition 'a' in '*a posteriori*' does not in this instance signify the *terminus a quo*; in this context '*a posteriori*' means '*per posterius*': through its consequence the *prius* is known. The absolute *prius*, however, is what has no *prius* from which it can be known. To be the absolute *prius* means, therefore, not to be known *a priori*.[24]

The relative *prius* is the a priori in its more or less conventional sense, the rich content of reason which thinking brings to experience and by means of which it understands experience. For Schelling, Kant is correct in showing that the a priori culminates in the idea of the *ens necessarium*, the idea of that being that, should it exist, exists necessarily or *as* God. The a priori is being-for-thinking. The a posteriori in its conventional sense is being that has been experienced. The absolute *prius* is neither thought nor experience; it is being itself irrespective of thought or experience. It is the groundless act at the basis of the sheer facticity of being, the reason why there is something rather than nothing. The task of positive philosophy, which we cannot go into in any detail here, is to prove that this primal and absolutely contingent actuality exists *as* God: being exists as the unfolding in time or historical revelation of the *ens necessarium*. Thus the *prius* (the *ens necessarium*) is known as factually existing *per posterius*, *through* the posterior or *through* experience. This is nothing short of a deconstruction of the traditional meanings of a posteriori and a priori, such that they come to mean their opposite: a posteriori now no longer means starting from the posterior, starting from experience: it means starting *above* experience (and in that sense *before* experience) and knowing something of that which cannot be directly experienced *through* experience, starting with the trans-experiential and returning to it via experience. The a priori no longer means starting with concept, reason and idea: it means starting with that which is absolutely prior, with that which therefore cannot be known merely through concept, reason and idea, because all of these are intentionally prior to that which they render intelligible; it means starting with the radically a posteriori.[25]

Positive philosophy is to be distinguished from negative philosophy, a philosophy that lays a claim to deductive power in so far as it remains within reason alone, and which, in Schelling's view, characterises most of the history of philosophy. The persistent power of negative philosophy, according to Schelling, resides in reason's secure possession of certain a priori truths, the principles of reason itself, which reason could only deny by performatively contradicting itself. Reason has a threefold structure, corresponding to the principles of identity, non-contradiction and excluded middle, which Schelling unpacks as 'the three potencies'. The first potency is –A, the principle of determinability or possibility. The second potency is +A, the principle of determination or actuality. The third potency is ±A, the principle of self-determination. –A is that which can be *anything* whatsoever because it actually is not anything in particular; +A is that which is fully actual and must be what it is for it has no possibility to be otherwise; ±A is that which is actual in one respect and possible in another. –A is potency without actuality; +A is actuality without potency; ±A is the synthesis of actuality and potency. The three potencies are expressed in every act of thinking as the parts of the judgement: –A is the subject of which something can be predicated – thus it is not in itself identical to any predicate; +A is the object which is predicated of a subject; ±A is the full act of predication, the subject which *is* in one way or another. The potencies are negative in the sense that they say nothing about the existence of non-existence of the positive, about that which exists outside of reason – really existing things, historical facts, freely acting persons and, above them all, the ungrounded act of being upon which they are all contingent – something that negative philosophy is continually forgetting. The principles of reason concern conceptual relations in abstraction from existence, possibilities and not concrete beings. Conceptual relations negatively determine what a being might be, how it can be conceived, but it cannot tell us whether or not it exists. As Spinoza put it, in a phrase made famous by Hegel, '*determinatio negatio est*'.[26] The three potencies would obtain even if nothing existed, but, if something exists, it must exist in terms of the potencies, that is, it must exist as a subject of which something can be said, or as that which could be said of a subject.[27]

Negative philosophy comes to its clearest expression in early modern rationalism and achieves its highest point in German idealism. It is not *refuted* by positive philosophy: on the contrary, without negative philosophy, there is no knowledge of positive philosophy, for two reasons. First, the positive can only be acknowledged as positive in so far as it is profiled against the negative. Without knowledge of the a priori nature of the conceptual, the a posteriori nature of the positive is missed altogether. Indeed, the philosophy of revelation presumes Kant's critique of knowledge and refuses to go back to a metaphysics that preceded it. Second, the only means philosophy has to think the positive are the principles and categories given with reason itself. The positive philosophy does not change the structure of reason but rather gives it something real, that is, existent, to think for the first time. Simply put, where the negative philosophy concerns necessary truths (the principles of reason), positive philosophy engages contingent truths, and the contingency of being itself. The negative philosophy understands the essences of things, the *quidditas* of whatever it is that can be thought, and does so with surety and conclusiveness, for its arena of operation is a priori; the positive philosophy is concerned with the contingent existence of things, the *quodditas* of that which is given thought to think. Here reason can only proceed fallibilistically, for nothing that is historically or factually given is necessary.

The beginning of positive philosophy is the metaphysical question 'Why is there something rather than nothing?' With this question, philosophy not only exposes itself to the contingency of being – for in the question itself, being is shown to be possible and not necessary (the questionability is only possible on the assumption that being need not have been) – philosophy also exposes the contingency of reason itself. The question 'Why is there something rather than nothing?' includes the questioner. However necessary the potencies are (necessary according to essence, even if contingent according to existence), none of them need be, for reason itself need not be. Schelling therefore supplements the metaphysical question first articulated by Leibniz with a yet deeper question that underlies it: why is there reason and rather not un-reason?[28] This point touches on what is so strikingly new in Schelling's later writings: his discovery, slowly realised over the second half of his career (two decades in which he ceased publishing), of the essential poverty of reason. This poverty is not simply a justification of scepticism, and neither is it a rediscovery of the phenomenal limits of reason. For reason does possess a world of its own that it can and has in the past inflated into a false absolute. This construct of reason is mythology, and in Schelling's own age Hegelian philosophy is no better: a confusion of the negative with the positive and a failure to recognise the real positive as such. The poverty of reason consists not only in its inability to think the truly divine God, but in its perennial susceptibility to substitute its own self-generated fiction for God. Contrary to his earliest assumption, the late Schelling discovers that reason cannot think the really existing God and so cannot fulfil itself. But this does not confine thought to correlationism; on the contrary, it sets it on an open-ended investigation of the emergent intelligibility of the universe. The insight into the poverty of reason does not lead to a deduction of the necessity of revelation, for that would leave philosophy in its negative moment dialoguing with the concepts that it produces out of itself. Rather, the impotence of idealism leads to philosophy's recognition of its dependence on an outside and the need for positive philosophy, which takes its point of departure not from concepts but from existence and, above all, from the truth mediated by certain extraordinary historical facts.

That reason is finite for Schelling means that it is *historical*: it need not exist and the necessity that drives its concepts is ultimately a virtual necessity, with at best a questionable relation to contingent reality. It is on these grounds that Schelling has been said to have returned to Kant and reasserted the limits of reason, albeit in a radically different way than Kant had.[29] Whereas the Kantian limits of reason are demarcated a priori, from within as it were, the Schellingian limits are demarcated a posteriori – demarked from without. It is not some arbitrary definition of knowledge as an a priori category filled out by sensible intuition that delimits reason; rather, the Kantian principles of knowledge remain as problematic for the late Schelling as they were for the early Schelling, bifurcating reality into two incommensurable domains of the phenomenal and the noumenal. For the late Schelling, what delimits reason is history. Reason can only grasp a priori an act which is preceded by potency, or a real that is determined by a concept. History, however, is an order that emerges out of unprethinkable events, acts that are not preceded by potency but which emerge literally out of nothing.

The beginning of the positive philosophy is not a concept, but a non-concept, not an existent that exists thus and so, or an essence, but an act of existence dirempted of essence. The act is not deduced from the negative philosophy, but rather willed by the reasoner who wants more than the negative philosophy, and who wills a philosophy of being, not just of reason. The negative philosophy ends and the positive begins when the philosopher says, 'I want that which is above being.'[30] Schelling calls the first principle of positive philosophy 'the inverted idea' (*die umgekehrte Idee*) and argues that it alone is the absolute *prius*. He distinguishes it from the relative *prius* (the a priori), which is a secure possession of reason. The relative *prius* is the triadic system of potencies, which cannot *not* be thought for they structure thinking itself. The absolute *prius*, however, is not a potency or an a priori truth – that is, it is not a being whose existence must be necessarily (logically) affirmed, even if its existence cannot be doubted a posteriori. The inverted idea, or the absolute *prius*, is not found within thought at all but is rather the presupposition of thought. And even more disturbing to reason, the absolute *prius* does not necessarily exist but is radically contingent. Only a being grounded in a concept can exist necessarily: the absolute *prius* is preceded by nothing: it is pure event, the event of being itself. That it has occurred is undeniable, but it need not have occurred. And *what* it ultimately is – the meaning of being, to speak the language of Heidegger – is not self-evident. Thus begins the work of positive philosophy, the open-ended, fallible and deeply historical investigation into the *nature* of existence.

Schelling is never more elusive than in his discussion of the absolute *prius*. He calls it the pure *that* (*das rein Daß*), the *actus purus*, A^0, unprethinkable being (*das unvordenkliche Sein*), being without potency (for it is preceded by nothing but is itself the absolute first), being which has a certain infinity about it (not because it exists necessarily but because it cannot be reduced to anything prior to it), and the absolutely transcendent being. As the absolutely first, the absolute *prius* is not experienced, at least not directly or immediately, for to experience anything at all is to experience something, a *that* which is given as a *what*. The question concerning the *prius* is a question that interrogates the being of being, the existence that precedes all essence, or the absolute fact that there is something rather than nothing. I will quote Schelling at some length for nowhere else in his corpus is his reasoning so close and inscrutable:

> The positive philosophy starts out just as little from something that occurs merely in thought (for then it would fall back into the negative philosophy) as it starts out from some being that is present in *experience*. If it does not start out from something that occurs in thought, and, thus, in no way from pure thought, then it will start out from that which is before and external to all thought, consequently from being, but not from an empirical being. For we have already excluded this, in that empirical being is external to thought only in the very relative sense, to the extent that *every* being that occurs in experience inherently carries with it the logical determinations of the understanding, without which it could never be represented. If positive philosophy starts out from that which is external to all thought, it cannot begin with a being that is external to thought in a merely relative sense, but only with a being that is *absolutely* external to thought. The being that is external to all thought, however, is just as much beyond all experience as it is before all thought: positive philosophy begins with the *completely transcendent being* and it can no longer be just a relative *prius* like the potency that serves as the basis of the science of reason. For precisely as potency – as *nonbeing* – it has the necessity to pass over into being, and, thus, I call it the merely relative *prius*. If that being from which positive philosophy proceeds were also merely relative then the *necessity* of passing over into being would inhere with its principle. Thus, through this principle, that being would be subordinated to the thought of a necessary movement and, consequently, the positive philosophy would fall back into the negative. If, therefore, the relative *prius* cannot be the beginning of the positive philosophy, then it must be the absolute *prius*, which has no necessity to move itself into being. If it passes over into being, then this can only be the consequence of a free act, of an act that can only be something purely empirical, that can be fully apprehended only a posteriori, just as every act is incapable of being comprehended a priori and is only capable of being known *a posteriori*.[31]

One of the many challenges in interpreting the above paragraph is that Schelling moves between two senses of being and does not always specify when he does so. He sometimes means being as essence (*quidditas* or *Washeit*) and at other times being as existence (*quodditas* or *Dassheit*). 'Some being (*Seiende*) that is present in experience' is an essence (*quidditas*) given as existent. 'Being' (*Seyn*) 'which is before and external to all thought' is existence (*quodditas*) without essence – not that *an existent* can exist without essence but that *existence* as such must be prior to any essence, for to assert otherwise, to assert the primacy of essence to existence, is to fall into contradiction, it is to say that *something* (some essence) *is* and *that* that something *is not* (does not exist) in the same respect at the same time. The potency that is a relative *prius* is not nothingness (*ouk on*), but rather 'non-being' in the sense of non-existent (the *me on* of Plato), an essence that is not yet determined as existing, or as a possible being. To think being as non-existent is not to fall into contradiction because being is here thought as the *possibility* of existing in some way or another. The relative *prius* (–A) 'has the necessity to pass over into being' not in the sense of the necessity to exist (for that way lies the ontological argument), but the necessity to be a possible *something*. –A cannot be posited alone but only in conjunction with +A, that is, –A (determinability or indeterminacy) *is* as the possibility to be *determined* (+A). But the absolute *prius* has no necessity to be a possible something because there is no possible being which it could be: as absolutely first, it is preceded by no possibilities by which it could be determined. Thus, it exists without prior determination; in other words, it is absolute contingency or event.[32] Hence its existence is a 'free act', and can only be known (inferred) a posteriori (but not experienced). 'The first beginning is expressly thought of as a contingent beginning. The first *being*, this *primum existens*, as I have called it, is, therefore, at the same time the first contingency (original coincidence). This whole construction therefore begins with the first contingency – which is not identical with itself – it begins with a *dissonance*, and must begin this way.'[33]

We can only think of the absolute *prius* as *being itself*, as sheer existence, being that is always presupposed in any act of thinking, for, according to Schelling's metaphysical voluntarism, 'it is not because there is thinking that there is being, but rather because there is being that there is thinking'.[34] –A can only be because there is something else that is not a potency or a thought, but is rather the act of being itself. The absolutely *prius* (A^0) is existence as really distinct from essence, and as the presupposition of all essences. But to single it out in this way, by 'remotion' as it were (for we do not posit being itself or define it, we rather isolate it as that which remains when we deny all predicates of it), is not to say anything about it at all. It is rather to say that it is prior to anything else, and to deny it is impossible, not because it exists necessarily, but because it is the presupposition of our own thinking about it. Being can be thought otherwise, to be sure, and such thought is expressed in the question 'Why is there something rather than nothing?' But it cannot be denied. We can think nothingness, but we cannot deny existence after the fact. In this recognition of the absolute facticity of being itself, reason is ecstatic, entirely outside itself, pointing beyond all concepts to that which is not a concept but which must *be* somehow if any concepts are:

> That which just – that which only – exists is precisely that which crushes everything that may derive from thought, before which thought becomes silent, and before which reason bows down; for thought is only concerned with possibility and potency; thus where these are excluded, thought has no authority. That which infinitely exists is precisely for this reason – because it is this – also positioned securely against thought and all doubt ... thus, indubitably exists – that which can never perish, abiding and necessary, which above all endures, come what may and regardless of what happens.[35]

We must not misread Schelling here, for he is not arguing for the necessary existence of God but for the indubitable, *existentially* necessary existence of being, which might or might not be God. 'But it is something completely different whether I say: God can only exist necessarily, or whether I say: He necessarily exists. From the First (He can only exist necessarily) only follows: therefore He exists necessarily. N.B. if He exists, but it does not at all follow that He exists.'[36] God exists, Schelling says, in the end of the positive philosophy, but he exists contingently, not necessarily, and therefore knowledge of his existence is provisional and fallibilist: we are only warranted in affirming that being exists as God in so far as we experience and continue to experience being as unfolding in a divine way, that is, as ordered, intelligible and directed towards the revelation of love.

In this 'ecstasy of reason', Schelling finds the solution to the problem of modern philosophy, which is the problem of the narcissism of reason, or idealism. It is not a logical solution but an ethical one, for, on the level of logic, idealism is entirely consistent. One must rather *engage* one's own existence and *decide* to put oneself into question in order to step outside the correlationist circle of the a priori. This existential engagement and decision indicates the act of will that undergirds the argument and places it on the terrain of the ethical. We can reconstruct Schelling's line of thinking here as a reversal of Descartes's argument for the existence of God in the Fifth Meditation. Schelling's argument is compressed into the following passage:

> That which just is [*das bloß Seyende*] is being [*das Seyn*] from which properly speaking, every idea, that is, every potency is excluded. We will, thus, only

be able to call it the inverted idea [*die umgekehrte Idee*], the idea in which reason is set *outside* itself. Reason can posit being in which there is still nothing of a concept, of a whatness, only as something that is absolutely *outside itself* (of course only in order to acquire it thereafter, a posteriori, as its content, and in this way to return to itself as the same time). In this posting, reason is therefore set outside itself, absolutely ecstatic.[37]

In Cartesian terms, this amounts to a reversal of the *cogito ergo sum*, thus an anti-*cogito*. Descartes doubts everything outside his own thinking and endeavours to proceed from within thought itself to the establishment of an outside. In that way, he performs the narcissism of reason, the refusal of exteriority. Schelling doubts the existence of thinking itself and proceeds from that which is absolutely outside thought. Descartes discovers within reason a rich world of possibilities, innate ideas, which he assumes he has produced himself. The ontological argument is then used to build a bridge between the idea of the infinite to the exterior and bring about the transition from essence to existence on the level of essence, the move from the negative to the positive without ever leaving the negative. We will not discuss here Levinas's important observation that, already in the Third Meditation, Descartes discovers that his *epoché* is an impossibility because the *existence* of the idea of the infinite present within his thinking is already an indication that he did not produce himself but depends upon an exterior.[38] Along this line, Descartes discovers that a suspension of all existence claims is not in fact possible. For the sake of the argument, we will assume the textbook Descartes, the father of idealism, the one who proves that reason is sovereign over itself and apparently contains within itself all that it needs to begin, the whole world of ideas, as its own immediate content. What Schelling demonstrates is Descartes's overlooking of being, the forgetting of the *sum* in his argument *cogito ergo sum*. Thinking may be given and self-productive in the *cogito*, but *the being* of the thinking is not produced by thinking but is rather the presupposition of thought.

> This *sum cogitans* cannot ... mean that it is as though I were nothing but thinking, or as if thinking were the substance of my being. ... Thinking is, therefore, only a determination or way of being. ... The *sum* which is contained in the *cogito* is, therefore, only *sum qua cogitans*, I am as thinking, i.e., in that specific way of being which is called thinking. ... The *sum* that is contained in the *cogito* does not, then, have the significance of an absolute 'I am', but only of an 'I am in one way or another' namely as just thinking, in that way of being which one calls thinking.[39]

I do not need to climb through the ideal to find the real (which is in any case impossible); I am already in the real in so far as I regard myself not merely as abstract reason, as disembodied thinking, but as that which exists, that is, as a will. Now I posit, that is, I intend (or better, *I will*) that

I am what I am, not that upon which all depends, the infinite being, but nothing more than the finite being that I experience myself as, the one who wants and wills because he does not possess the fullness of the real. The presupposition of this act of will is the possibility that I not intend myself as finite but rather mis-take myself as sufficient unto being, as infinite and first. Thus, I posit myself as that which depends on something that is not myself, as the I that depends on being in order to be able to say 'I am'.

This positing of the willing self is not a logical movement but a decision, that is, it is not a process that occurs logically in thinking but an act of willing. I could in fact posit myself otherwise. By abstracting from my existence, I could posit myself as reason itself, as pure possibility – after all, I am also a reasoning being and not merely a willing being, and in so far as I am a reasoning being, I possess the image of being (the three potencies) as my own content. However, if I did so, that is, if I followed modern idealism, then I would remain within negative philosophy – not in the kind of negative philosophy that knows itself as such, but rather in a negative philosophy that disavows its own negativity, chooses not to know that reason is always the reasoning of a finite willing existent, and so can consistently take reason to be identical to the real. To know negative philosophy as negative is only possible for one who has already posited the positive: thus, whereas negative philosophy has a logical priority to positive philosophy, positive philosophy has an existential priority to negative philosophy. Since it would still be I, the really existent finite being that I am, that would, with Descartes, posit itself as reason as such, the negative philosophy's disavowal of its own negativity can only be an *epoché* of the real – which it is in Descartes – a suspension of the spontaneous and everyday judgement that things *are* and that they exist outside myself.

Since I now posit myself as real, which means since I *will* and know myself in my willing, I am already in the real. As Schelling writes, 'pure thought, in which everything develops of necessity, knows nothing of a decision, of an act, or even of a deed'.[40] But how do I posit myself as finite, that is, how do I posit myself without at the same time absolutising myself, without intending myself as the absolute? How do I empty myself and thus stay in the act of willing *on the outside* and resist the siren call of reason to enfold itself in itself and become absorbed in its own inner world? I do this, not by positing myself as such, that is, not by asserting myself, willing myself and insisting *I am*, but rather by willing another, and thereby negating myself, saying, 'It alone is, I am as though I were nothing.' To get to this moment of *kenosis*, Schelling introduces an intermediate step, no less ecstatic than the recognition of the truly existing God, but not yet asserting the latter as such. There must be a purely philosophical transition from the narcissism of reason to the ecstatic recognition of being. I do not posit myself directly, but only indirectly, performatively, by deciding, acting and judging not that *I am*, but that *that being*, which is not me, and upon which I depend, truly *is* and cannot not be (because it factically is). Not that being exists necessarily – for being is the primarily contingent, it is contingency itself – but that it exists factically and indubitably, for if it were not, neither would I be. I posit not the I but the sheer reality of being upon which the I depends for its existence, the being that has no priority in concept: unprethinkable being (*das unvordenkliche Sein*). I posit this purely negatively at first, as that which I am not in so far as I can conceive myself and so have an a priori notion of myself; I posit that which has no apriority in thinking, which is the *prius* absolutely and, in that sense, the groundless being, and which I presuppose in any assertion of my own being.

Notice, it is not an *experience* of being with which positive philosophy begins: I do not *experience* sheer existence, the pure *that*; rather, I *posit* it as that which is without any prior potency determining it. If it were an experience, sheer existence would be in part conceived since nothing can be experienced without some degree of conceptualisation. And if it is in part conceived, then the being that is so conceived is not the unprethinkable being, the being that is wholly outside of reason, but rather a being that has an a priori concept adequate to it in reason. The pure *that* is in a way the *intentum* of an *intentio*, but a very peculiar intention, one that renounces a priori possession of its *intentum* and thus the intention of the non-conceptual, and to that degree it is an inverse intention (the inversion of intentionality). In this act, reason empties itself and gestures to that which it does not and cannot contain in itself, that is, it gestures to the factical condition of its own possibility. In the ecstasy of reason, thinking thinks itself as product, not producer, by endeavouring to think that which cannot be thought and thus renouncing its claim to totality. In this decision, reason experiences itself as inadequate to the real, which is to say, reason experiences itself *as real*, that is, as existing by means of an act that is not its own.

Conclusion

Idealism is therefore the presupposition of Schelling's ecstatic realism and an essential stage in the encounter with the real. We could say that correlationism is the presupposition of positive philosophy, not because it is true, but rather because it is false, and, in its failure, reveals the real. Only one who possesses something, or at least *could* lay claim to possession, can empty himself. A *tabula rasa* cannot empty itself before the real. The idealist's presupposition of the triadic structure of reason is confirmed to some degree by revelation, only this ideal content is now revealed to be a virtual real, one that must be qualified by the really existing God. The late Schelling's position strikes a middle ground between idealism and realism as they were understood up until then. With the idealists, the a priori is made instrumental to cognition. With the realists, the truth is held to be irreducible to innate ideas. Revelation is a disruption of the a priori by the a posteriori (which is no longer identified simply with sense data): it is an encounter with the real, not a deduction of it. A priori reasoning, however necessary, is merely negative; the real is excluded from it. Schelling's positive philosophy begins from the assumption that reason is only fully rational when it is 'ecstatic', outside itself and *receives* the truth of that which it did not itself generate.

The paragon of such an interruption is biblical revelation. The Hebrews are distinguished from the Greeks in that they never claimed to possess any philosophical or mystical insight into the God who reveals Himself in history. The First Commandment forbids the Hebrews any mythic image or even visualisation of God. In effect, the Hebrews are denied a consciousness of God (God cannot be objectified) and are forbidden to think of him in any terms other than his own. Jehovah can be known only in so far as he reveals himself in history. In the history of ancient peoples, the Hebrews are unique, for they were never localised by a mythic tradition, a historical consciousness of the divinity, which would produce a cult of local deities, and consequently never became a people or a nation (*ein Volk*) in the strict sense of the term.[41] Hebrew theology is a repetition and an interpretation of what God Himself has said about Himself. According to Jacobi, the acknowledgement of the otherness of truth is the most reasonable thing the human knower can do.[42] But Schelling goes much further than affirming with Jacobi the extra-mental reality of the revelation. The late Schelling held that revelation, received a posteriori, will become the foundation for a new mode of philosophy, positive philosophy, when its truths are appropriated by reason.

Readers of Meillassoux might well ask, with his argument that realism must be foregrounded in idealism or negative philosophy, how does the late Schelling avoid the charge of correlationism? Meillassoux defines correlationism as 'the idea according to which we only ever have access to the correlation between thinking and being, and never to either term considered apart from the other'.[43] Schelling would not agree that we never have access to being 'considered apart' from thinking, but neither would he presume to speak of being without considering how we access it. Schelling would not want to simply negate correlationism and take up an anti-correlationist stance, for he believes that the desired realism of being can only be accessed *through* thinking, but being is not therefore reducible to being that is thought. The whole problem, he would think, is, at least on Meillassoux's terms, deeply confused. No doubt, a being that is nothing other than a being-for-thinking is inadequate to the metaphysical demand (we want that which is 'above being', that is, that which is not merely correlative to being-for-thought); but, because we do not possess an infinite reason, the access point to the really real will always inevitably be through and by means of the ideal, which is not to say that what is thereby accessed is necessarily correlative to thinking. We access being neither a priori nor a posteriori but *per posterius*. Idealism renders access to being a priori and only ever knows being-for-thought. Empiricism renders access to being a posteriori and only ever knows being-for-sensation. Schelling's *per posterius* method ventures to think being-in-itself, sheer being, *das rein Daß*, actuality which is not preceded by potency (being that is not correlative to thought), but to do so it must deploy thinking, that is, it must deploy the *a priori*. But the being which Schelling thereby thinks is not correlative to thought. He knows it by means of the a posteriori and in correspondence to the a priori, but what he thereby knows is neither an experience nor a concept.

The failure of correlationism to reveal existence is positive philosophy's clue to the uncorrelated or unprethinkable origin of being. Neither the ideal nor the real can be revealed apart from the other: the reality of the real reveals itself in contrast to the ideal, and, conversely, the ideality of the ideal is revealed in the experience of the real. This humiliation of reason before the real, Schelling argues, has already occurred: it is nothing less than the history of religion, which is far more deeply entwined with Western rationality that most philosophers have recognised. Thus, in its final act, German idealism comes full circle and returns to the point of its inception, the notion of self-mediated reason, only to emphatically deny it. Reason does not mediate itself in the writings of late Schelling; rather, reason is mediated by history, which is never reducible to reason. The late Schelling sees the abyss of nihilism that history opens before the feet of reason, and he denies its ultimacy. Chaos is indeed older than order but not therefore the last word. The *Philosophy of Revelation* is in many ways a sustained argument for why it is better that there is something rather than nothing. Its starting point is the ecstatic recognition that *something* is, and it is not simply reason or thinking, but rather the non-rational condition of its possibility.

Notes

1. See Frederick C. Beiser, *German Idealism. The Struggle against Subjectivism, 1781–1801* (Cambridge, MA: Harvard University Press, 2002), which has become a standard

record-straightening account. Some of the material which appears in the first section of this chapter was first published in a different form as Sean J. McGrath, 'German idealism', in Paul Ennis and Peter Gratton (eds), *The Meillassoux Dictionary* (Edinburgh: Edinburgh University Press, 2014), pp. 80–2. The literature on Schelling is growing, but the late Schelling is still largely unknown in the English-speaking world. See Tyler Tritten, *Beyond Presence: The Late F. W. J. Schelling's Criticism of Metaphysics* (Boston: De Gruyter, 2012) and Sean J. McGrath, *The Ecstasy of Reason: The Philosophical Theology of the Late Schelling* (Edinburgh: Edinburgh University Press, forthcoming). On the beginnings of Schelling's late realism in the theory of the unconscious in his middle works, see Sean J. McGrath, *The Dark Ground of Spirit: Schelling and the Unconscious* (London: Routledge, 2012).

2. It is only matched by the history of British idealism (philosophy in Britain between 1870 and 1930). British idealism (F. H. Bradley, T. H. Green, B. Bosanquet, J. M. E. McTaggart, R. G. Collingwood) is even less known today and in serious need of re-examination, rife as it is with truly ingenious speculative and logical alternatives to the atomistic empiricism, logical positivism and analytical philosophy of language that buried it. On British idealism, see James Bradley, 'Hegel in Britain Part 1', *Heythrop Journal*, vol. 20, no. 1 (1979), pp. 1–24; 'Hegel in Britain Part II', *Heythrop Journal*, vol. 21, no. 2 (1979), pp. 163–88; Iain Hamilton Grant and Jeremy Dunham, *Idealism: A History* (London: Routledge, 2010); William J. Mander, *British Idealism: A History* (Oxford: Oxford University Press, 2011).

3. F. W. J. Schelling, 'Erlanger Vorträge', SW 9, pp. 207–52; 'Reden in den öffentlichen Sitzungen der Akademie der Wissenschaften in München', SW 10, pp. 377–507; *Grundlegung der positive Philosophie: Münchener Vorlesung WS 1832/33 und SS 1833*, ed. H. Fuhrmans (Turin: Bottega d'Erasmo, 1973). SW refers to the standard fourteen-volume edition of Schelling's *Sämtliche Werke*, ed. K. F. A. Schelling (Stuttgart: J. G. Cotta, 1856–61).

4. Note from Kierkegaard's journal, cited in Michelle Kosch, *Freedom and Reason in Kant, Schelling, and Kierkegaard* (Oxford: Oxford University Press, 2006), p. 105.

5. F. W. J. Schelling, *Urfassung der Philosophie der Offenbarung*, ed. Walter E. Ehrhardt (Frankfurt am Main: Meiner, 2010).

6. I have examined the relation of Schelling's early nature-philosophy to the positive philosophy in 'Is the late Schelling still doing nature-philosophy?', *Angelaki*, vol. 24, no. 4 (2016), pp. 121–41. The phrase 'the indivisible remainder' (*der nie aufgehende Rest*) is from Schelling's 1809 *Freedom* essay: F. W. J. Schelling, *Philosophical Inquiries into the Essence of Human Freedom*, trans. Jeff Love and Johannes Schmidt (Albany: State University of New York Press, 2006), p. 29. The expression 'unprethinkable being' (*unvordenkliches Sein*) is from the positive philosophy. See F. W. J. Schelling, *The Grounding of the Positive Philosophy: The Berlin Lectures*, trans. Bruce Matthews (Albany: State University of New York Press, 2008), pp. 178–9.

7. See Schelling, *Urfassung* and *Philosophie der Offenbarung 1841/42*, ed. Manfred Frank (Frankfurt am Main: Suhrkamp, 1977).

8. See F. W. J. Schelling, *Historical-critical Introduction to the Philosophy of Mythology*, trans. Mason Richey and Markus Zisselsberger (Albany: State University of New York Press, 2007).

9. See Schelling, 'Einleitung in die Philosophie der Mythologie (Darstellung der rein rationalen Philosophie)', in Karl Friedrich Anton Schelling (ed.), SW 11, pp. 253–572.

10. See F. W. J. Schelling, 'Vom Ich als Prinzip der Philosophie', SW 1, pp. 149–244, esp. p. 163: 'The last ground of all reality is namely a something which is only thinkable via itself, i.e., thinkable via its being, which is thought only in so far as it is, in short, that in which the principles of being and of thinking coincide.'

11. See Immanuel Kant, *The Critique of Pure Reason*, trans. Norman Kemp Smith (New York: Palgrave Macmillan, [1787] 2003), B xxvi; B34/A20.

12. Schelling, 'Von Ich', p. 84.

13. Karl Leonhard Reinhold, *Über das Fundament des philosophisches Wissen* (Hamburg: Meiner, [1791] 1978).
14. Schelling, 'Vom Ich'.
15. F. W. J. Schelling, *First Outline of a System of the Philosophy of Nature*, trans. Keith R. Peterson (Albany: State University of New York Press, [1799] 2004), pp. 13–19.
16. G. W. F. Hegel, *The Difference between Fichte and Schelling's System of Philosophy*, trans. H. S. Harris and Walter Cerf (Albany: State University of New York Press, [1801] 1988).
17. Ibid. p. 155.
18. See G. W. F. Hegel, *Hegel's Phenomenology of Spirit*, trans. A. V. Miller (Oxford University Press, [1807] 1977), pp. 7–9.
19. See Arsenij Gulyga, *Schelling: Leben und Werk* (Stuttgart: Deutsche Verlags-Anstalt, 1989), pp. 141–2.
20. F. W. J. Schelling, 'System of philosophy in general and of the philosophy of nature in particular', in Thomas Pfau (ed.), *Idealism and the Endgame of Theory: Three Essays by F. W. J. Schelling* (Albany: State University of New York Press, 1994), pp. 139–94.
21. This is the thesis of Schelling's 1804 short work, *Philosophie und Religion*, reprinted in SW6. A translation exists: F. W. J. Schelling, *Philosophy and Religion*, trans. Klaus Ottmann (Putnam, CO: Spring Publications, 2010).
22. F. W. J. Schelling, *On the History of Modern Philosophy*, trans. Andrew Bowie (Cambridge: Cambridge University Press, 1994), pp. 136–63; *Grounding*, pp. 129–33.
23. Schelling, *Grounding*, p. 181.
24. Ibid. p. 180.
25. See John Burbridge's account of Schelling's late method in his *Hegel on Logic and Religion: The Reasonableness of Christianity* (Albany: State University of New York Press, 1992), p. 66: 'The positive philosopher asks: Within experience itself does one encounter the features specified in reason's hypothesis? This is not strictly an argument a posteriori. One does not move from the particulars of experience to an inductive generalization. Schelling calls it a proof *per posterius*. The consequent of a hypothetical statement is experienced as true. A priori reasoning has already shown that one or other of two contraries is necessarily implied by the one condition that is in question. That condition had in fact been in doubt because both contraries could have been false. The fact that one has been experienced as true thus establishes the truth of that condition. "Through its results is the priori known." At each stage in the positive philosophy, then, the following logical pattern occurs. Two givens that have a definite logical order are acknowledged. The first principle plus whatever has already been derived from it *per posterius* has a logical priority; it is a possible condition. The task is to find a middle term which is both the immediate consequent of the condition and sufficiently determinate to entail a difference in the actual world. When that difference is found independently to hold true in the world, the truth of the middle term is confirmed, and it can then be added to the set of logically prior terms.'
26. Benedict de Spinoza, *The Correspondence of Spinoza*, ed. and trans. Abraham Wolf (London: George Allen & Unwin, 1966), letter L.
27. For a solid exposition of the potencies, see Tritten, *Beyond Presence*, pp. 91–136.
28. Schelling, *Grounding*, p. 94; *On the History*, p. 147.
29. See Axel Hutter, *Geschichtliche Vernunft: Die Weiterführung der Kantischen Vernunftkritik in der Spätphilosophie Schellings* (Frankfurt am Main: Suhrkamp, 1996).
30. Schelling, *Einleitung in die Philosophie der Mythologie*, p. 570.
31. Schelling, *Grounding*, pp. 178–9.
32. Tritten has therefore argued that contrary to Meillassoux's argument for the necessity of contingency, the late Schelling argues for the contingency of necessity. See Tyler Tritten, 'After contingency: toward the principle of sufficient reason as *post factum*', *Symposium*, vol. 19, no. 1 (2015), pp. 24–38.
33. Schelling, 'Reden', SW 10, p. 101.

34. Schelling, *Grounding*, p. 203n.
35. Schelling, *Grounding*, pp. 202–3.
36. Schelling, 'Reden', SW 10, p. 15.
37. Schelling, *Grounding*, p. 203.
38. See Emmanuel Levinas, *Of God Who Comes to Mind*, trans. Bettina Bergo (Stanford: Stanford University Press, 1998), p. 64: 'The placing in us of an unencompassable idea overturns this presence of self which is consciousness. . . . It is thus an idea signifying within a significance prior to presence, to all presence, prior to every origin in consciousness, and so an-archic, accessible only in its trace.' See also ibid. p. 66: 'The Infinite affects thought by simultaneously devastating it and calling it; through a "putting it in its place", the Infinite puts thought in place. It wakes thought up.'
39. Schelling, 'Reden', SW 10, p. 10.
40. Schelling, *Grounding*, p. 211.
41. See Schelling, *Historical-critical Introduction*, p. 110: 'The knowledge of the true God is with one single race, which has remained outside of the peoples. For humanity has not merely divided itself into peoples but rather into peoples and non-peoples, although admittedly, the latter are by no means completely what the still homogeneous humanity was – like when milk curdles, the non-curdling part is also no longer milk. Precisely this "not having partialized themselves" becomes for them a particularity, as the universal God to which they cling now indeed has become *their* god. . . . The true religion, as well as the revelation, thus will be found neither in humanity nor in a people but rather in a lineage that remained distant from the path of the peoples and believes itself still bound to the God of the primal time.'
42. Friedrich Heinrich Jacobi, 'On faith and knowledge in response to Schelling and Hegel' [1803], in Ernst Behler (ed.), *Philosophy of German Idealism* (New York: Continuum, 2002), pp. 142–57.
43. Quentin Meillassoux, *After Finitude: An Essay on the Necessity of Contingency*, trans. Ray Brassier (New York: Continuum, 2009), p. 5.

Chapter 3

Before Infinitude: A Levinasian Response to Meillassoux's Speculative Realism

Lee Braver

And so, once again, the real. Lacan might be on to something – it does always return, though, strangely, we never seem to be able to settle the matter. Never definitively achieved, never left behind – such is the reality of philosophers.

A number of years ago, a brash young philosopher wrote that the history of continental philosophy is largely a history of anti-realism.[1] Since its birth, this headstrong go-getter argued, continental philosophy has been working on and working out its Kantian heritage, in particular, the notion that our access to the world is always mediated, essentially oblique. This makes the notion of 'the world itself' rather problematic, for what can we say when we try to address it directly? What, after all, can we say about this 'it' itself if we are always limited to what we can say about it? That same year, another philosopher, in a far more concise (and far better-selling) work, wrote that twentieth-century philosophy has been dominated by what he called 'correlationism'.[2] This view holds that we can only think about being as it is thought about, that is, in correlation with consciousness or some variation thereof: Dasein, language, *Geist* and so on.

Now, if Derrida is right, any telling of the history of philosophy (indeed, any text at all, though we will stick with the weaker claim) can be read in multiple, often (always?) incompatible ways. If he is right,[3] this would mean not that these anti-realist or correlationist readings are wrong, but neither are they exclusively, definitively, exhaustively correct. Any telling of the history of philosophy will ignore undercurrents of alternate histories flowing through the same stream. In this case, it would mean that continental philosophy can also be told as largely a history of realism (and analytic philosophy as predominantly anti-realist, but that is a different project). I'd like to spend this paper doing a bit of fishing in one of these undercurrents, the undercurrent of continental realism.[4]

There is no question that the shadows of Kant and Hegel, idealists of one stripe or another, loom large over continental thinkers. But, of course, one of the ways to deal with an overwhelming influence is to fight it, and one of their greatest critics is Emmanuel Levinas. Levinas was, like Quentin Meillassoux, a committed enemy of correlationism, although he did not believe it to be confined to the twentieth century. No, for Levinas, correlationism defined philosophy through and through (aside from a very few exceptions, such as moments in Plato and Descartes). However, his analysis, and his critique, are quite different from Meillassoux's, and in this essay I want to set up a dialogue between these two great opponents of correlationism.

Meillassoux defines correlationism as the necessary connection between thought and reality, the idea that 'we only ever have access to the correlation between thinking and being, and never to either term considered apart from the other'.[5] Conceding the seductiveness of this idea,[6] he ultimately finds the notion tremendously limiting as it rules out all contact with a reality that exceeds our experience, thus deflating the very realness of reality. For Levinas, beginning as he did from phenomenology and, in a certain sense, never leaving it, this kind of correlation is inescapable. Although he never stops seeking the transcendent, Levinas does not think of it as something wholly outside our awareness, repeatedly insisting on 'the interdiction against seeking the beyond as a world behind our world',[7] rejecting 'the factitious transcendence of worlds behind the scenes'.[8] Meillassoux does not think of the Absolute this way either, conceiving of it instead as fundamentally independent of human awareness. Levinas, however, remains loyal to a version of Husserl's 'principle of all principles' that any evidence for claims must be brought to experience in *some* way just for us to speak and think about them.[9]

Meillassoux lays out two arguments against correlationism in *After Finitude*: a quick, easy one and a long, complex one. Here, I will focus on the former, the so-called, 'problem of ancestrality',[10] with a few passing remarks on the latter. Meillassoux's basic question concerns the time before humans were around, what he calls 'ancestral' reality. The problem follows from 'this simple observation: today's science formulates a certain number of ancestral statements bearing upon the age of the universe, the formation of stars, or the accretion of the earth',[11] which, he holds, cannot lie down peacefully with any form of idealism. Now, this issue has been raised before, for example, in the question about the age of the sun that A. J. Ayer purportedly put to Bataille and Merleau-Ponty in 1951 in a bar in Paris in a conversation that 'continued until three o'clock in the morning'.[12]

The standard correlationist response is that any 'before-us' must necessarily 'be-for-us'. All temporal measurements and relations employ concepts and ways of measuring that are always ours, bringing them within our ways of thinking, which they can never escape: these matters are, as Kant put it, transcendentally ideal. There is the sphere of human experience, outside of which ancestral time takes place, but this outside must in turn occupy a position inside a larger space of human time – not the time of actual human lives, but of human understanding. Were we not speaking of matters that we can in principle comprehend, we could not even make sense of claims that they transcend our comprehension. This move replaces all assertions concerning that which precedes us with an anti-realist, scare quote version of them: evolution happened 'before' humans, certainly, but in a before-us-for-us-and-so-in-a-more-sophisticated-sense-after-us. Given the way we think about time, date fossils and so forth, stars certainly existed long before any clearing of human awareness, but this entire process of establishing and understanding such claims takes place *within* a clearing, our present scientific one in particular. Thus, as Nelson Goodman and Heidegger (both early and late[13]) would have it, various things 'pre-existed' our version *within* our version, what Meillassoux calls '*a retrojection of the past on the basis of the present*'.[14] Talk about the child being father to the man! Ancestral time gets swallowed up within the larger context of temporal comprehension; as our progenitor, time remains within our family tree.

Meillassoux fully understands and appreciates the force of this response, what he calls 'the apparently unanswerable force of the correlationalist circle', yet he rejects it because – in the short argument – of 'its irremediable incompatibility with ancestrality (contrary to the correlationist)'.[15] Whereas the correlationist believes that she accommodates ancestral statements about reality before humans, and hence before the correlation between reality and thought was set, Meillassoux finds this highly tempting attempt a failure.

The correlationist resorts to fancy hermeneutic footwork to assimilate ancestral claims. Yes, she says, there was a sun before humans, but we must place scare quotes around that 'before' because even radical befores only occur contemporaneously with us; befores can only get a temporal foothold 'after' we come on the scene and establish them. Meillassoux finds it short work to point out that a before us that must occur after us is not a genuine before, so the correlationist has not preserved the scientist's ancestral claim but has distorted it, fatally compromised it, leaving out precisely that which makes it ancestral. In supposedly translating the scientist, the correlationist has left out her meaning, patronisingly telling us what she really meant, what she *must* have meant, what she could only have meant. This is, quite simply, a mistranslation:

> An ancestral statement only has sense if its literal sense is also its ultimate sense. If one divides the sense of the statement, if one invents for it a deeper sense conforming to the correlation but contrary to its realist sense, then far from deepening its sense, one has simply cancelled it. This is what we shall express in terms of the ancestral statement's *irremediable* realism: either this statement has a realist sense, and *only* a realist sense, or it has no sense at all.[16]

Despite protests that she fully respects science, the correlationist regresses into archaic ways of thinking: fideism, Ptolemaic astronomy, even fundamentalist creationism.

Now Levinas would agree that twentieth-century philosophy has been one of correlationism, but only because that is true of the entire history of philosophy.[17] The trend has, perhaps, accelerated since Descartes's epistemological turn to subjectivity, German idealism's emphasis on the subject's role in constituting reality, and phenomenology's refusal to speculate about reality as it falls outside the purview of our experience (do the brackets ever truly get removed?), but the basic idea goes back a bit further, to Plato and Plotinus. 'The Soul and, in our times, the incarnate Soul, man, are interpreted as unavoidable moments in the play of Being itself.'[18] Indeed, Levinas often uses the very term chosen by Meillassoux: 'as manifestation, consciousness of . . . can be expressed in terms of subjectivity as well as in terms of being; there is strict correlation here.'[19]

The reason correlationism can be found throughout philosophy is that it is embedded in 'the structure of all thought, which is correlation. . . . To appear, to seem, is forthwith to resemble terms of an already familiar order.'[20] Expressing the same appreciation of its force as Meillassoux, Levinas writes that 'idealism imposes itself like a tautology: what appears as being – appears, and consequently is found directly or indirectly within the limits of consciousness. What exceeds the limits of consciousness is absolutely nothing for that consciousness.'[21] It is the nature of thought and knowledge to bring about a particular kind of relationship between reality and thinking, which differs from the one that Meillassoux diagnoses. Levinas is worried about an experiential correlation, where the very notion of reality depends on coming into contact with our awareness, presumably thinking of comments such as these by Husserl:

> It must always be borne in mind here that *whatever physical things are* – the only physical things about which we can make statements, the only ones about the being or non-being, the being-thus or being-otherwise of which we can disagree and make rational decisions – *they are as experienceable physical things*. It is experience alone that prescribes their sense.[22]

Our very ability to determine what something is, or that it is, depends on our ability to experience it in some way, making it 'counter-sense' to claim that something that exceeds or precedes our experiential capacities is real. Not causally, but conceptually does reality depend on our bestowing the sense 'real' on to it. Having the meaning 'real' is, almost tautologically, what it means to be real, and meaning can only be given by the being who makes meaning – us. The title of the chapter from which Husserl's quote is taken is: 'The Natural World as a Correlate of Consciousness'.

Levinas began his career as a phenomenologist, studying with Husserl and Heidegger and writing some of the first works on both in French, and, while he certainly stretched and strained the school's precepts, he never abandoned them. Near the beginning of *Totality and Infinity*, he writes that 'the presentation and the development of the notions employed owe everything to the phenomenological method'.[23] And towards the end of his other great work, *Otherwise than Being*, he says that his 'analyses claim to be in the spirit of Husserlian philosophy. . . . Our presentation of notions . . . remains faithful to intentional analysis, insofar as it signifies the locating of notions in the horizon of their appearing.'[24] In particular, he sticks to the phenomenological commitment to find 'concrete' instantiations of abstract notions within actual experiences: 'This way of approaching an idea by asserting the concreteness of a situation in which it originally assumes meaning seems to me essential to phenomenology. It is presupposed in everything I have just said.'[25] For example, if we are to philosophise about God, as he does, it can only be of the 'God who comes to mind', in the words of the title of one of his books – the holy being as it enters the clearing – for otherwise how could we speak of such matters?[26] Here begins the theological turn in French phenomenology.

Thus, Levinas qualifies as a correlationist in Meillassoux's sense. His commitment to the spirit of phenomenology means that he will only philosophise about the world that we can have some experience of, for experiences are the only 'data' on which we can base analyses. Absent all awareness, we would not even know that there was something to talk about, much less what to say about it. But that does not mean that he was a faithful disciple. It seems a quasi-Hegelian law governing the history of ideas that those original thinkers who most want obedient followers attract strong thinkers who end up using the tools given them by their intellectual masters to slay them, a fate that befell Husserl repeatedly. As Derrida, one of Levinas's first and best readers, writes, Levinas uses phenomenology against itself[27] by finding something in experience that overturns or exceeds experience. This occurs above all in what Levinas calls 'experience preeminently',[28] 'experience par excellence'[29] and 'the great experience':[30] the experience of the face.

This particular concrete encounter is so central to his thought that Levinas often speaks of a phenomenology of the face somewhat the way

Husserl might consider 'phenomenology of consciousness' to be a pleonasm. This is the experience that alters the very notion of experience – along with concomitant concepts such as consciousness, intentionality, concepts. What makes this experience paradigmatic is that, in a certain sense, it is not an experience, at least not in any traditional sense, that is, not in any sense that still clings to making sense. Phenomenology claims that all experiences in principle must make some kind of sense since they appear within a horizon, that is, within a collection of concepts that fit it into an intelligible order, similar to how Newtonian physics and Euclidean geometry structure and limit the space of possible experience for Kant.

The encounter with the face is certainly an encounter with a phenomenon – it must appear to us in order for us to become aware of it, in order for it to make any impact upon us whatsoever ('for the Other cannot present himself as Other outside of my conscience'[31]) – but it is a phenomenon that subverts the structure of phenomenality. The face of the other, paradoxically, appears as not appearing,[32] as infinitely exceeding all appearances; she is not the aspects that manifest themselves, but neither is she some further being hiding behind a merely phenomenal façade. The experience of the other escapes, even violates, the concepts that phenomenology deems necessary for experience. We cannot make sense of the other because the sense of the other is to exceed all sense we make of her, making any sense we make of her a counter-sense, in Husserl's sense. Her sense is to be a counter-sense, which forms the very sense of ethics.

> Ethical language, which phenomenology resorts to in order to mark its own interruption . . . is the very meaning of approach, which contrasts with knowing. No language other than ethics could be equal to the paradox which phenomenological description enters when, starting with the disclosure, the appearing of a neighbour, it reads it in its trace, which . . . cannot be synchronised in representation.[33]

Whereas idealism, ontology and phenomenology all rest on a tautology, Levinasian ethics is constructed on a contradiction.

This experience overturns the fundamental structure that has governed the understanding of knowledge, truth, experience, being and other fundamental ideas for millennia. That nearly ubiquitous governing structure has been correlationist, but in a very different sense than Meillassoux's. Instead of viewing it as the bare connection between reality and our awareness that defines correlationism for Meillassoux – something that, as we have seen, Levinas, the heretical phenomenologist, still accepts – correlationism is for Levinas a more restrictive relationship. He argues that the West's relationship between thought and being imposes a homogeneity between the two. If we are to think and, even more, know being, then being must be thinkable and knowable – a simple tautology (in Meillassoux's formulation of what he calls the circle of correlation: 'if you think X, then you *think* X'[34]). This means that being must be digestible by our mental processes. The world has to fit into our thought-holes if we are to think it, and if the world does not, as is the case with Kant's things-in-themselves, then we either filter it out or force it in by shearing off all the knobbly noumenal bits that stick out.

> Generally speaking, truth means the adequation between representation and external reality. . . . The fact that being unveils itself, that it shines forth, that its being consists in being true, implies that the contours of being fit into the human scale and the measures of thought.[35]

On this model, being – the only being that we can say or think that it is – must be thinkable; it must match up with our capacity to think, or else we would not know that it was, even to declare it unthinkable. But that effects a massive reduction in what reality may be, for it is not allowed by us to exceed us. This ratchets up Kant's 'highest principle of all synthetic judgments . . . that the conditions of the *possibility of experience* in general are likewise conditions of the *possibility of the objects of experience*',[36] since his formulation still distinguishes the world-for-us from how it is in-itself, which behaves very differently. Hegel's version of Kant's highest principle removes this restriction: 'logic therefore coincides with Metaphysics'.[37] The world is as our minds are, for we cannot pull the two apart: the mind knows not the unminded world. We cannot, in John McDowell's image, see mind and world sideways-on to sift them out, but only frontways, inescapably viewing the world through our mental apparatus. This is why, for Heidegger, 'only as phenomenology, is ontology possible' because 'our investigation . . . asks about Being itself in so far as Being enters into the intelligibility of Dasein'.[38]

For Levinas, these more overt, sophisticated versions of idealism just spell out what was implicit in ontology and epistemology from the beginning (despite his admiration for early Heidegger, he ends up seeing him as extending the tradition rather than escaping or overthrowing it). As soon as the Greeks conceived of being and knowing in terms of light, presence and, yes, correlation, Western thought was set on its path; these recent systems represent merely accelerations, not a change in course. What Levinas wants is to find something that is correlated in the sense of being our experience, without being correlated in the sense of fitting into our ways of understanding, and he finds it in the experience of the face (along with God).

What we can now see is that correlation divides into two kinds. There is the weak kind that simply depends upon some form of awareness – let us call this kind correlation$_a$ – and the stronger, more restrictive kind consisting in knowing being, which we can call correlation$_k$. Now, Levinas's entire philosophical project is to find an experience, broadly conceived, that exceeds the bounds of knowledge, broadly conceived, and therefore does not have to be cut down to the scale of what we can comprehend. It must still be an experience, contra Meillassoux, because of his commitment to one of the fundamental intuitions informing phenomenology: we must be aware of something in order to talk about it at all. But his innovation is the claim that not everything that we can become aware of must play by the rules of understanding or intelligibility. In other words, Levinas bases his thought on a direct contradiction of Kant's highest principle of all synthetic judgements: the conditions of our faculties of processing experience do not determine the limits of all possible objects of experience. Impossible experiences, that is, experiences that violate and rupture our concepts, are possible: we can run across non-Euclidean shapes, non-Newtonian events. Indeed, we come across them every time we see another's face, every time we open the door for another, every time we say, 'Bonjour!', that is, in 'the extraordinary and everyday event' of encountering others.[39] These encounters, which he calls infinite because they cannot be contained, are paradigmatic experiences because they truly come to us from without; they come upon us by absolute surprise without the possibility of transcendental anticipation. 'The idea of infinity exceeds my powers (not quantitatively, but, we will see later, by calling them into question); it does not come from our a priori depths – it is consequently experience par excellence.'[40] To put this in my terms, we have an experience which is hence correlated$_a$, that breaks free of our comprehension, thus escaping correlation$_k$: 'The relationship with the Infinite then no longer has the structure of an intentional correlation.'[41] The former correlation is necessary; the latter limiting, distorting, like Procrustes' bed. An experience that threads the needle by satisfying the former while avoiding the latter overturns twenty-five centuries of ontological oppression and exclusion. 'Transcendence designates a relation with a reality infinitely distant from my own reality [that is, violating correlation$_k$ – LB], yet without this distance destroying this relation [that is, preserving correlation$_a$ – LB] and without this relation destroying this distance.'[42]

What is interesting about this conceptual formation is that it is the reverse image of Meillassoux's innovation, for he seeks something that satisfies correlation$_k$ while escaping the supposed need for correlation$_a$, that is, knowledge we can achieve that in no way depends upon the human capacity for awareness. Meillassoux finds this in the evidence for the 'ancestral', what he calls the 'arche-fossil': 'any reality anterior to the emergence of the human species'.[43] Since it wholly precedes awareness, ancestral reality can in no way, not even conceptually, depend upon awareness, thus escaping correlation$_a$. What breaks us out of correlation$_a$, then, for Meillassoux, is scientific knowledge of the arche-fossil. He insists on 'mathematical discourse['s ability] to describe a world where humanity is absent; a world crammed with things and events that are not the correlates of any manifestation; a world that is not the correlate of a relation to the world'.[44] Meillassoux's thought, in a certain sense, inverts Heidegger's: it is the search for our *not*-being-in-the-world, Dasein's authentically *not*-being-there. And it is mathematics, the paradigm of knowledge since Plato, that lets us peer over the horizon of our own clearing, enabling us to become aware of that which precedes all awareness. For Meillassoux, mathematical knowledge exceeds awareness: correlation$_k$ gets us out of correlation$_a$.

For Levinas, on the other hand, certain experiences – ethical experiences of the Other – exceed the possibilities of knowledge, reason, concepts: correlation$_a$ breaks us free of correlation$_k$. He's quite insistent on this contrast: 'what is produced here is not a reasoning, but the epiphany that occurs as a face.'[45] This is because Levinas sees an incompatibility between knowledge and otherness: to know something is to reduce it to our ways of knowing, a horizon of already present concepts, which removes whatever does not fit them: 'When the Other enters into the horizon of knowledge, it already renounces alterity. . . . It infinitely overflows the bounds of knowledge.'[46] Where Meillassoux's exteriority only finds expression in mathematical science,[47] Levinas's only comes out in ethics.

Meillassoux finds correlationism claustrophobic. For too long, it has forced us to study being only as it appears to us, ruling out anything else as conceptually incoherent. This creates

> a strange feeling of imprisonment. . . . If this outside seems to us to be a cloistered outside, an outside in which one may legitimately feel incarcerated, this is because in actuality such an outside is entirely relative, since it is – and this is precisely the point – relative to us. . . . In actuality, we do not transcend ourselves very much by plunging into such a world. . . . Contemporary philosophers have lost the *great outdoors*, the *absolute* outside of pre-critical thinkers: that outside which was not relative to us, and which was given as indifferent to its own givenness to be what it is, existing in itself regardless of whether we are thinking of it or not [correlation$_a$]; that outside which thought could explore with the legitimate feeling of being on foreign territory – of being entirely elsewhere.[48]

The external world of the correlationist$_a$ is not genuinely external, he says, but merely a projection we carry around with us which we can never escape, no more than you can see past the edge of your visual field by turning your head or get to the other side of the rainbow.

Levinas uses many of the same metaphors; one of his first works is titled 'On Escape' and the last chapter of *Otherwise Than Being* is called 'Outside'. He too spies a false opening actually keeping us locked within an interior: 'Focusing on being, [thought] is outside itself, but remains marvelously within itself, or returns to itself. The exteriority or otherness of the self is recaptured in immanence. . . . One learns only what one already knows.'[49] The difference is that what Meillassoux uses as the key to escape – knowledge – is precisely what Levinas casts as the bars keeping us in. One says that 'what is mathematizable cannot be reduced to a correlate of thought',[50] whereas the other claims that 'the alleged sovereignty of objectifying thought . . . in fact imprisons the thinker within himself and his categories'.[51] Levinas, too, seeks 'the experience of something absolutely foreign',[52] but he thinks that trying to escape the legacy of Kant's transcendentalism through mathematics and science, the very disciplines Kant's transcendentalism is built to protect and the forms of knowledge Kant hard-wired into the ways we become aware of anything, is exactly the wrong solution.[53] 'We are so habituated to the language of knowledge that we even state that which breaches presence in terms of knowledge.'[54] To quote Hume's dry critique of Descartes's appeal to the reality of God in order to legitimate our trust in our senses, such an argument is 'surely making a very unexpected circuit'.[55]

Knowledge is not the solution, for Levinas; it is the problem. It cannot get us outside of ourselves since it is the beating heart of our homogenising clearing, as Heidegger also argues: 'science always encounters only what its kind of representation has admitted beforehand as an object possible for science'.[56] In Levinas's words, for this way of thinking, 'an entity counts only on the basis of knowing'.[57] Meillassoux objects that, for the correlationist, 'to be is to be a correlate, a term of a correlation',[58] but Levinas would argue that he retains this formulation, merely changing the final term to 'mathematical', turning the correlation$_a$ into a correlation$_k$. Any prescription of what reality must be in order for it to be is an example of correlation$_k$, which does not get free of subjectivity's assimilation. The great outdoors Meillassoux plants his flag in, this 'absolute outside' is nothing of the kind, for it must speak the language of mathematics in order to be recognised as such. It still depends on recognition by our cognition, our bestowal of sense, just via mathematics.

Continental philosophers are not misologists or haters of science, as they are sometimes caricatured, but they do frequently express wariness of reason and science, a concern for what it leaves out and what it represses. One of the refreshing features of Meillassoux's work is the way he embraces them and warns of the dangers involved in their dismissal. Nevertheless, from a Levinasian perspective, this embrace compromises the very externality he seeks, since the outside must still conform to our mathematical and scientific expectations and requirements in order to count as outside. This sets ourselves up as the judges of externality, the Ptolemaic centres of the universe, which has the effect of domesticating any foreignness before one can even be established. In other words, correlation$_k$ stops the trip to the great outdoors before it can even begin.

Levinas and Meillassoux would both accuse the other of remaining within a hall of mirrors where one only sees reflections of oneself, employing criticisms that form mirror images of each other. Meillassoux would say that, since Levinas anchors his work on experience, no matter how broadly conceived, he never breaks free of the gravitational field of awareness, never reaches a true outside of human consciousness. Levinas would respond that Meillassoux tries to get out of human awareness by using a tool that actually extends humanity's touch as surely as Kant's transcendental ego phenomenologises all noumena that it encounters. This is 'because of the universality of knowledge ... and the impossibility for anything to be on the outside'.[59] Just as Meillassoux condemns what Levinas considers a necessary tool – experience – so Levinas proscribes Meillassoux's chosen instrument: 'knowledge never encounters anything truly other in the world. This is the profound truth of idealism.'[60] Precisely where Meillassoux finds the gift of realism, Levinas sees the poison of idealism, raising the same objection of the false outside:

> As knowledge, thought bears upon the thinkable called being; bearing upon being, it is outside of itself, to be sure, but remains, marvelously, in itself. The exteriority, alterity, or antiquity, of what is 'already there' in the known, is taken up again into immanence: the known is at once the other and the property of thought. Nothing pre-exists.[61]

This mention of the past brings the two thinkers into another interesting proximity, since it is ancestral reality, the time before humans were around and hence anterior to awareness, givenness, clearing and so on, that motivates Meillassoux's argument (the first, simple argument of *After Finitude*, as I specified above; I am not discussing here the second, complicated argument about the necessity of contingency). And yet Levinas seems to be brashly denying the past, just as Meillassoux predicts: any philosopher wedded to correlation$_a$ must deny the past, if she were being honest or, at any rate, literal. In fact, however, Levinas is not denying a deep past, but recasting it, as he did with experience.

Levinas's critique of knowledge as a way out (he is not rejecting knowledge wholesale, of course) is that it works by subsuming new facts or individual events under familiar, general concepts: 'The achievement of knowledge consists of grasping the object. Its strangeness is then conquered. Its newness, the opening up of its otherness, is reduced to the 'same', to what has already been seen, already known.'⁶² In his oft-repeated phrasing, it reduces the other to the same because we re-cognise old ideas in new phenomena: 'Oh, I see, that's just another one of that kind of thing.' Besides eliminating the unique features of each entity, which is 'violent' and unethical when done to people, it is a power play. We tame the threatening, unsettling wilderness of the unknown by setting ourselves up in intellectual control of the situation by comprehending it, encompassing it within our grasp. Understanding it, we stand over it, 'lords and masters' of the situation intellectually, even if it actually overpowers us:

> The detour of ideality leads to a coinciding with oneself, that is, to the certainty which remains the guide and guarantee of the whole spiritual adventure of Being. That is why the 'adventure' is not exactly an adventure. It is never dangerous. It is always a self-possession, sovereignty, *arche*. What arrives of the *unknown* is already disclosed, open, manifest, cast in the mold of the *known*, and can never come as a complete surprise.⁶³

Meillassoux's daring adventure into the great outdoors, for Levinas, is merely camping in his parents' backyard with all the comforts of home within arm's reach because he clings to the essentially familiar forms of mathematics and science as his guide. With their aid, Meillassoux retrojects his awareness into the ancestral past, *à la* Berkeley (a low blow, I realise), by following the trail of our re-cognisable notions of time and causality back into the past, an understandable anterior and so correlated$_k$ interior. His ancestral past is transparent to comprehension, thereby pushing the boundary of our clearing back to encompass it rather than getting clear of it.

The only way to get out of this homogenising power grasp of all experience is to dislocate the self at the centre of the web of knowledge, to introduce experiences or 'concepts' that undermine and disrupt the forms we use to structure a reassuring, stable system.

> Everything depends on the possibility of vibrating with a meaning that is not synchronised with the speech that captures it and cannot be fitted into its order; everything depends on the possibility of a signification that would signify in an irreducible disturbance . . . a time, a plot, and norms that are not reducible to the understanding of being.⁶⁴

One of these counter-concepts is, of course, the face: 'our relation with the other certainly consists in wanting to comprehend him, but this relation overflows comprehension . . . because in our relation with the other, he does not affect us in terms of a concept'.⁶⁵ Another is the infinite. Indeed, in an argument that parallels Meillassoux's complex argument, which turns our supposed ignorance of reality itself due to our finitude into a positive knowledge of its chaotic nature,⁶⁶ Levinas argues that 'what was taken as an imperfection of human knowledge measured by a certain ideal of self-evidence and certitude becomes a positive characteristic of the approach of a certain type of reality'.[67]

Time is another counter-concept. Meillassoux and Levinas are continental philosophers, so it was inevitable that the issue would come down to their conceptions of time, which, oddly enough, both call by the same name: diachrony (Meillassoux inserts a hyphen after 'dia'). Levinas creates an innovative account of time to accommodate the infinite experience of the other. Instead of its traditional definition of a series of now-points where the past is a moment that previously was a now but is presently gone and the future is a now that has not yet happened, Levinas speaks of a past that was never present, which he calls a trace, as well as a future that will never come (or that, as Derrida puts it, forever remains 'à venir', to come). Once again, he locates a phenomenological basis for this view in an experience: when the other looks at me, I find myself bound by a responsibility to her even though I never agreed to it, guilty before her even if I have not offended her. The moment of contracting responsibility for/to the other, like the social contract, never actually happened, yet we live in the wake of this non-event as we find ourselves bound to the other. The sin that makes us guilty before the other might never have happened but, like original sin, we are nevertheless tainted by it and responsible for it. We live forever in the after-effects of moments that never took place, after a before that never was but which makes the present what it is. The trace is a before-us that would not be-for-us.

Correlatively, there is a future that is not a present-that-will-arrive, but the time after my death which, like Heidegger's being-toward-death (in this sense, at least), retroactively infuses my present:

> The Future for which such an action acts must from the first be posited as indifferent to my death. As different from play and from computations is the Work being-for-beyond-my-death. . . . To envisage this triumph in a *time without me*, to aim at this world without me . . . to be *for* a time that would be without me, *for* a time after my time, over and beyond the famous 'being for death', is not an ordinary thought which is extrapolating my own duration; it is the passage to the time of the Other.[68]

This is the time of my child who both is and is not me, undermining identity. I will live through my child, loosening Heidegger's restrictive emphasis on *Jemeinigkeit* and the end of my projects in death, but of course it will not be me living that life. My identity, my investment, my selfhood, get spread out in a way that cannot be recovered and re-collected into a stable, substantial self.

Meillassoux's dia-chrony – the ancestral past and scientifically projected future after humans are gone, as well as the time after my own death – employs our familiar notions of time as one damn moment after another, merely extending them into the distant past or future. This is well past where we normally trace or project them but these very understandable concepts – one of the forms of intelligibility and mathematics for the original correlationist, Kant[69] – illuminate an intelligible path into this dimming gleam, letting us see past where we would normally see. Mathematics becomes a chronoscope, so to speak, extending our awareness instead of pushing past it. This approach obeys what Levinas calls 'ontological thought, where the eternal presence to oneself subtends even its absences in the form of a quest . . . always aris[ing] anew as the principle of what happens to it'.[70] To extend knowledge to the past is literally to re-present it: 'it would draw up the temporal disparity into a present, into a simultaneousness',[71] which means a homogenising correlation$_k$. Meillassoux seeks 'not the time of consciousness but the time of science';[72] Levinas does not recognise this distinction. Meillassoux believes 'that it is science which grants us access to a time that cannot be captured by any correlation',[73] but we can now see that it remains captured within correlation$_k$. Whereas Meillassoux thinks that the moral of the Galilean–Copernican–Cartesian revolution is that 'what is mathematizable cannot be reduced to a correlate of thought',[74] Levinas argues that

> whatever be the extension of my thoughts, limited by nothing, the Other cannot be contained by me: he is unthinkable – he is infinite and recognised as such. This recognition is not produced again as a thought, but is produced as morality.[75]

Levinas's diachrony unsettles the categories we make sense of the world with – before, after, self, other, free choice, external imposition – in a slightly similar way to some French readings of Nietzsche's eternal recurrence. Instead of re-establishing our intellectual control over even that which precedes and exceeds us, the trace unravels our powers, showing us the inescapable heteronomy lurking beneath all autonomy. Interestingly, given Meillassoux's disdain of fideism and in particular of creationism,[76] Levinas contrasts continuous, intellectually recuperable time with 'creation *ex nihilo*'. Not that he believes in its literal truth, which he dismisses as myth or superstition; rather, absolute creation serves as an analogy of 'a passivity that does not revert into an assumption'.[77] A being created out of nothing could not have been there to play any role in, nor to have conceptual categories to anticipate and make sense of, such an event, inabilities that mark all of the paradigmatic experiences.

> Thus Levinas insists on correlation$_a$, but as a way to resist correlation$_k$: The Infinite does not enter into a theme like a being to be given in it [correlation$_k$], and thus belie its beyond being. Its transcendence, an exteriority,

more exterior, more other than any exteriority of being, does not come to pass save through the subject that confesses or contests it [correlation$_a$].[78]

Correlational transgressions only happen in the correlation, but they do not remain within it, similar to Meillassoux's argumentative strategy: 'it's always from the inside that I try to defeat the correlationist'.[79] Experiences of the Infinite overpower our attempts to comprehend, 'thus undoing all the structures of correlation',[80] that is, of correlation$_k$, which inevitably enforces idealism and compromises realism. 'The idea of being does not therefore suffice to sustain the claim of realism, if realism is equivalent to affirming an alterity outside the Same. Only the idea of the infinite renders realism possible.'[81] Such encounters do not confirm the structures of knowledge I already possess, but rather unsettle my self. This is how Levinas gets what Meillassoux wants: 'to achieve what modern philosophy has been telling us for the past two centuries is impossibility itself: *to get out of ourselves*'[82] – by cracking open the self's filtering concepts to allow in the unthinkable, the genuinely other, the real. 'For the claim of realism – the recognition of another than I – to be possible, it is necessary that I myself am not originally what I remain even in my explorations of the obscure or the unknown.'[83]

The other than I is not bound by the forms with which I render the world intelligible; it is what confounds them. That is what makes it other; that is how I know it is real and not merely my projection. Knowing the other, on the other hand, compromises her otherness.

> Being is immanent in thought and thought does not transcend itself in knowledge. ... The transcendent or the absolute, claiming, as it does, to be unaffected by any relation, can in fact bear no transcendental sense without immediately losing it: the very fact of its presence to knowledge signifies the loss of transcendence and of absoluteness. ... Intentionality signifies an exteriority in immanence and the immanence of all exteriority.[84]

Whereas Meillassoux pursues reality in independence from thought, Levinas finds it in violations of thought; Meillassoux prizes indifference whereas Levinas looks for disobedience. Whereas Meillassoux wants 'to think a world without thought – a world without the givenness of the world',[85] Levinas seeks 'a thought destined to think more than it thinks' because 'the paradoxical, formal feature of this idea [of infinity], contain[s] more than its capacity and ... break[s] ... the noetico-noematic correlation'.[86] Levinas believes that we break free of correlation 'only if thought finds itself *faced* with an other refractory to categories'[87] because such an experience '*infinitely* overflows the bounds of knowledge'.[88] It is only 'an irreducible otherness [that] is strong enough to "resist" this synchronization of the noetico-noematic correlation'.[89] When found, 'correlation is broken'.[90]

One reason for Meillassoux's reliance on mathematics and science is his need to give content to the Absolute, that is, reality uncorrelated$_a$.[91] He argues that the correlationist is forbidden from discussing what the world might be like outside of our thought of it, except for the basic claim that it could be radically different.[92] 'If I don't have a rational procedure to discover specific properties of the Real, those properties threaten to be arbitrarily posited.'[93] As we have seen, Levinas thinks that no 'rational procedure' can encounter the Real as what is other to reason since it inevitably sifts what it finds through a homogenising rationality, just as Kant's transcendental ego cannot but find a spatial, temporal, causal world. But the strategy I have explained gives Levinas a rejoinder to Meillassoux's worry here. Because Levinas grounds his thought in a heretical form of phenomenology, basing his views on experiences of concrete encounters, his analyses of the face are rigorous and non-arbitrary, even though they contravene our ways of making things intelligible. Indeed, his claim would be that he is being far truer to the spirit of phenomenology than Husserl since the things themselves are no longer restricted to human intelligibility. Whereas Meillassoux comes up with what he calls figures of contingency or factuality,[94] that is, aspects of absolute reality that we can derive from the fact that only contingency is necessary (the fundamental conclusion of his complex argument), Levinas is able to determine a number of features about the other from our encounters with her: our relation with her is asymmetrical, the other places unsatisfiable ethical demands on us, she possesses inexhaustible, incomprehensible depth, and so on. It is his preservation of correlation$_a$, that is, his reliance on experience, that avoids the mystical hand-waving about true reality that for Meillassoux amounts to fideism and results in arbitrary characterisations.

In fact, I would argue that Levinas is actually in a stronger position than Meillassoux. The latter says that

> it is because I can conceive the non-being of the correlation [which the correlationist is forced to admit in order to avoid full-blown idealism, even though her whole thought prevents her from truly thinking it – LB] that I can conceive the possibility of an in-itself essentially different from the world as correlated to human subjectivity.[95]

As we have seen, Levinas would argue that this uncorrelated$_a$ world remains correlated$_k$ to human subjectivity through Meillassoux's use of mathematics to map it, thus never actually getting free of human entanglement. His in-itself is not 'essentially different from the world as correlated to human subjectivity' since it remains correlated to mathematics. Levinas's thought, on the other hand, avoids the arbitrariness Meillassoux criticises in other correlationist philosophies while establishing the actuality, not just the possibility, that reality is essentially different from the one we think. He achieves both by grounding his thought in experiences, that is, by preserving Meillassoux's mortal enemy, correlation$_a$, and showing how it reaches a truly other reality, a reality we do not return to in familiar recognition, but rather discover in the wondrous awe before incomprehensible infinitude.

Notes

1. Lee Braver, *A Thing of This World: A History of Continental Anti-Realism* (Evanston: Northwestern University Press, 2007).
2. Quentin Meillassoux, *After Finitude: An Essay on the Necessity of Contingency*, trans. Ray Brassier (London: Continuum, 2007).
3. If Derrida is right, one might be able to read Derrida's own works this way as well, such that they are claiming that all works, including his own, can only be read as making a single, univocal claim, but I am not clever enough to pull off that antideconstructive deconstruction.
4. I have been exploring this undercurrent in other recent works. See Lee Braver, 'A brief history of continental realism', *Continental Philosophy Review*, vol. 45, no. 2 (2012): pp. 261–89; 'On not settling the question of realism', *Speculations IV*, 2013, <http://www.speculations-journal.org/storage/Braver_OnNotSettling_Speculations_IV.pdf>; 'Transgressive realism in art', *Methode*, vol. 4, no. 5 (2015): pp. 18–29, <http://www.methode.unito.it/methOJS/index.php/meth/article/view/144>; 'Thoughts on the unthinkable', *Parrhesia: A Journal of Critical Philosophy*, vol. 24 (2015): pp. 1–16, <http://www.parrhesiajournal.org/parrhesia24/parrhesia24_braver.pdf>.
5. Meillassoux, *After Finitude*, p. 5.
6. Ray Brassier, Iain Hamilton Grant, Graham Harman and Quentin Meillassoux, 'Speculative realism', *Collapse III* (2007): pp. 306–449, here p. 409. See also Graham Harman, *Quentin Meillassoux: Philosophy in the Making* (Edinburgh: Edinburgh University Press, 2011), pp. 3, 9, 55, 164.
7. Emmanuel Levinas, *Basic Philosophical Writings*, ed. Adriaan T. Peperzak, Simon Critchley and Robert Bernasconi (Bloomington: Indiana University Press, 1996), p. 60.
8. Emmanuel Levinas, *Otherwise Than Being, or Beyond Essence*, trans. Alphonso Lingis (Pittsburgh: Duquesne University Press, 1981), p. 4.
9. Edmund Husserl, *Ideas Pertaining to a Pure Phenomenology and to a Phenomenological Philosophy: First Book*, trans. F. Kersten (Boston: Kluwer Academic, [1913] 1982), §24.
10. Meillassoux, *After Finitude*, p. 26.
11. Ibid. p. 10.
12. Andreas Vrahimis, *Encounters between Analytic and Continental Philosophy* (Palgrave MacMillan, 2013), p. 87.
13. In my view, Heidegger continues to hold this view throughout his writings. See Braver, *A Thing of this World*, ch. 6.
14. Meillassoux, *After Finitude*, p. 16.
15. Ibid. p. 27.
16. Ibid. p. 17. One wonders what Derrida would have made of Meillassoux's repeated insistence on literal meaning, which is also at the heart of his more complicated argument (see, for instance, Brassier et al., 'Speculative realism', pp. 436–7; Meillassoux,

After Finitude, pp. 51, 121), especially in a text that employs so many metaphors (ancestral, the great outdoors, etc.). A related objection could be raised concerning Meillassoux's embrace of radical contingency, according to which the laws of nature have 'no reason, because they are *not* necessary' (Brassier et al., 'Speculative realism', p. 441). This hardly strikes me as what most scientists mean when they speak of physical laws, despite the fact that just such a violation of the literal meaning of scientific proclamations, of 'the scientist's own conception of her discipline', is the heart of his first argument against correlationism (Meillassoux, *After Finitude*, p. 13; see also ibid. p. 28; Brassier et al., 'Speculative realism', pp. 329, 439). Meillassoux very briefly addresses this point at Harman, *Meillassoux*, p. 172.

17. Levinas, *Otherwise Than Being*, p. 132: 'Phenomenality, the exhibition of being's essence in truth, is a permanent presupposition of the philosophical tradition of the West. Being's *esse*, through which an entity is an entity, is a matter of thought, gives something to thought, stands from the first in the open. . . . [Being] has recourse to a receptivity necessary to its sort of life, if we can put it that way.'
18. Levinas, *Basic Philosophical Writings*, p. 13. See also *Otherwise Than Being*, p. 131: 'That one could think being means, indeed, that the appearing of being belongs to its very movement of being, that its phenomenality is essential, and that being cannot do without consciousness, to which manifestation is made.' See further *Basic Philosophical Writings*, pp. 4–5; *Otherwise Than Being*, pp. 17, 28, 61, 103, 179; *Discovering Existence with Husserl*, trans. Richard A. Cohen and Michael B. Smith (Evanston: Northwestern University Press, 1998), p. 113.
19. Levinas, *Otherwise Than Being*, p. 71.
20. Levinas, *Basic Philosophical Writings*, p. 67.
21. Levinas, *Discovering Existence with Husserl*, p. 127. Compare with Kant: 'that x (the object) which corresponds to [the manifold of representations] is nothing to us – being, as it is, something that has to be distinct from all our representations' (Immanuel Kant, *Critique of Pure Reason*, trans. Norman Kemp Smith (New York: St. Martin's, [1781] 1965), A105). And with Hegel: 'what is not present for consciousness as something existing in its own right, i.e. what does not appear, is for consciousness nothing at all' (G. W. F. Hegel, *Phenomenology of Spirit*, trans. A. V. Miller (New York: Oxford University Press, [1807] 1977), p. 151/§249).
22. Husserl, *Ideas I*, §47, p. 106.
23. Emmanuel Levinas, *Totality and Infinity*, trans. Alphonso Lingis (Pittsburgh: Duquesne University Press, 1969), p. 28. See also Emmanuel Levinas, *Entre Nous: Thinking-of-the-Other*, trans. Michael B. Smith and Barbara Harshav (New York: Columbia University Press, 1998), p. 197.
24. Levinas, *Otherwise Than Being*, p. 183.
25. Levinas, *Entre Nous*, p. 227; see also Emmanuel Levinas, *Of God Who Comes to Mind*, trans. Bettina Bergo (Stanford: Stanford University Press, 1998), p. xiv.
26. Levinas, *Otherwise Than Being*, pp. 44–5, 68, 156; see also *Totality and Infinity*, p. 78; *Basic Philosophical Writings*, pp. 25, 29; Emmanuel Levinas, *Is It Righteous to Be? Interviews with Emmanuel Levinas*, ed. Jill Robbins (Stanford: Stanford University Press, 2001), pp. 222, 236. In his long-awaited book *The Divine Inexistence*, Meillassoux writes of a God who may come someday. Harman, *Meillassoux*, ch. 3, Appendix.
27. Jacques Derrida, *Writing and Difference*, trans. Alan Bass (Chicago: University of Chicago Press, 1978), pp. 118, 133, 141, 312 n. 14. See also Braver, *A Thing of This World*, pp. 281–2 n. 100. Levinas, *Is It Righteous to Be?*, p. 271: 'I almost always begin with Husserl or in Husserl, but what I say is no longer in Husserl.'
28. Levinas, *Totality and Infinity*, p. 109.
29. Ibid. p. 196.
30. Levinas, *Is It Righteous to Be?*, p. 234.
31. Levinas, *Totality and Infinity*, p. 232; see also p. 26. Note that the French word

'conscience' means both conscience and consciousness, an interesting ambiguity for Levinas's thought since he believes that consciousness emerges from conscience.
32. There are considerable similarities here with Heidegger's notions of appearing as withdrawing. See Lee Braver, *Heidegger: Thinking of Being* (Cambridge: Polity Press, 2014); *Heidegger's Later Writings: A Reader's Guide* (London: Bloomsbury Books, 2009).
33. Levinas, *Otherwise Than Being*, p. 193 n. 35.
34. Brassier et al., 'Speculative realism', p. 413.
35. Levinas, *Basic Philosophical Writings*, p. 13; see also ibid. pp. 36, 67, 74, 99, 154; *Entre Nous*, pp. 69, 126, 200.
36. Kant, *Critique of Pure Reason*, A158/B197.
37. G. F. W. Hegel, *Hegel's Logic*, trans. William Wallace (Oxford: Clarendon Press, [1830] 1975), p. 36/§24.
38. Martin Heidegger, *Being and Time*, trans. John Macquarrie and Edward Robinson (Oxford: Blackwell, 1962), H. 35, 152.
39. Levinas, *Basic Philosophical Writings*, p. 117; see also *Otherwise Than Being*, p. 141. Here we can see the importance of Kant's ethics, where each act of goodness exempts us from the phenomenal, deterministic order of self-interested inclinations. One way to look at Levinas's work is that he transposes this ethical violation into the broader order of phenomena, though still for ethical purposes.
40. Levinas, *Totality and Infinity*, p. 196.
41. Levinas, *Basic Philosophical Writings*, p. 77.
42. Levinas, *Totality and Infinity*, p. 41; see also ibid. p. 80; *Basic Philosophical Writings*, pp. 19, 55.
43. Meillassoux, *After Finitude*, p. 10.
44. Ibid. p. 26.
45. Levinas, *Totality and Infinity*, p. 196.
46. Levinas, *Basic Philosophical Writings*, p. 12.
47. Meillassoux, *After Finitude*, pp. 11, 26, 113, 117, 131 n. 12; see also Harman, *Meillassoux*, p. 53.
48. Meillassoux, *After Finitude*, p. 7. Compare Levinas's description of the face: 'its wonder is due to the *elsewhere* from which it comes and into which it already withdraws' (*Basic Philosophical Writings*, p. 60).
49. Levinas, *Entre Nous*, p. 125; see also Emmanuel Levinas, *The Theory of Intuition in Husserl's Phenomenology*, 2nd edn, trans. Andre Orianne (Evanston: Northwestern University Press, 1995), pp. 43, 88, 125, 150.
50. Meillassoux, *After Finitude*, p. 117.
51. Emmanuel Levinas, *Time and the Other*, trans. Richard A. Cohen (Pittsburgh: Duquesne University Press, 1987), p. 65. For Husserl, standing in for the entire tradition, 'there exists no knowing but of oneself. . . . Nothing can enter it, everything comes from it. . . . In its inner recesses, the subject can account for the universe. . . . The subject's coexistence with something other, before being a commerce, is a relation of intellection' (Levinas, *Discovering Existence with Husserl*, p. 82; see also pp. 85, 129).
52. Levinas, *Totality and Infinity*, p. 73; see also *Entre Nous*, p. 69.
53. Meillassoux very briefly and, by his own admission, inadequately addresses this point at Harman, *Meillassoux*, pp. 167–8.
54. Levinas, *Is It Righteous to Be?*, p. 269.
55. David Hume, *Enquiries*, 3rd edn, ed. P. H. Nidditch (Oxford: Clarendon Press, [1748–51] 1975), p. 153.
56. Martin Heidegger, *Poetry, Language, Thought*, trans. Albert Hofstadter (New York: Harper & Row, 1971), p. 170.
57. Levinas, *Otherwise Than Being*, p. 80.
58. Brassier et al., 'Speculative realism', p. 409; see also Meillassoux, *After Finitude*, p. 28.
59. Levinas, *Time and the Other*, p. 65.

60. Ibid. p. 68. Compare with Hegel, who describes 'an otherness which is superseded in the act of grasping it', which means that 'otherness as an *intrinsic being* vanishes' (Hegel, *Phenomenology*, pp. 143/§237, 140/§233).
61. Levinas, *Time and the Other*, p. 125.
62. Levinas, *Is It Righteous to Be?*, p. 191.
63. Levinas, *Basic Philosophical Writings*, p. 80; see also *Otherwise Than Being*, p. 99.
64. Levinas, *Basic Philosophical Writings*, pp. 67–8.
65. Ibid. p. 6.
66. Brassier et al., 'Speculative realism', pp. 433, 445–6; see also Meillassoux, *After Finitude*, p. 82.
67. Levinas, *Discovering Existence with Husserl*, p. 68; see also pp. 93–4; *Is It Righteous to Be?*, p. 252; *Basic Philosophical Writings*, pp. 14, 26; *Entre Nous*, p. 71. Levinas, *Of God Who Comes to Mind*, p. 65: 'The not-able-to-comprehend-the-Infinite-by-thought is, in some way, a positive relation with this thought.' Interestingly, a Cantorian, non-delimitable infinity plays an important role in Meillassoux's complex argument.
68. Levinas, *Basic Philosophical Writings*, p. 50. Meillassoux also directs his thoughts about time after one's own death against Heidegger's analysis: 'death cannot fight Heidegger because death is a correlate of being-in-the-world and *Dasein*. So there is no being-toward-death, because if you want being-toward-death you have to conceive an event able to survive you. You have to conceive a time able to survive you' (Brassier et al., 'Speculative realism', p. 437).
69. Brassier et al., 'Speculative realism', p. 439.
70. Levinas, *Otherwise Than Being*, p. 113.
71. Ibid. p. 133; see also p. 165.
72. Meillassoux, *After Finitude*, p. 21.
73. Ibid. p. 131 n. 12.
74. Ibid. p. 117.
75. Levinas, *Totality and Infinity*, p. 230.
76. Meillassoux, *After Finitude*, p. 18.
77. Levinas's thought here resembles Meillassoux's analyses of what he calls advents: events of absolute novelty being introduced into the universe, such as matter, life, thought and (perhaps) justice. See Harman, *Meillassoux*, ch. 3, Appendix. His thoughts on a divine justice to come are what lead him to make the astonishingly Levinasian claim that, 'the essential stakes of both Eastern and Western thought consists entirely in a single question: how can we think the unity of Jewish religion and Greek reason' (quoted in Harman, *Meillassoux*, p. 228), though I don't see how this is of particular importance to Eastern thought.
78. Levinas, *Otherwise Than Being*, p. 156.
79. Brassier et al., 'Speculative realism', p. 439; see also pp. 426, 436; Harman, *Meillassoux*, pp. 6, 9.
80. Levinas, *Otherwise Than Being*, p. 148.
81. Levinas, *Basic Philosophical Writings*, p. 21.
82. Meillassoux, *After Finitude*, p. 27.
83. Levinas, *Basic Philosophical Writings*, p. 15.
84. Emmanuel Levinas, 'Beyond intentionality', in Alan Montefiore (ed.), *Philosophy in France Today* (Cambridge: Cambridge University Press, 1983), p. 106.
85. Meillassoux, *After Finitude*, p. 28.
86. Levinas, *Of God Who Comes to Mind*, pp. 67, 184 n. 4; see also pp. 70, 151; *Basic Philosophical Writings*, pp. 76, 155.
87. Levinas, *Totality and Infinity*, p. 40.
88. Levinas, *Basic Philosophical Writings*, p. 12.
89. Levinas, 'Beyond intentionality', p. 108.
90. Levinas, *Basic Philosophical Writings*, p. 77.
91. Brassier et al., 'Speculative realism', p. 440.

92. This is the absolute contingency that even the correlationist must admit, which forms the basis for Meillassoux's complex argument.
93. Brassier et al., 'Speculative realism', p. 435; see also Meillassoux, *After Finitude*, pp. 44–6.
94. Meillassoux, *After Finitude*, pp. 80–1; see also Brassier et al., 'Speculative realism', p. 435.
95. Brassier et al., 'Speculative realism', p. 431.

Part II
Convergences and Correctives

Chapter 4

Kantian Realisms: The Noumenal, Causation and Grounding

Alison Assiter

When one gets beyond a certain 'age' in academic life, one comes to see that the intellectual world, no less than clothing, art or music, is subject to fashion. These 'fashions' may have some sort of extra theoretical 'ground', to use a contemporary term, unlike, for example, that for punk or for beards, but there are nonetheless parallels with these. One fashion that is current at the moment, in certain philosophical circles, is a predilection for a certain type of materialism or realism as well as a return to ontology and metaphysics following a decline in interest in these domains in the mid-twentieth century. The 1930s verificationists, to take the most outrageous example of the contrary view, had proclaimed for a number of years that metaphysical claims constituted literal nonsense. As someone who was a die-hard realist when a non-realist form of postmodernism was all the rage, I welcome this recent move. However, in this chapter, I would like to offer a certain redress, a move back to the epistemic, not in order to deny this realism, but in order to suggest that reading Kant through Lacan or through the lens of Laruelle or Meillassoux or indeed through the lens of a certain form of critical realism, may fail to do justice to a crucial dimension of his thought. It may be, indeed, that the recent debates about Kant's work are themselves filtered through discussions that were taking place in the work of the post-Kantian German idealists who read his thought as leading to scepticism.[1] Indeed, I will suggest that one can find a strong realist argument in Kant's *Critique of Pure Reason*.

In the first section of the chapter, I will respond to a variant of a certain type of realist critique of Kant. I will also suggest, more controversially, that, if one takes seriously Kant's notion of 'spontaneous causation', it may be possible to offer a Kantian defence of the 'grounding' of the phenomenal in the noumenal. This notion of 'grounding' is important for a number of reasons, one of which is that it can allow for a change in the terms of reference of certain debates on freedom of the will. Although this chapter will not spell out the arguments for the latter view, I will lay out in the final paragraphs how the latter argument might be developed. The second section of the chapter will be a discussion of Bhaskar's 'transcendental realism' versus Kant's 'transcendental idealism'. I will suggest that although Bhaskar's arguments are not as strong as Kant's, they can indeed be developed into a robust defence of realism.

Some recent defences of realism

Despite their differences, there is some commonality between Meillassoux's search for the 'great outdoors' and Bhaskar's defence of the 'transcendentally real'. Each of them opposes something Meillassoux labels Kant's 'correlationism' and Bhaskar his 'empirical realism'. Meillassoux has claimed, in a vivid phrase, that much of 'pre-meta-physical' contemporary philosophy – by which he means phenomenology and 'various currents of analytic philosophy'[2] – has lost 'the *great outdoors*, the *absolute* outside'.[3] This metaphor, for him, conveys the idea of an 'outside' that is not relative to human beings, a domain of reality that exists in itself whether or not we are thinking it. By 'correlationism', then, Meillassoux refers to the view that the only reality that exists is one that is, in some sense, a construction of the subject. He writes: 'By "correlation" we mean the idea according to which we only ever have access to the correlation between thinking and being, and never to either term considered apart from the other.'[4] For Meillassoux, Kant is the paradigmatic proponent of this view, and Bhaskar expresses a similar concern. 'Empirical realism', which includes the philosophy of Kant, inappropriately denies, according to Bhaskar, the existence of the 'real' world of rocks, stars and tides.[5] According to Bhaskar, empirical realism thus also denies the existence of some form of the 'great outdoors', and, in contrast to it, Bhaskar labels his own position 'critical realism'.

For both Bhaskar and Meillassoux, then, the Kantian view that the world is derived from the forms of space and time as well as the concepts that we, as finite beings, deploy to 'create' appearances renders natural objects like stones incapable of an existence independent from the creative powers of such limited beings as ourselves. By contrast to this Kantian 'correlationist' perspective, the recent realists seek to defend a conception of Being, or the Absolute or Nature, that exists whether or not there are any beings like us to experience 'it'. Described in this way, their attempts invite the retort: is this not exactly Kant's noumenal world? The contemporary realists, however, argue that the noumenal is like having your cake and simultaneously eating it: Kant's noumenal, they contend, is both required for experience to be possible and such that we are unable to say anything about what it is. We experience the world through the spectacles of space and time. The noumenal is supposed to be outside these and yet it is also expected to play the role of grounding experience. They would argue that the faculty of sensibility, for Kant in the Transcendental Aesthetic, 'receives' representations and these must emanate from the noumenal, yet the noumenal is constructed in such a way that it cannot itself cause anything to happen. The noumenal cannot fulfil this function when it is outside the conditions – the principle of causation, for example – that are required for this 'grounding' to make sense.[6]

At this point, I would like to defend what I will characterise as the 'epistemic' Kant against these recent views that see him as falling prey to this objection. For a statement of the position I will critique, I would like to take as my point of departure the work of two recent scholars – one an interesting presentation and paper by Kirril Chepurin,[7] and the other a paper and an excellent book by Dustin McWherter.[8] The two writers approach Kant from different perspectives, but they have in common a particular view of his philosophy. Both Chepurin and McWherter defend a view of Kant that runs a little like the above characterisation: Kant, they claim, both requires the 'noumenal', which, in their eyes, is equated with the 'real', and simultaneously denies that this 'reality' exists in the form in which it is required. To quote from Chepurin: 'German idealism has an excessive Utopian structure and Utopian core, and it is this Utopian structure that first makes it "idealist" . . . or makes it into a non-realism.'[9] Also, Chepurin writes:

> Idealism, I will argue, is a non-realism insofar as, in its Kantian origin which then mutates in post-Kantian German Idealism, it 'suspends' the real and proceeds from *not relating* to the real, from denying its own emergence from the real (from the environment, from nature, from the in-itself). Idealism, then, of which Kant's transcendental idealism is the original example, is indifferent to its emergence from the real.[10]

Chepurin, quoting Kant, writes that, for the latter: 'if one does not assume this kind of ideality of time and space [the realm of appearance as the ideal], nothing else remains except *Spinozism*, in which space and time are essential definitions of the first being [*Urwesen*, God] itself'.[11] Kant, then, gestures towards the in-itself being the 'ground' (A380) and 'cause' (B567) of appearance, while refusing to explain that further. To attempt to paraphrase Chepurin, his claim seems to be that Kant both requires a strong version of realism and is unable to provide it, since the way in which he characterises the noumenal prevents it from functioning as the causal ground of appearances. In effect, Kant's position involves a 'suspension' of what Chepurin labels Kant's conception of the 'real'.

McWherter, in turn, while offering a range of interesting arguments about the ontological status of Kant's various claims, also makes reference to the above assertion. He writes, after arguing that Kant attempts to 'circumvent ontology with epistemology' and that the non-ontological status of appearances can only be secured if ontological status is located elsewhere:

> However, as transcendental idealism's earliest critics famously protested, it is exactly this location of an 'elsewhere' in things-in-themselves that Kant deprives himself of the right to identify in virtue of his restriction of the objective validity of the categories to appearances. For example, claiming that things in themselves actually exist uses the category of existence beyond its domain of legitimate application.[12]

I would like to pose a question about this: why should we equate the noumenal with the real? One reason that might be offered for equating the two is that Kant labels the world we know, the world of material objects in space and time, the world of 'appearance'. Presumably, there would have to be some separate world – the world of 'things-in-themselves' – that would ground this domain of 'appearance'. But this latter world, to reiterate, fails to meet the criteria it would have to meet in order to fulfil its role of grounding the former since it is unknowable, outside of space and time, and beyond the reach of the principle of causation.

However, another reading of Kant suggests that the noumenal world is not the 'real' world. Kant contrasts his own transcendental idealism – an idealism about whether or not the world we know is the only possible way of knowing – with the realism of some of his predecessors. For Leibniz, for example, the world we know is equated with the 'real' world, but Kant imagines the possibility of beings who might see the world differently from us. Such beings would inhabit some possible world, but claims about the actual world we live in are different. It is very important for Kant that we refrain from simply speculating about the way the actual world might be since he intended his claims about the world of objects in space and time to be provable and to rest on solid grounds. So, when Kant characterises the 'noumenon' negatively, he means that it is 'something I know not what'. This, of course, could be read as implying that it is some *thing* that is unknowable in principle by beings like us. But it might be alternatively characterised as implying simply that there are many possible worlds out there – we might call them 'noumenal' worlds but they are not equivalent to the actual world that we finite, limited beings know. Indeed, the notion of a positive noumenon makes more sense when the noumenal is read this way since it is described as the object of a 'non-sensible' intuition. In other words, if there were some Being or being who had direct access to the ultimate possible world, then this being would know the noumenal. We can hypothesise the existence of such a Being but we cannot know of its existence.

It is also important to note that although Kant uses the word 'appearance', to describe the world we know, he famously does not intend this word to be understood in an empirically idealist manner. He explicitly distinguishes 'appearances' from their subjective counterparts – 'intuitions' and 'concepts'. 'Appearance', he notes, is the 'undetermined object of an empirical intuition'.[13] However, in several places, but specifically in the 'Refutation of Idealism' section of the first *Critique*, Kant also sets out to prove that there must be objects existing in 'space outside me'[14] in order for me to be conscious of my own existence in time. Indeed, in that section, Kant aimed to show that 'material idealism', in both its problematic and its dogmatic forms – that is, idealism that 'declares the existence of objects outside us to be either doubtful and indemonstrable or false and impossible' – is false. He shows that we could not have a sense of our own experiences in time unless there were something outside these experiences. The consciousness of myself, he argues, which is required in order for us to think or to imagine anything at all, requires the possibility that something exists outside me. I could not identify any of my thoughts as thoughts of redness or thoughts of fire, for example, unless something existed outside me on the basis of which I could have a coherent thought.

Moreover, Kant contrasts the 'transcendental' employment of a concept, which consists in its application to things in general and 'in themselves', with its empirical employment, which consists in its application to objects of a possible experience.[15] It is a criterion of a concept's having application that we have both the 'logical form of thought in general' and the possibility of giving it an 'object to which it applies'. So Kant is, in this limited sense, already a realist, and a realist about the independent existence of rocks and stones, despite the fact that the label he gives for this 'reality' is 'appearance'. He gives it this label because it is important for him that he offers grounds for any claim he makes about the world that is knowable to such limited, finite beings as ourselves. Hence, it is possible to argue that equating the noumenal with the 'real' is both textually wrong and ignores the epistemic claims made by Kant. We might also argue that, contrary to Bhaskar's claim that the world of rocks and stones does not, for Kant, exist independently of the subject, that this is not true for an individual self. In general, beings like us create the conditions that make knowledge of any kind possible and these conditions, for Kant, actually require the relative independence of 'things outside me' from my own experiences.

What of the other assertion made by Chepurin and McWherter, the claim that the noumenal is supposed to 'ground' the phenomenal and that Kant makes it impossible for this to happen since we know nothing about this noumenal world and causation lies within the phenomenal?[16] At this point, I would like to suggest an alternative view of the relation between the noumenal and phenomenal that will, I hope, avoid this objection while retaining what is important in the epistemic reading outlined earlier. This alternative reading draws on two notions in Kant's writings. In particular, Kant distinguishes between causation and the 'ground'/'consequent' relation. The latter allows for an alternative relation between noumena and phenomena to the causal one defended in the Second Analogy. It allows specifically for the 'self-positing' notion of causation defended by Kant in the Third Antinomy. In this section of the first *Critique*, he defends a notion of a 'first cause' or an 'absolute spontaneity' – a cause that begins of itself. He argues that if we assume the notion of a causal series that applies with unlimited universality, we are faced with a self-contradiction. If the principle of universal causation were to be applied in such a fashion, then there would be no beginning of the series and therefore no completion of it. For this reason, there must be a first cause or an 'absolute spontaneity'.

In the Antithesis of this Antinomy, Kant argues the opposite. But, he claims, thesis and antithesis can both be true. The principle of universal causation can apply in the phenomenal world and the notion of an 'absolute spontaneity' in the noumenal. He argues, for instance, that I have freedom in this latter sense: 'By freedom, on the other hand, in its cosmological meaning, I understand the power of beginning a state *spontaneously*.'[17] As a noumenal self, or as he puts it in *Religion within the Limits of Reason Alone*,[18] a 'person', I can be shaped by my will. The self as a 'person' in this sense lies outside the domain of operation of the universal principle of causation defended in the Second Analogy. Alongside the notion of freedom of the will is a conception of the 'grounding' of the whole phenomenal world. Given this, there need be no contradiction between the noumenal 'grounding' of appearances and the fact that the principle of causation applies universally in the phenomenal world. Kant would, on this new hypothesis, be a realist about noumenal powers, the spontaneous powers of noumenal agents and about the ground of the whole phenomenal world but he would be only a speculative realist. We would be able to make speculative claims about this reality but we could not say that it must be this or that way. We need, the claim would be, the phenomenal world – Meillassoux's 'correlationist' world – to be grounded but we cannot know what this ground is like.

In *The Critique of Judgment*, Kant elaborates on the possibility of an atemporal ground of the whole of nature in parallel to the 'spontaneous will' of the rational and moral agent. There, he famously defends a teleological notion of causation, albeit one that is only regulatively construed. A tree is cause and effect of itself and constitutes, effectively, a self-regulating system, even though this is only regulatively the case for us. Moreover, the ultimate exemplification of 'purposiveness' for Kant is 'man' acting as a moral agent.[19] We rational beings have to suppose, for the understanding of morality, that 'man' is the ultimate purpose. More precisely, 'man' acting as a moral agent is the purpose against which we judge the purposiveness of everything else. Kant writes:

> Man is indeed the only being on earth that has understanding and hence an ability to set himself purposes of his own choice, and in this respect he holds himself lord of nature; and if we regard nature as a teleological system then it is man's vocation to be the ultimate purpose of nature, but always subject to a condition: he must have the understanding and the will to give both nature and himself reference to a purpose that can be independent of nature, self-sufficient, and a final purpose.[20]

This final purpose, then, would be a noumenal ground of the whole, or some version of a God. It would operate outside time and, as such, it could not function in the temporal fashion that is presupposed by the example of the tree. Yet, like the tree, this final purpose could be both cause and effect of itself – it would be responsible for producing nature but it could also be construed as being, in some alternative sense, identical with nature. There is, therefore, a way of construing the relation between the 'noumenal ground' of the whole and the phenomenal world that does not lead to the self-contradiction suggested in the criticism of Kant presented earlier. Kant would be, to reiterate, a realist about the ground of the natural or phenomenal world, but we cannot know what this ground is like. In the third *Critique*, as we have seen, he describes this ground as God. Yet it is clear that he has argued that we cannot know of God's existence.

Transcendental idealism versus transcendental realism

Opposing the transcendental idealism of Kant, Roy Bhaskar defends what he calls a transcendental realist position. In his work *A Realist Theory of Science*, Bhaskar offers a transcendental analysis, using a Kantian form of argument, for the conditions of the possibility of experimental activity. In short, he argues that the conditions that make experimental activity possible require transcendental realism. Unless we assume a transcendental realist position, experimental activity, which is a crucial requirement for the possibility of science, would make no sense.

Experimentation, then, according to Bhaskar, is a significant feature of the natural and (in some cases also) the social sciences. This is the initial premise of his argument, and he proceeds to articulate the required conditions in order for this premise to make sense. He claims (and this is the crucial feature of his 'critical' realism) that in order for experimentation to make sense, there must be something that is absolutely independent of humans. As he puts it:

> We can easily imagine a world similar to ours, containing the same intransitive objects of scientific knowledge but without any science to produce knowledge of them. In such a world, which has occurred and may come again, reality would be unspoken for and yet things would not cease to act and interact in all sorts of ways.[21]

In support of this claim, Bhaskar argues that it is necessary to draw a distinction between the regularities of succession generated by scientists in an experimental context and the causal laws these regularities describe. If this distinction were not made, then we would have to draw the implausible conclusion that scientists themselves generate causal laws. This would in turn commit one to the absurd view that scientists cause and generate the laws of nature.

However, one might inquire from a Kantian perspective: how is it that we know that natural scientists do not themselves generate causal laws? How can we be sure that scientists do not produce the laws of nature? Moreover, is it not also the case that all that is required for Bhaskar's argument to get off the ground is that the laws are independent of the particular scientists' or group of scientists' experimental activity? To answer this question, Bhaskar offers a second argument: if scientists did indeed generate causal laws, then there would be no point to their activity. Indeed, the whole point of experiential activity would be lost since scientists would be producing the laws rather than investigating them. Once more, though, it would be perfectly possible for a Kantian to complain that, although this scenario would indeed be implausible and would render scientific activity somewhat odd, the argument has not shown that the distinction between the activity of scientists in generating causal laws and the laws themselves must be made.

I would like to present one caveat to Bhaskar's argument. In particular, Bhaskar wants his 'critical' realism to apply both to the natural and to the social sciences. In the latter context, he writes: 'in rejecting this ontology (that of empirical realism) and sociology, transcendental realism also situates the possibility for a new *critical naturalism* . . . Such a naturalism . . .

can sustain the *transfactuality* of social structures, while insisting on their *conceptuality* (or concept dependence).'[22] If Bhaskar means that social structures must be conceived as independent of social scientists who study them while at the same time being conceptually constructed by those same social scientists, then the question would arise of how this differs from Kant's empirical realism. One might further ask, even if the social structures were not constructed by the social scientist, it is nonetheless obvious, given that they are *social* structures, that they cannot be independent of humans in the way outlined in relation to the objects investigated by the natural sciences.

At this point, I would like to consider whether or not it is possible to develop arguments for a realist position that might reflect the spirit of Bhaskar's thinking about the natural sciences, if not his actual arguments. I will do this by suggesting a possible realist approach inspired by Bhaskar as well as responses to it from a Kantian perspective. In general, Bhaskar is clear that he is deploying a broadly Kantian form of argument – a transcendental argument – that proceeds by suggesting the conditions for the possibility of X being the case. The question arises, however, whether or not the use of this argument form, even if we accept his strong premise concerning the natural sciences, carries the same weight outside its original Kantian context. After all, in deploying the form of argument, Kant is primarily concerned with describing the conditions necessary for the possibility of experience. Operating in a context where Hume's discussion of causation had famously 'awoken him' from his 'dogmatic slumber', he set out to demonstrate, among other things, that, if Hume's conclusions were true, then no experience would be possible at all: if the world were constantly changing, as it might be on Hume's view, then we could not even have the kind of experience that Hume presupposes. We could not, in other words, have the kind of experience that is required for us to make a claim about, for example, the sun and whether or not it will rise tomorrow. In order for us to be able to make such claims, we need to assume a relative degree of stability both in our own consciousness and in the world that contains the sun. These claims are made in various forms in the three Analogies section of the *Critique of Pure Reason*, and particularly in the Second Analogy. Against Hume, Kant argues there that, while individual causal sequences are not themselves necessary, the principle of causation must be presupposed in order for us to distinguish, among our temporally successive experiences, those that represent objective succession from those that represent objective coexistence.

At the moment, I am not assessing the extent to which Kant is right about these claims. The point in question is the strength of the argument, if he is right. If he is right, then there are certain conditions that are required in order for such finite beings as ourselves to think or to have conscious experience or any knowledge at all. In contrast to Kant, Bhaskar appears to be making a far weaker claim. Even if we accept – a point that is controversial – that experimentation is ubiquitous in science, and even if we accept all the steps of Bhaskar's argument, we will not have produced an argument that is as strong as that of Kant. Such an argument will be weaker because describing the conditions necessary for the possibility of experience is stronger than describing the conditions necessary for experimentation in science. Denying that something is necessary for scientific experimentation to be possible has less drastic consequences than denying the conditions necessary for experience to be possible. The former actually requires the latter. If no experience were possible, there could be no scientific experimentation; however, it is not the case that, if there were no scientific experimentation, there could be no experience. Therefore, even if I were to accept Bhaskar's premise and his argument for that premise, his argument would not constitute a refutation of Kant's transcendental idealism and a proof of transcendental realism. Indeed, it is possible to accept his premise and simply claim that there might be no scientists and therefore no scientific experimentation.

We might claim, then, that it is perfectly possible for beings like us to survive without scientific experimentation. The lack of scientific experimentation would not imply that we would cease to have experience. Kant, as is well known, set out to outline the underpinning conditions that, he argued, were required in order for Newtonian science to be possible. But he equated this with the possibility of knowledge in general or with experience in general. Bhaskar, even if we were to concede his premise concerning the conditions of possibility of experimentation in the natural sciences, would not have shown that there must be a world that is absolutely independent of beings like us. He would have shown only that it is a requirement of the natural sciences that we must assume such a world. To refute Kant's transcendental idealism, he would also have to have shown, something that, to my knowledge, he did not show, namely, either that we could not survive without natural science or that a reality independent of humans is necessary for the possibility of experience in general.

In the remainder of the chapter, I will consider whether or not different arguments can be offered for some form of realism that is stronger than 'empirical realism' and also than the form of realism defended in the first section of this chapter. Kant himself, as noted, demonstrated the necessity of something existing independently of our combined sensory and conceptual states in order for us to be aware of these states. Someone sympathetic to Bhaskar, however, could argue that, if the world of trees, fields, rocks, planets and stars were only a construct of the human forms of experience, through the human frame of time, space and causation, then these things would fail to fulfil the conditions Kant himself requires of them. Kant requires that something exist independently of the consciousness of an individual self, in order for this consciousness to make sense to the self. So, if the tree in my garden were purely a construct of my sense experience combined with my conceptual apparatus, then it would strictly fail to exist independently of me, and thus it would fail to meet the criteria laid down by Kant for the elements of my stream of consciousness making sense.

It is possible to suggest, moreover, in a stronger challenge to Kant, that he, on his own premises, is unable to account for the coming into being of the temporal – if such a view makes sense. Using an argument that is similar to one presented by Meillassoux, we could suggest that the transcendental conditions that are required for experience to be possible, on Kantian premises, themselves need to come into being. Meillassoux has suggested that the transcendental subject needs to come into being. If it didn't come into being, then it would violate the conditions for the 'essential finitude of the subject'.[23] One might claim, then, either that time has always existed in which case it would be difficult to account for change, or that time came into being, in which case, time could not be the form of inner sense of beings like us. On this argument, then, there would be a reality – a temporal one – that pre-existed beings like us, and out of which we emerged. The argument would not show quite what Bhaskar would like, but it would at least demonstrate that there must be something that existed *anterior* to beings like us.

The argument could take the following form: in order for the spatiotemporal conditions that we deploy to construct experience to make sense, there must be something permanent against which we engage in this construction. Otherwise we would be spinning in a void. Indeed, and ironically, it is possible to read Kant's first Analogy in a fashion that lends support to a strong realist position analogous to this one. In the first Analogy, Kant describes 'appearances' as being in time. He writes: 'All appearances are in time; and in it alone, as substratum (as permanent form of inner intuition), can either co-existence or succession be represented.'[24] He goes on to note that time itself cannot be perceived and that therefore there must be something else, something 'permanent', a 'substratum', to represent time. Now Kant has been represented by respected commentators, on this matter, as confusing a principle of the conservation of matter with some transcendental condition of the possibility of experience.[25] It has been argued, by Peter Strawson, in particular, that no absolute permanence is required as a transcendental condition of the possibility of experience. What Strawson argues is necessary instead is 'that we should be able to identify places, and hence objects or processes, as the same at different times'.[26] All that is needed, on this view, is a relative degree of independence from the elements of my consciousness and a relative degree of permanence.

However, it is possible to interpret Kant, rather, as noting the above realist point about time. It is possible, in other words, to claim that he is arguing here that we need a permanent temporal order in which to locate experience. Since we cannot perceive time itself, there needs to be something within the spatio-temporal frame that is independent of our experience and that acts as a proxy for this permanent frame. Kant labelled this something 'permanent substance'. Indeed, such a substance must be more fundamental than Bhaskar's rocks and stones, since these come into being and perish. Henry Allison further notes that Kant argues, in the *Metaphysical Foundations of Natural Science*,[27] for a principle of the conservation of matter. However, as Allison recognises, this derivation requires empirical premises and is thus at a different level of argument from the need for the transcendental principle. According to Allison's interpretation of the first Analogy, Kant is here making an epistemic point. To this extent, Allison is in agreement with Strawson and others. Where he differs from the latter is that he argues that the perception of change requires a permanent and unchanging backdrop. While this is indeed an epistemic point, it also has ontological consequences. A permanent and unchanging 'substrate' cannot be created, through the framework principles of space and time, by us since it is precisely a requirement of the argument that the permanent is that – that it persists though all change. It therefore persists through the coming into being and going out of existence of the transcendental self. It is important to note, at this point, that this way of reading Kant is not necessarily incompatible with time being the form of inner sense since the permanent 'substrate' is not time itself but some representative of time. However, such an interpretation does push Kant in a stronger realist direction than 'empirical realism' or the form defended in the first section of this chapter. The permanent substance noted here would exist, by virtue of this permanence, independently of the experience of particular groups of beings like us, but it would nevertheless be found within the phenomenal realm. Kant himself identified this permanent through the frame of Newtonian science but, as noted, it would not have to be identified this way.

A limitation of the argument, though, is that a realist like Meillassoux would require that time itself – and not merely some proxy for time – exist independently of beings like us. It is difficult for Kant both to hold that time exists outside the frame of beings like us, in order for us to be able to come into being, and that it is the form of inner sense of beings like us. On the other hand, as Kant himself has made us aware, we cannot know that we did come into being. Žižek, making a parallel point, reads Kant as unable to resolve the dualisms between the phenomenal and the noumenal, or between freedom and determinism. Yet he does not see this as a failure; rather, he argues that Kant has brought to our attention the inevitability of paradox. Our understanding the world and our acting in it are impossible outside the production of antinomies that are incapable of conceptual resolution.[28] As Steven Shakespeare has put it: 'These antinomies are not the unfortunate outcome of a deficiency in thinking – the encounter with an impassable limit – but the productive force that engenders the very possibilities of conceptual thought, moral action and aesthetic judgment.'[29] Conceptual thought is impossible without a recognition that there are limits to this thought, and moral action is, in Shakespeare's account of Kant, inseparable from the paradox that freedom occurs within a mechanical, causally determined world. For Kant, then, it is important to recognise that there is always something that is outside a certain form of conceptual thought.

There are good grounds for some kind of realist position, then. However, the realist cannot provide a conclusive reason that would be as strong as Kant's own arguments within transcendental idealism. It is intrinsic to Kant's transcendental view that this cannot be the case, since we cannot step outside of ourselves and find conclusive proof that the 'outside' takes on a certain character. Although it seems undeniable that, for example, there must have been a time that is independent of 'our' framework principles, in which beings like us came about, it is difficult to prove this. For Kantian reasons, then, any realist proposal will be speculative. If we assume such a proposal to be about 'permanent substance' or about 'things' and 'powers', this will remain a speculative hypothesis. The German absolute idealists each made some sort of assumption about Being as a whole that Kant would claim they cannot prove to be the case.

Conclusion

In this chapter, I have defended Kant against two 'realist' charges against him. First of all, I have suggested that his epistemic claims deserve more attention than some of the realists give them and that his 'empirical realism' involves him in moving somewhat in the direction of his realist critics. Secondly, I have argued that Kant is able to give a defence of the notion of the 'grounding' of the phenomenal in the noumenal that does not involve him in extending the principle of causation defended in the second Analogy beyond its legitimate sphere of operation. Thirdly, I then moved to discuss the force of Bhaskar's 'critical realism' over Kant's transcendental idealism. While I have questioned the strength of Bhaskar's own key argument, I have suggested that some support can be given to the idea that there is a reality that is absolutely independent of the human and indeed that Kant himself developed an argument for such a position. However, contrary to the claim of Bhaskar in particular, one cannot show that this reality must be a certain way. Rather, claims about the nature of any reality outside the human will be speculative hypotheses.

I would like to add one concluding comment. The critical realist wants some clear conception of the nature of the 'outside' that is independent of ourselves as finite beings. But, for Kantian reasons, this is a demand that cannot be met. This is not to say that there is no such reality – there almost certainly is a 'reality' of some kind 'out there' – but this reality cannot be conceptualised in the way some realists appear to require and any characterisation of its nature will necessarily be speculative. Here, I am using the same word as Meillassoux. For me, as indeed is the case for him, the use of this word does not mean that it involves pure speculation and that no reasons can be given for the hypothesis. It rather means that we cannot be sure that we are right about it not only because someone cleverer or more imaginative might come up with reasons why we are wrong, but rather because we are operating at the very limits of the capacities of thought of beings like ourselves. Indeed, thinking about the nature of the 'real' may generate paradoxes.

I do have one caveat to this, however. Although I accept that the notion of paradox adumbrated here is important, there is one significant dimension of human interaction that Kant sees as paradoxical that I would like to suggest need not be paradoxical in the way he imagines it to be. This is the aforementioned distinction between freedom and determinism. This distinction, it seems to me, is rendered paradoxical by Kant in a way that it need not be because of the assumptions he makes about his world of 'appearance' – his world of Newtonian substances that interact externally upon one another. He assumes, in the first *Critique*, that causes are related externally to their effects and that each cause sufficiently determines its effect. Something close to this assumption seems to me, indeed, to be common in some contemporary literature on freedom/determinism. This Kantian view of reality, although it is not usually spelt out, is sometimes taken for granted as the way the world must be. Though a detailed discussion will have to wait for another time, let me briefly outline the issue.

In the first *Critique*, as I have argued above, Kant defended a notion of self-causation. In so doing, Kant differentiates this conception from the causal principle defended in the second Analogy. The notion of 'absolute spontaneity' is radically distinct from the principle of causation that operates in the phenomenal world. A number of contemporary philosophers, however, have doubted that there can be any such thing as 'spontaneous causation' or 'self-causation' or, therefore, freedom of the will.[30] In his third *Critique*, however, Kant offers a different notion of self-causation. There, he defends the idea that a tree is cause and effect of itself in the sense that the seed gives rise to the tree and the tree, in its turn, to further trees. If the laws of nature, overall, then were characterised in terms of the powers of objects, as Kant does here (although, as noted, for him this notion of a causal power is only regulatively conceived), then there would be room for a less radical separation of freedom from determinism. Self-causation, then, could instead be understood in terms of the powers of objects. Each and every object, then, might be endowed with a rudimentary notion of self-causation in this limited sense, as the power to act. While the notion of radical self-causation might operate to characterise the ground of the whole of nature, a less drastic conception, like the relation between a seed and a tree, might function within the natural world.

The suggestions made in these final remarks would involve a challenge to the Kant of the first *Critique* that is different from the realist challenge examined in the body of this chapter. It would involve questioning the view that there is a radical separation between 'nature' on the one hand, which is said to be governed by natural causal laws, and freedom on the other, where a different conception of causation is supposed to operate. The claim would rather be that humans are part of nature, that their causal powers are analogous, rather than wholly distinct from, the powers of objects in the natural world, including other animals and at least some natural objects. Indeed, in the third *Critique*, Kant's arguments about the causal powers of such living beings like trees do seem to lead in this direction. Because of his Newtonianism, however, he was unwilling to accept the 'real existence' of causal powers. Yet, his detailed account of how it is that the power of a seed to become a tree could not be accommodated within a regularity of succession and Newtonian model of causation plausibly leads in the direction I am suggesting.[31]

Notes

1. Fichte, to take one example, saw Kant's project as leading to absolute scepticism. See Johann Gottlieb Fichte, *The Vocation of Man*, trans. Peter Preuss (Indianapolis: Hackett, 1987).
2. Quentin Meillassoux, *After Finitude: An Essay on the Necessity of Contingency*, trans. Ray Brassier (London: Continuum, 2007), p. 6.
3. Ibid. p. 7.
4. Ibid. p. 5.
5. See Roy Bhaskar, *A Realist Theory of Science* (London: Verso, [1975] 1998).

6. This is, indeed, a version of an argument earlier put forward by Hegel. According to him, the Kantian 'thing-in-itself' is self-contradictory. It is supposed to cause sensation but it cannot do this since causation is a category of our minds. Moreover, the whole conception of an unknowable existence is self-contradictory anyway since if we know that a thing exists, then we have some knowledge of it, which itself therefore involves a self-contradiction. See G. W. F. Hegel, *The Science of Logic*, trans. A. V. Miller, foreword by J. N. Finlay (London: Allen & Unwin, 1969), p. 121.
7. Kirril Chepurin, 'Utopia in excess, political theology as critique in Kant and Fichte', paper delivered at conference on Political Theology, Liverpool Hope University, July 2015. This is a very interesting and wide-ranging paper and I do not claim to do justice to the whole paper. I am, rather, considering only the initial assumptions made about the phenomenal/noumenal distinction.
8. Dustin McWherter, *The Problem of Critical Ontology: Bhaskar Contra Kant* (London: Palgrave, 2013).
9. Ibid. p. 1.
10. Chepurin, 'Utopia in excess', p. 2.
11. Immanuel Kant, *Critique of Pure Reason*, trans. Norman Kemp Smith (London: Macmillan, 1970). Chepurin, 'Utopia in excess', p. 2.
12. McWherter, *The Problem of Critical Ontology*, p. 51.
13. Kant, *Critique of Pure Reason*, A20/B34.
14. Ibid. B276.
15. Ibid. A239/B298.
16. One interesting interpretation of the 'grounding' of appearances is given by Beth Lord. She suggests that it is the productive understanding that makes the conditions for the production of knowledge possible. Hers is an interesting reading but it may result in Kant becoming too much like a Berkeleyan idealist. See Beth Lord, *Kant's Productive Ontology: Knowledge, Nature, and the Meaning of Being* (Doctoral dissertation), Warwick University, 2004; available at <http://wrap.warwick.ac.uk/36683/1/WRAP_THESIS_Lord_2003.pdf> (last accessed June 2015).
17. Kant, *Critique of Pure Reason*, A533/B561.
18. Kant, *Religion within the Limits of Reason Alone*, trans. Theodore M. Green and Hoyd Hudson (New York: Harper & Row, 1960).
19. Immanuel Kant, *Critique of Judgment*, trans. Werner S. Pluhar (Indianapolis: Hackett, 1987).
20. Ibid. p. 318, Ak. 431.
21. Bhaskar, *A Realist Theory*, p. 22.
22. Roy Bhaskar, 'Transcendental realism and the problem of naturalism', in Gerard Delanty and Piet Strydon (eds), *Philosophies of Social Science: Classic and Contemporary Readings* (Maidenhead: Oxford University Press, 2003), p. 447.
23. Meillassoux, *After Finitude*, p. 24.
24. Kant, *Critique of Pure Reason*, B225.
25. Indeed, Henry Allison claims that 'virtually all the commentators' read Kant this way. See Allison, *Kant's Transcendental Idealism: An Interpretation and Defence* (New Haven and London: Yale University Press, 2004), p. 242.
26. Peter Strawson, *The Bounds of Sense: An Essay on Kant's* Critique of Pure Reason (London: Methuen, 1966), p. 129.
27. Kant, 'The metaphysical foundations of natural science', in *Theoretical Philosophy after 1781*, trans. Michael Friedman (Cambridge: Cambridge University Press, 2002).
28. Slavoj Žižek, *The Parallax View* (Cambridge, MA: MIT Press, 2009), p. 22.
29. Steven Shakespeare, *Kierkegaard and the Refusal of Transcendence* (Basingstoke: Macmillan, 2015), p. 169.
30. For some examples of such contemporary thinkers, see Galen Strawson, 'The impossibility of moral responsibility', *Philosophical Studies: An International Journal for*

Philosophy in the Analytic Tradition, vol. 75, no. 1/2, *Free Will, Determinism, and Moral Responsibility* (1994): pp. 5–24.
31. I am grateful to Bob Stern and Charlotte Alderwick for helpful comments on earlier drafts of this chapter.

Chapter 5

Pessimism, or The Importance of Indifference, Time and Suffering in Realist Ontologies

Rick Elmore

Pessimism has only recently begun to be seen as a truly robust philosophical position. This is in part because pessimism is generally read as an account of human psychology.[1] It is commonplace to figure pessimism as a dour worldview articulated by those disenchanted with existence. Even in the case of a thinker such as Schopenhauer, who undeniably articulates a philosophical pessimism, the question of temperament is never absent, as if it were impossible to be a pessimist without harbouring a personal distaste for life, happiness or joy.[2] However, there is a growing body of work that attempts to reclaim pessimism as a philosophical position, a position central to the development of modern philosophy and, as I will show, to the re-emergence of realism within continental philosophy.[3] In particular, thinkers such as Joshua Foa Dienstag and Eugene Thacker argue that pessimism is a philosophical stance that, for Thacker, challenges the limits of philosophy and, for Dienstag, offers a persuasive counter-tradition to mainstream political theory. In addition, the growing interest in the work of H. P. Lovecraft and object-oriented ontology, alongside the rise of black metal theory, bleak theory, the dark enlightenment and eliminative nihilism, not to mention accelerationism, suggests that there is a certain, darker tradition in contemporary theory, one that arises alongside the re-emergence of realism in contemporary thought. It is this connection between realism and pessimism that I develop in this chapter. More precisely, building on the work of Dienstag, Thacker and Ligotti, I show how pessimism is best understood as an anti-correlationist realism, its concern for the unhappy and suffering-laden character of human life emerging from an ontological commitment to a world indifferent to and independent from human life. In addition, I argue that, in contrast to many current continental realisms, pessimism connects the assertion of a realist ontology to questions of suffering, violence and time, highlighting the dangerously ideological character of optimistic or anti-realist metaphysics. It is this emphasis on realism as ideology critique that, I contend, marks pessimism's key contribution to our understanding of realism. More specifically, I argue that pessimism provides a unique and pivotal account of the stakes of asserting a realist ontology, showing how a certain thinking of ideology, suffering and time is requisite for any realism that wishes to avoid falling back into idealism. I begin by outlining pessimism's realist ontology, an ontology that emerges from a concern for indifference.

Pessimism is a realism

The defining claim of pessimism is that true human happiness is largely impossible. From Leopardi, Rousseau and Schopenhauer, to Camus, Zapffe and Ligotti, pessimists assert that this world is not one in which humans can expect any lasting joy or satisfaction. This is because, for pessimists, the universe is fundamentally indifferent to human wants or desires. As Thacker puts it, pessimism 'is the difficult thought of the world as absolutely inhuman, and indifferent to the hopes, desires, and struggles of human individuals and groups'.[4] For many pessimists, this indifference is rooted in the human experience of linear time and the contradictory nature of consciousness: humanity's finite and temporal existence assures that the satisfaction of our desires is, at best, fleeting and, at worst, unattainable. Desire drives us to want what we do not have, and, even if we get it, we quickly move on to new desires, a cycle that shows human existence to be a questing after something that ultimately cannot be achieved or maintained. Hence, pessimism assets a basic teleological indifference of the universe towards humans, one that assures us little possibility of lasting happiness. It is on the basis of this teleological indifference that pessimists lament the fallen and suffering-laden character of human life, and it is perhaps this focus on human unhappiness that in part explains the tendency to read pessimism as a worry over the situational and psychological plight of humans. However, this concern for the universe's teleological indifference towards humans is, in pessimism, justified ontologically.

Although pessimists are certainly concerned with the plight of humans, it is important to recognise that the justification for their bleak account of the human condition is first and foremost ontological:

> Pessimism, as a theory, is interested in the prevalence of human unhappiness. . . . But this is of course very different from the theory itself having its origins in a particular disposition within its authors. Indeed, fundamentally, the pessimistic account of the origins of unhappiness . . . has little to do

with psychology itself but with a claim of ontological misalignment between human beings and the world they inhabit.[5]

For pessimists, the plight of humans is not the result of contingency, bad luck or a certain psychological perspective; rather, it is an effect of the ontological structures of the universe. In particular, pessimists see an ontological misalignment between humans and the universe, one that leads directly to human unhappiness and suffering. This 'ontological misalignment' takes a variety of forms within pessimist discourses, the most prominent of which involves the inability to square the consciousness of linear time with any possibility for human life to be ultimately meaningful. In other words, our ontological entanglement with time grounds our inability to achieve, in a lasting sense, any of our desires or wants. We shall return to pessimism's account of time shortly. However, what is central to my argument here is that pessimism's assertion of a teleological indifference, and its diagnosis of the human condition, is grounded ontologically, the universe's indifference to human ends being nothing but the expression of a deeper ontological indifference. As Thomas Ligotti puts it, pessimism entails the recognition that '[n]othing in nature needs us'.[6] For pessimists, we live in a world not made for us, a world that does not align with human wants or desires because it is ontologically inhuman. As we will see, this insistence on indifference is an all or nothing proposition, and the indifference of the universe constitutes a complete depriviledging of the human in cosmic affairs. However, it is also this indifference that, I argue, shows pessimism's ontology to be fundamentally realist.

In his ground-breaking work *In the Dust of this Planet*, Eugene Thacker develops the implications of pessimism's commitment to ontological indifference, contending that it challenges us to think not simply the world that stands in opposition to the human or to human consciousness, 'the world-for-us' versus 'the world-in-itself', but, far more radically, 'the world-without-us', the world as completely unrelated and unrelatable to the human.[7] This is, for Thacker, the fundamental insight of 'cosmic pessimism', and he traces this thinking of the 'world-without-us' through black metal, demonology, mysticism, philosophy and horror fiction, showing how this indifference manifests across an array of discourses and fields.[8] At stake in this reading is not only pessimism's positing of an ontological disjunction between the material world and the world of human consciousness, ideas and language (a claim one finds in many ontologies), but, more importantly, its positing of the world as ontologically non-recuperable to the sphere of human life. In pessimism, the world exists ontologically independent from all things human, which is to say that pessimism asserts a fundamentally realist ontology. One sees the depths of this commitment to realism, pessimism's relentless insistence on the ontological independence of the world from the human, in its critique of progress and temporality.

In his award-winning study, *Pessimism: Philosophy, Ethics, Spirit*, Joshua Foa Dienstag shows how pessimism contests our modern understanding of time and its inherent commitment to progress.[9] For Dienstag, pessimism is a child of modernity, in the sense that pessimism is 'marked out from the start by a belief in linear time and non-cyclical historical narrative'.[10] Like modernity, pessimism entails a non-cyclical account of time in so far as circularity implies that everything, including human existence, ultimately repeats or cycles, a logic that flies in the face of pessimism's rejection of any necessary, structural role for humanity within cosmic affairs. In circular temporality, the repetition of human existence would give humans a definitive place in the structures of the cosmos, even if that place were simply that of repeating the same sad and unhappy existence over and over.[11] Hence, for Dienstag, pessimism's ontological commitments entail a linear conception of time, as non-linearity gives too much potential importance to the human. However, while linear, pessimism's conception of time is also non-progressive.

The notion of progress is a primary corollary of modernity's shift to conceiving time linearly, the notion of linear time going hand in hand with the idea that things not only change, but develop, and, at least potentially, improve. Dienstag presents progress as perhaps the most lasting and powerful legacy of the shift from a cyclical to linear time-consciousness, despite the fact that it has so often been critiqued: '[t]hough supposedly slain many times . . . this beast [progress] continues to rise from the ashes for the simple reason that, first, it helps us to make sense of the linear time of our calendar and second, there is no easy substitute for it'.[12] Progress is a difficult notion to let go, as it both coheres with our experience of time, and abandoning it presents the challenge of marking change without implying development or advancement. This in part explains the persistence of progressive thinking, even in discourses that explicitly reject cultural, historical or temporal progress in a grand sense. Yet, it also explains the relatively poor fate of pessimism. In fact, for Dienstag, pessimism is nothing less than the shadow of progressive thinking, an alternative to progress that 'asks us to rethink our sense of time . . . challeng[ing] our notions of order and meaning in dramatic ways'.[13] More specifically, pessimism demands that we think 'a non-progressive yet linear view of human existence', a conception of time that denies the comforting and ultimately humanising logic of either circularity or progress, denying the dream that humans are or could become happy and important in this universe.[14] Hence, pessimism demands that we think a notion of time and the universe that does not harbour the implicit hope that human life is or could become integral or important, a universe that on an ontological, teleological and temporal level does not either reassure or return to us, a universe completely and forever inhuman. Dienstag will go on to work out the ways in which various pessimists from Rousseau and Leopardi to Nietzsche and Freud have understood this ontological and temporal character of the universe, insisting along the way that such a conception does not entail political quietism. Dienstag does not develop his critique in the direction of realism, yet what his analysis shows, I argue, is just how deep and thoroughgoing pessimism's ontological deprivileging of the human is. For pessimists, the universe needs us not at all, and it is this claim that not only makes pessimism a realism, but also marks its deep commonality with other recent continental realisms and, specifically, the critique of correlationism.

Pessimism and the critique of correlationism

Although there are a wide array of recent continental realisms, ranging from the speculative materialism of Quentin Meillassoux and the object-oriented thinking of Graham Harman and Levi Bryant to the transcendental materialism of Adrian Johnston and the vitalism of Jane Bennett and Karen Barad, what these positions generally have in common is a resistance to what Quentin Meillassoux calls 'correlationism', the belief that the human–world correlate forms the central element of philosophical investigation.[15] Meillassoux defines correlationism as 'consist[ing] in disqualifying the claim that it is possible to consider the realms of subjectivity and objectivity independently of one another'.[16] For Meillassoux, then, correlationism is the belief that one can never have access to subjects or objects, thinking or being separately. On his account, continental philosophy since Kant has tended to be correlationist, disavowing any form of 'naive realism' that would hold that one can have direct access to the objectivity of the world, which could be apprehended independently of its constitutive relation to subjectivity.[17] At stake in this critique of correlationism, then, is the question of to what degree philosophy remains fundamentally idealist and also humanist, in the sense of seeing human thought as necessary to, and constitutive of, the world. If one can never access the world except in relation to thought, then without thought there can be no experience of the world and, in fact, no world at all, in the sense that we can say nothing about the world outside thought. This is the claim that many recent continental realisms contest, each arguing in their own way that there is a world that exists independently of human thought and that we can philosophise about that world. It is this assertion of a world independent of the human that, in a minimal sense, marks the realism of these critiques. Yet, it is also this claim that aligns these realisms with pessimism, in so far as pessimism too insists on the ontological claim that the universe exists without any fundamental relationship to the human. In fact, like pessimism, the critique of correlationism asserts an ontological indifference of the universe towards humans.

Included in the critique of correlationism is the notion that the world must be ontologically indifferent to human existence, since to argue otherwise would be to concede that one cannot have objectivity separate from subjectivity. For thinkers such as Meillassoux, this indifference is based on the fact that the world existed long before humans and, therefore, cannot be understood in terms of a constitutive or dependent relationship to the human. This is not to suggest that humans do not affect their environment or that, from the perspective of human life, thought may not be requisite to our experience of the world; rather, it is to recognise that ontologically and teleologically, we have a non-reciprocal relationship to the universe. Or, as pessimists would contend, it is to recognise that we live in a universe not made for us. It is this claim of indifference that, as Catherine Malabou has argued, marks the radicality of the critique of correlationism, challenging fundamentally the anti-realist tendencies of philosophy after Kant.[18]

Although philosophy has long critiqued the relation between thought and the world, the critique of correlationism challenges us to ask whether these critiques (for instance, those of deconstruction, phenomenology, critical theory and post-structuralism) have stopped short of abandoning the privileged correlation of thought and the world, a refusal that would seem to condemn these approaches to an essential idealism and humanism. For realists, correlationism, although showing us the limits of thought and subjectivity, always, in the end, recuperates the importance of thought and the human. Or, to put this in pessimistic terms, correlationism remains always optimistic, always ultimately committed to the constitutive importance of thought and the human even in its critique of this importance. Hence to follow thinkers such as Malabou, if the radicality of the critique of correlationism rests on its commitment to the indifference of the universe, the world's unrecuperable and 'radical otherness' to all things human, then it follows that the radicality of this critique lies precisely in its pessimism, in its commitment to the ontologically inhuman character of the universe. At stake in this connection between continental realism and pessimism will be the question of what it means to philosophise the ontological indifference of the universe and to what degree this kind of realism commits one to certain pessimistic conclusions regarding not only ontology and teleology but also time and, as we will see, suffering and violence. Yet, it also requires that we directly address the complications of asserting a realist ontology from the side of thought, the paradoxical logic of marking the real, ontological limits of thought from within thought itself. In pessimist discourses, this paradoxical logic emerges in the structures of human consciousness.

Despite the fact that pessimism presents human existence as fundamentally meaningless, nearly all pessimists argue that human life is exceptional in one sense: its ability to comprehend its own meaninglessness. As the German pessimist Julius Bahnsen puts it, humans are 'self-conscious Nothings'.[19] Self-consciousness allows us to see our mortality and, ultimately, our insignificance: we know that we will one day die and that, given our place in the universe, everything we do between this moment and that one must logically amount to the same thing – nothing. This is the truth of ontological indifference from the beginning, and it is, for pessimists, consciousness that shows us this truth. This capacity for self-consciousness will, for nearly all pessimists, mark the difference between humans and the rest of the natural world as well as motivate pessimism's tendency towards antinatalism.[20]

Although self-consciousness gives humans knowledge of their mortality and, subsequently, their insignificance in cosmic affairs, it also ironically hides this knowledge from them. As Thomas Ligotti puts it, 'consciousness has forced us into the paradoxical position of striving to be unself-conscious of what we are – hunks of spoiling flesh on disintegrating bones'.[21] The insight that we are irrelevant, although revealed to us through consciousness, is, however, radically unpalatable to consciousness, since it suggests that, although we might feel like our actions matter, it actually makes no ultimate difference what we do. It is important to note that this is as true for each of us as individuals as it is for our species, since, in the end, our species will also perish either by its own hands or by the death of our sun. Even if, by some profound stroke of luck, humans colonise other worlds, thereby avoiding extinction from our sun's death, the eventual end of everything we have ever done seems logically assured. Here again we see pessimism's focus not simply on individual perception (the question of whether my life matters or whether I feel my life to matter) but on the greater question of humanity's ontological place in the universe, a place marked by indifference. Yet, for pessimists, there is something in the structures of consciousness that pushes us to deny this indifference, to deny the very insights provided by consciousness. There are various accounts of this denial. For some pessimists, it is an evolutionary development: optimism about existence being an adaptive advantage in the game for survival.[22] For others, it is the logical result of the self-conservative nature of systems, as from the side of life or consciousness these qualities surely seem superior to their alternatives. However, in all of these accounts, there is a recognition that the attempt to carry through the insight of ontological indifference necessarily involves a structural 'forgetting' or 'denial' of the very truths given to us by this insight. The assertion of ontological indifference, thus, stumbles on a certain self-conservative mechanism within consciousness. The recognition of this self-conservative logic shows that pessimism is far from a naive realism, taking head on the complex and paradoxical implications of thinking the limits of thought and humanism. However, it also shows that pessimism is not simply a denial of the importance of life, but rather questions what is at stake in the affirmation of life and in the ontologies that sustain such affirmations. This question of the stakes of affirming life is further developed in the pessimist refutation of suicide as the logical outcome of pessimistic thinking.

A common critique of pessimism is that if one truly espouses the conviction that life is meaningless, then one must be logically committed to suicide as the only rational response. As Ligotti puts it, 'some critics of pessimism often think they have his back to the wall when they blithely jeer, "if that is how this fellow feels, he should either kill himself or be decried a hypocrite"'.[23] Some version of this argument is often presented as a justification for pronouncing pessimism a philosophical pseudo-problem, the failure of pessimists to kill themselves – not to mention their penchant for writing books about the meaninglessness of existence – showing pessimism to be logically inconsistent from the outset. There are a number of problems with this argument, not the least of which is that it falsely assumes a logical connection between a belief in the meaninglessness of life and the necessity of suicide. Ligotti again: 'simply because someone has reached the conclusion that the amount of suffering in this world is enough that anyone would have been better off never having been born does not mean that by force of logic or sincerity he must kill himself'; rather, it means only that one has 'concluded that the amount of suffering in this world is enough that anyone would have been better off never having been born'.[24] However, pessimists also contend that this argument misunderstands the logic of suicide, since, while suicide might appear the ultimate denial of any meaning to life, it, in fact, harbours precisely the fantasy that life is meaningful: the fantasy of life as something worth denying. Pessimists like Leopardi and Ligotti argue that there is perhaps no greater affirmation of life than suicide, suicide being 'the final way in which we let ourselves be dominated by the pursuit of happiness'.[25] From this perspective, the logic of suicide confers rather than denies meaning to life, showing how 'every negation is adulterated or stealthily launched by an affirmative spirit'.[26] Here we return to the same paradoxical logic found in the structures of consciousness, the affirmation of indifference and meaninglessness reverting into their contraries. However, what the account of suicide illustrates is that at stake in the paradoxical logic of consciousness is a deeper concern for the ideological character of affirming of life, consciousness and the human found in much modern thought, an affirmation that, as we will see, is linked to suffering and violence. However, one will also note the deep affinities here between pessimism's suspicion of the structures of consciousness and the critiques of conceptualisation, subjectivity and systematicity found in much nineteenth- and twentieth-century European philosophy.

From Nietzsche to Adorno, Heidegger to Derrida, there is a long tradition of critiquing the idealist tendencies of Western philosophy and insisting that this critique involves a certain structural paradox. For example, one finds in Nietzsche the notion that while consciousness opens up the world to analysis, this opening is made possible only by foreclosing any immediate access to the materiality of the world and particularly that of our own bodies.[27] For Nietzsche, consciousness paradoxically only gives us access to consciousness, a set of conceptual metaphors that never represent fully the objects they claim to represent.[28] Similarly, the German philosopher and sociologist Theodor Adorno argues that conceptualisation (and by extension consciousness as such) works through a reduction of objects to those characteristics they share with other objects, a reduction that leads consciousness to exclude necessarily the unique time and space of each object's material existence.[29] Heidegger's notion of truth as the movement of revealing and concealing, Derrida's conception of meaning as the product of a fundamental play of differences – all of these are critiques of conceptualisation, subjectivity and systematicity that understand these operations as fundamentally paradoxical endeavours that have deep metaphysical and ontological stakes. For example, one finds in these critiques, as in pessimism, the conviction that consciousness entails a logic of 'forgetting', limiting our access to the non-conceptual while simultaneously occluding this limiting. Hence, pessimism is a tradition that bears much in common with the nineteenth- and twentieth-century critiques of metaphysics and fundamental ontology found in deconstruction, critical theory and phenomenology, and, like these other traditions, it challenges us to ask what is at stake in this paradoxical character of existence. Where does this paradox leave us ontologically? For pessimists, the answer to this question has everything to do with their concern that optimism implies an ontology in which humans must have some potential importance within cosmic affairs, an ontology that would remain essentially idealist and humanist in so far as it grants some ontological privilege to human thought. Thus, pessimism suggests that a truly thoroughgoing critique of idealism and humanism requires a realist ontology (a claim shared by all critiques of correlationism). However, pessimism also contends that the stakes of denying this realism are that it risks perpetuating an ideological denial of suffering and violence. I would argue that it is this second claim that differentiates pessimism from many recent accounts of realism, pointing to what makes pessimism valuable to our thinking of realism. In what remains of this chapter, I explore pessimism's worry over suffering and violence as well as its foregrounding of the importance of time as ways in which pessimism expands and contributes to the discourses of continental realism.

Realism, suffering and time

Although pessimism is one among several traditions that assert a realist ontology based on the indifference of the universe towards all things human, no other account of realism gives such a central place to suffering. As Ligotti puts it,

> whether a pessimist urges us to live 'heroically' with a knife in our guts or denounces life as not worth living is immaterial. What matters is that he makes no bones about *hurt* being the Great Problem it is incumbent on philosophy to observe.[30]

Although pessimists draw different conclusions about how one ought to live in the face of the ontological indifference of the universe, pessimists see the stakes of this indifference and our response to it as necessarily entangled with suffering. This suffering is the direct result of humanity's 'ontological misalignment' with the universe. The recognition and fear of death, the constant change and perishability of things, and the way in which this ontological transience and perishability gives existence 'a sense of unreality' all mark the sites at which pessimists see suffering as built into the ontological structures of existence.[31] As Dienstag states, 'central to the entire pessimistic tradition' is the conviction that time-consciousness leads directly to human suffering, in so far as it 'magnifies the trifling sufferings of animal existence into something much greater'.[32] Time-consciousness, by allowing us to see our inherent, ontological meaninglessness, necessarily 'magnifies' the small pains and frustrations of existence by showing these pains to be themselves meaningless. For pessimists, suffering is always a suffering for suffering's sake and thus a suffering that cannot lead to any benefit or greater good. It is on the basis of this account of suffering that pessimism often aligns itself with antinatalism, the refusal to reproduce that is posited as a resistance to the further propagation of life's meaningless suffering. However, what is key here is that pessimism identifies an essential link between suffering and the ontological indifference of the universe on two interrelated levels: (1) that suffering is a structural fact of the ontological misalignment between human life and an indifferent universe, and (2) that optimism constitutes a denial of this suffering, a covering over of the structural suffering exposed by pessimism's realist ontology.

What we see in pessimism's emphasis on suffering is a general concern for the way in which anti-realist, optimistic accounts of ontology both occlude and perpetuate suffering. As Schopenhauer writes in *The World as Will and Representation*: 'I cannot hold back from declaring here that optimism . . . strikes me as not only absurd, but even a truly *wicked* way of thinking, a bitter mockery of the unspeakable sufferings of humanity.'[33] Given the fact that consciousness shows our existence to be ontologically unimportant, optimism, or the denial of this ontological fact, amounts to a denial of suffering, a disavowal not only of the ontological insights of realism but also of the suffering that realism shows to be tied up in our 'ontological misalignment' with the universe. Here we see yet again a link between pessimism and discourses such as deconstruction, which insist on the structural or 'originary' violence of all systems of meaning, representation and metaphysics, as well as on the mechanisms of 'reparatory' violence that attempt to cover over these forms of structural violence.[34] The oft-stated clichés that 'what doesn't kill us makes us stronger' or that 'suffering builds character' are just the most public versions of the general optimistic ideology in which the suffering of existence is recast as positive and ultimately meaningful. It is this recasting that, for pessimists, marks not just the ideological import of optimism, but also, I would argue, its anti-realism: the insistence that suffering can be meaningful entails an ultimately correlationist metaphysics in which human beings would be anything but unimportant within cosmic affairs. In addition, given pessimism's association of this optimistic perpetuation of suffering with human reproduction, one can see that this concern with optimism has much in common with resilience discourse, optimism's denial of suffering emerging as an insistence that humans make their suffering, damage and trauma not only positive or productive but ultimately reproductive through the continuance of the species.[35] This link to resilience discourse also points to a collusion between optimism and capitalism, the pressure to be a cheerful, productive member of society complementing the expansion of capitalist labour and the forces of affective labour. In fact, pessimism suggests that optimism is primarily an ideology of affective labour, insisting that one not only make one's suffering productive but smile while one does it. Hence, pessimism allows us to see that the assertion of realist or anti-realist ontologies cannot but entangle us in questions of suffering and ideology, a point that differentiates pessimistic realism from much recent continental realism.

In addition, pessimism's association of questions of ontology and metaphysics with those of suffering and ideology connects pessimism with discourses such as feminism, critical race theory and queer theory, discourses that have long questioned the 'neutrality' of philosophy, metaphysics and ontology and the way in which this supposed 'neutrality' works to privilege certain figurations of thought, consciousness and subjectivity over others. Hence, pessimism positions realism at the intersection of ideology and suffering, an intersection that remains relatively underdeveloped in many realist ontologies, and one that suggests a fundamental link between realism and politics. It is beyond the scope of this chapter to detail all the implications of this connection between realism, suffering and ideology. However, pessimism suggests that one of the primary sites of this concern emerges around the question of temporality within realist ontologies.

The question of time is inseparable in pessimism from those of ontology and suffering. As outlined above, nearly all pessimists see time-consciousness as central to the ontological misalignment between humans and the universe and the suffering-laden character of human existence. For pessimists, our relationship to time positions us as ontologically paradoxical, out of joint with the universe, and subject to suffering as a result. This is not to suggest that all pessimists assert a shared or even compatible conception of time or time-consciousness. For some pessimists – like Schopenhauer, for example – linear time is an illusion of human consciousness, reality being ontologically and in itself timeless. For others – like Leopardi and Rousseau – linear time is an ontological fact to which humans must adapt as best as they can.[36] Yet, for all pessimists, time is an essential aspect of their ontology. In fact, realism requires an account of time because, as Peter Gratton argues, without an account of time, realism ends up falling back into idealism.

In his critical introduction to continental realism, *Speculative Realism: Problems and Prospects*, Gratton contends that recent continental realisms have, in general, failed to give an adequate account of 'real time'.[37] For Gratton, these realisms, and particularly object-oriented ontology, remain implicitly committed to a more or less static account of the real, a commitment that risks undermining the anti-idealist nature of these accounts: 'I hope to show that speculating on the reality of time is [something ...] those in speculative realism should take on, lest they give themselves over to the idealism of objects, mathematics, and so on.'[38] The presentation of the real as static risks idealisation in the sense that it re-enacts the longstanding tendency of Western philosophy to present its accounts as if from a 'standpoint outside of time', which is to say, from a standpoint of assumed timeless universality.[39] This risk of idealisation is, for Gratton, hardly limited to philosophy, as one finds it also in traditions of physics and neurobiology that take time to be 'illusory'.[40] Hence Gratton argues that the desire to critique the idealising tendencies of Western thought (the basic critique of correlationism) requires a thinking of the real dynamism of time. It is, for Gratton, the critique of the metaphysics of presence that offers resources for thinking this real dynamism of time.[41] Specifically, he argues that Derrida's notion of writing, as both difference/deferral, provides a model for thinking the dynamism of real time, tracing a 'pivot' from a 'temporality' of specific text or contexts (moments) to a 'real time' that makes possible these particular instances but is not reducible to them.[42] Now Gratton's account is only schematic, but it is this notion of time as a 'real pivot' that is central to his account, since it is this real pivoting that prevents time from becoming either a static foundation or a mere construct of human consciousness, an inaccessible and ultimately idealist thing-in-itself.

Across a number of quick, dense pages, Gratton outlines what he sees as Derrida's notion of real time via readings of Levinas, Heidegger and Aristotle. This argument hinges on Derrida's well-known account of the trace structure of writing as a temporal and spatial othering: writing is both a temporal deferral (one never has the pure presence of any object or trace) and a spatial difference (a trace being always other than that of which it is a trace).[43] Following this logic, Derrida will argue that both the temporal present (moment) and the spatial other (object) always come to us from the future, a logic that shows space and time to be what they are only by being other than what they are. Now one might be tempted to read this logic as correlationist or even idealist, Derrida suggesting that we never have access to a real time or space except through the mediation of writing, language or conceptualisation.[44] However, Gratton argues – and this will mark the key move of his argument – that this temporal and spatial logic of the trace, this coming from the future, must be real, since otherwise it would never truly be other to the conceptual or linguistic:

> this trace would link us to a thinking of the trace of the Other that always interested Derrida, an Other that would come to us not 'as if' from the future, but as the future of what can never be present, here and now.[45]

The trace structure cannot be merely an 'as if,' a conceptual or metaphorical futurity or a time correlated to the schemas of language or concepts, since this would undermine its radical otherness. For the other to come from the future, this coming must be real, and it is this necessity that, for Gratton, shows the 'realness' of Derrida's account of time. This is not to suggest that the real is straightforward in Derrida's work or that Gratton's account does not leave certain questions unanswered. However, what is compelling about Gratton's argument is that it identifies the necessity of reading Derrida's account of temporality, whatever other implications it may have, as real, since, without such a reading, one cannot make sense of his account of the future, the other and the trace structure generally. This seems right to me. However, in a wider sense, Gratton's argument begins the work of detailing what it means to give a realist account of time, an account that he argues is not only necessary to avoid falling into idealism, but that also aligns the real with a certain 'absolute danger' and 'monstrosity', an alignment that brings us back to pessimism.

Having laid out Derrida's realist account of time, Gratton writes, 'we have [here] an argument that to speak to the real is to speak to what is timely and works backwards from there – in the face of a future that may be monstrous'.[46] What Gratton finds in Derrida's logic of writing is an account of real time that would not be a metaphysics of presence precisely because it denies the comfort of a fixed point around which the stability of one's reading could be grounded or secured. It is this resistance to stability, this insistence on the incalculability of the future that makes this account of time real and anti-correlationist, but it is also this incalculability that associates it with the monstrous, the non-recuperability of time to the human leaving us totally outside the safety of the human. Now this is just a passing reference in Gratton's account, and one that will be familiar to readers of Derrida's work, as he constantly associates the undecidability of the future with 'the worst'. However, read in the context of my account of pessimism, this reference suggests that Derrida's account of 'real time' would be akin to pessimism's account of time as necessarily linear and non-progressive in so far as the emphasis in these accounts is on the way in which the real must necessarily reject the comfort of progress or circularity, difference and deferral. Both these accounts remind us that the real, to be real, must be something that cannot be recuperable to the human and could thus always end badly. It is this reminder, this insistence that there is necessarily something unnerving and idealist about a realism that would not speak to time that is brought out in both pessimism and in Gratton's account of real time, and it is the relentless following through of this insight in connection to the role ideology and suffering play in realism that, I argue, marks the primary contributions of pessimism to the discourses of realism.

Conclusion

Although often understood as merely an account of human psychology or temperament, I have argued that pessimism is better read as a realist and anti-correlationist ontology, a following out of the assertion of an ontological indifference of the universe towards the human. Yet, more than perhaps any tradition of continental realism, pessimism insists that the assertion of a realist ontology is entangled with suffering and time, and that the failure to take seriously these aspects of realism works to idealise and humanise, on an ideological basis, not only the existence of human suffering but ontology and metaphysics more generally. Hence, pessimism suggests that, if the radicality of realism resides in its assertion of a radical indifference of the universe, an otherness that remains always and forever non-recuperable to the human, then pessimism would name not only the assertion of this ontological otherness, but also the worry for the way in which the denial of this otherness – whether in the form of correlationism, optimism or anti-realism – entails the ideological denial of suffering. It would suggest that realism must not assume to be beyond ideology, politics or violence, as it is precisely this assumption that has always marked the most profound moments of idealism and humanism within the Western philosophical tradition. In fact, pessimism suggests that being a realist means precisely engaging in the critique of ideology, a critique of real suffering and real time, lest we lose sight of why realism matters. For real.

Notes

1. Joshua Foa Dienstag, *Pessimism: Philosophy, Ethic, Spirit* (Princeton: Princeton University Press, 2006), p. 4.
2. Ibid. p. 17.
3. In addition to the work of Dienstag, see Eugene Thacker, *In the Dust of this Planet* (Winchester: Zero Books, 2011) and *Cosmic Pessimism* (Univocal Publishing, 2015); David Peak, *The Spectacle of the Void* (USA: Schism, 2014).
4. Thacker, *In the Dust*, p. 17.
5. Dienstag, *Pessimism*, p. 33.
6. Thomas Ligotti, *The Conspiracy against the Human Race* (New York: Hippocampus Press, 2010), p. 221.
7. Thacker, *In the Dust*, p. 5.
8. See also Eugene Thacker, *Starry Speculative Corpse* (Winchester: Zero Books, 2015); *Tentacles Longer Than Night* (Winchester: Zero Books, 2015).
9. Dienstag, *Pessimism*, p. 5.
10. Ibid. p. 9.
11. For Dienstag's subtle and detailed account of his aligning of pessimism with modernity, see *Pessimism*, pp. 9–19.
12. Dienstag, *Pessimism*, p. 5.
13. Ibid. p. 5.
14. Ibid. p. 5.
15. Levi Bryant, Nick Srnicek and Graham Harman (eds), *The Speculative Turn: Continental Materialism and Realism* (Melbourne: re.press, 2011), p. 3. See also Peter Gratton, *Speculative Realism: Problems and Prospects* (London: Bloomsbury, 2014).
16. Quentin Meillassoux, *After Finitude: An Essay on the Necessity of Contingency*, trans. Ray Brassier (London: Bloomsbury, 2009), p. 5.
17. Ibid. p. 5.

18. Catherine Malabou, *Before Tomorrow: Epigenesis and Rationality*, trans. Carolyn Shread (Cambridge: Polity Press, 2016), pp. 175–86.
19. Ligotti, *Conspiracy*, pp. 13–14. Also see Radoslav A. Tsanoff, *The Nature of Evil* (Nabu Press, 2011).
20. Antinatalism is a collection of philosophical and social views that see reproduction of the human species as undesirable. See David Benatar, *Better Never to Have Been: The Harm of Coming into Existence* (Oxford: Oxford University Press, 2006), p. 8; Jim Crawford, *Confessions of an Antinatalist* (Charleston: Nine-Banded Books, 2010).
21. Ligotti, *Conspiracy*, p. 28.
22. Ibid. p. 65.
23. Ibid. p. 50.
24. Ibid. p. 50.
25. Dienstag, *Pessimism*, p. 78. See also Ligotti, *Conspiracy*, p. 51.
26. Ligotti, *Conspiracy*, pp. 50–1.
27. Friedrich Nietzsche, 'Truth and lies in a nonmoral sense', in *Philosophy and Truth: Selections from Nietzsche's Notebooks, Early 1870's*, ed. and trans. Daniel Breazeale (New York: Humanities Press, 1990), pp. 79–80.
28. Ibid. p. 82.
29. Theodor W. Adorno, *Metaphysics: Concepts and Problems*, ed. Rolf Tiedemann, trans. Edmund Jephcott (Stanford: Stanford University Press, 2001), pp. 70–1.
30. Ligotti, *Conspiracy*, p. 64.
31. Dienstag, *Pessimism*, pp. 19–25.
32. Ibid. p. 25.
33. Arthur Schopenhauer, *The World as Will and Representation: Volume I*, trans. Christopher Janaway (Cambridge: Cambridge University Press, 2010), p. 352.
34. For an account of the essential role of violence in deconstruction, see my essay, 'Revisiting violence and life in the early work of Jacques Derrida', *Symplokē*, vol. 20, no. 1–2 (2012): pp. 35–52.
35. For a concise account of resilience discourse, see Robin James, *Resilience & Melancholy: Pop Music, Feminism, Neoliberalism* (Winchester: Zero Books, 2015), pp. 6–7.
36. Dienstag, *Pessimism*, pp. 19–25.
37. Gratton, *Speculative Realism*, p. 202.
38. Ibid. p. 202.
39. Ibid. p. 202.
40. Ibid. p. 203.
41. Ibid. p. 204.
42. Ibid. p. 208.
43. Ibid. pp. 214–15.
44. Ibid. p. 207.
45. Ibid. pp. 214–15.
46. Ibid. p. 216.

Chapter 6

Being (with) Objects

Anna Mudde

> I am a primitive Venus, a small fertility goddess with a naked alabaster body. ... A woman rather than a gazelle: Everything in me invokes flesh, not contemplation. And yet, he looks at me, he never stops looking at me, the instant he lifts his eyes from his page, the instant he begins to meditate and sets his long dark gaze upon me without seeing me. Other times, however, he scrutinizes me thoughtfully, trying to penetrate my immobile sculpture's soul, I can tell he is a whisker away from establishing contact, from guessing, conversing, and then suddenly he gives up and I have the exasperated feeling that I have just attended the performance of a man who is looking at himself in a two-way mirror, never suspecting for a moment that from behind the mirror, someone is observing him ... and this is the way it is for him with the flesh and blood creatures who cross his path in life, they are absent from memory when he turns his back upon them and, when once again they enter the field of his perception, they offer him a presence he cannot grasp. ... His watchful, intelligent eyes are separated from what they see by an invisible veil that hinders his judgment ... and the veil is that of the distraught autocrat, with his perpetual anxiety that the person opposite him might turn out to be something other than an object he can dismiss from his vision at leisure.
>
> <div align="right">Muriel Barbery, <i>Gourmet Rhapsody</i></div>

In *The Quadruple Object*, Graham Harman argues that phenomenology has an ambivalent relationship with the 'philosophy of access', or correlationist philosophy. At once drawing upon Husserl and Heidegger as phenomenologists who 'take objects seriously', Harman also argues that phenomenology is irretrievably idealist.[1] In its place, Levi Bryant writes, object-oriented ontology (OOO) insists on the decentring of the human,[2] shifting away from accounts of the world in which being is always 'reduced' to what being is for 'us' (that is, human beings).[3] One of the central commitments of OOO theorists is to worldly, real object-things, which exceed and operate independently of the human capacity to encounter and know them. There is a 'world out there', doing its own thing, that is both philosophically rich and worthy of philosophical attention. In this vein, Harman proposes a new *respect* for objects, asking us to notice how objects 'withdraw' from their engagements with other objects, and exceed the other's 'distort[ions], caricature[s], and transformation[s] of the hidden reality of things'.[4]

In this chapter, I explore some of the ambivalent potential of Harman's post-humanist object-oriented ontology for thinking about human beings as objects, and for how to be with human beings as objects. In particular, I consider the work of feminist phenomenologists attuned to objectification[5] as both having a tradition of object-orientation and as already contesting the idealist tendencies opposed by Harman. Like Harman, they are often centrally concerned with worldly particularities, with the 'churning' of reality,[6] and with philosophically salient experiences that are inseparable from that churning. Objectified human beings inhabit a site of ontological duality, often knowing themselves as objects for others, who thus experience the ontological and epistemological *disruptions* that can emerge from the human activity of objectification. Absence of these analyses[7] in OOO constitutes an important oversight since such analyses draw attention not only to object relations among human beings, but thereby also point to ways of understanding human relations with non-human objects.

I began with an epigraph by novelist Muriel Barbery because the passage provides an entry point for thinking about the ways human relations with objects are coextensive with inter-human relations. Particularly relevant here are the ontological *effects* that can come from knowing oneself to be an object for others, namely: how being objectified affects the ways knowers can understand both the 'respect' and 'withdrawal' of objects.[8] Given some of Harman's central commitments to re-envisioning human beings, like other beings, as worldly objects, he provides glimpses of what it would be like to move around in the world, respecting other things, understanding our contact with them to be partial and limited, always a 'distortion', 'caricature' or 'objectification' of their withdrawn reality. Yet it is peculiar not to see sustained consideration of what it is like to be a thing-respected, to be a thing-withdrawn, a thing-distorted or thing-caricatured. That matters, I will suggest, because it can lend itself to the utterly misinformed position that assumes, on the one hand, that the ways things withdraw are somehow of their own design, choice, or nature and, on the other hand, that distortions and caricatures 'just happen', that they are not produced in part by the ways the *perceiver* is shaped, trained and broadly enculturated to perceive objects and kinds of objects. It misses, then, key ways in which human objects, at least, can get things wrong as ontologists and can be unwilling or unable to be corrected by the world, a central commitment in most forms of metaphysical realism. In this respect, I suggest that the experience and analysis of embodied objectification provides an indispensable rejoinder to any ontology that is object-oriented.

Attending to how one/we attend(s) to objects is becoming a central ecological exercise for thinking, being and responding differently; Harman and other OOO theorists, as part of the highly variegated group of speculative realists, draw us to this in a particular way. Primarily ontological and epistemological, and by extension political and ethical, such an exercise is pressingly non-optional for responsible, thoughtful forms of human life. Yet it is and has been a feature of many critically engaged philosophies of the twentieth century – indeed, forms of 'guerrilla metaphysics' have been operational for decades.[9] The ones I am interested in in this chapter attend specifically to objectification, a metaphorical description of the ways some human beings are attended to by others, and of what it is like to be seen-as object. An underlying assertion in this chapter is that, in contrast with the sense of novelty one might find reading work in OOO, there are long-standing, if often marginalised, bodies of work on the ways we attend to objects and to human beings as objects.

The objectification(s) of certain human bodies is not only present as sexual objectification but, more generally, as a pervasive lived way of being and being perceived by key others. Indeed, if one wants a sense of 'what it is like to be a thing' vis-à-vis human perception, asking about such objectification is a good place to start. Drawing on feminist phenomenological analyses of embodied knowledge, I suggest that those who learn 'first and best' how to live as *objectified* often know what it is to 'withdraw' from the perceptions and conceptualisations of another, to exceed the distortions and caricatures of knowers engaged in the sort of project of access Harman (and others) worry about. Although I do not propose that objectification is wholly equivalent to Harman's 'respect' for objects, I do propose it both as a 'gateway' and as a cautionary account revealing that *how* we are with and as objects is at least as important as *what* we theorise objects to be. There are particular epistemological and ontological risks that arise when human beings attend to objects, and those risks shift, but do not disperse, when the ontological centrality of human beings is challenged.

Prehension

In keeping with the descriptive epigraph I borrowed from Muriel Barbery, the embodied, 'carnal'[10] experience of being objectified can not only leave a person with a lived sense of what it is like to be a thing for others, it can also provide reasons to attend to objects and to ways of attending to objects. Analyses of objectification often describe being a thing for human others as, in part, being withdrawn and mysterious, unintelligible, cut off from and by the thing that is perceiving oneself. We see an early version of this in Simone de Beauvoir's articulation of the myths of woman in *The Second Sex*:

> Of all these myths, none is more anchored ... than the feminine 'mystery'. It has numerous advantages. At first it allows an easy explanation for anything that is inexplicable; the man who does not 'understand' a woman is happy to replace his subjective deficiency with an objective resistance; instead of admitting his ignorance, he recognizes the presence of a mystery exterior to himself: here is an excuse that flatters his laziness and vanity at the same time ... And thanks to the mystery, this negative relation that seemed to Kierkegaard infinitely preferable to positive possession is perpetuated; faced with a living enigma, man remains alone: alone with his dreams, hopes, fears, love, vanity; this subjective game ... is for many a more attractive experience than an authentic relation with a human being.
>
> Surely, in a way, woman is mysterious, 'mysterious like everyone', according to Maeterlink. Each one is a subject only for himself; each one can grasp only his own self in his immanence; from this point of view, the other is always a mystery ... [but] as she is mystery for man, woman is regarded as mystery in herself.[11]

It might already be clear from this passage why the OOO appeal to withdrawal and hiding, to inherent distance and the mystery that ensues, might provoke dis-ease among some readers, especially when the experiences of things-objectified are not part of the discussion.[12] But to draw out the point, when reading Harman, I cannot help but 'hear' faint echoes of Beauvoir and of other objectified people in ways I will explore in the following sections.

In an early paper, challenging what he sees as *the* disappointingly perpetual philosophical question – about how to 'bridge the gap' between subject and object, or, about the subject's 'access' to worldly objects – Harman turns to Alphonso Lingis's *Foreign Bodies* for an alternative approach. Extrapolating from Lingis, Harman writes that, rather than assuming that gap, we can instead understand objects to be 'making room for one another':

> objects contest each other, seduce each other, empower or annihilate each other. Commanding one another by way of the reality of their forces, the objects exist as imperatives. Like fish hunting food or dogs playing with balls, it is possible that gravel and tar, cloth and magnesium wage war against one another, compress one another into submission, command respect from one another.[13]

Leaving aside what I think is a telling assumption about respect as involving command and submission, it is helpful to notice that, in refusing the gap between subject and objects, Harman appeals to Whitehead, who describes things, objects, as 'prehending' one another.[14] Harman elsewhere writes: 'This word [prehension] designates the mutual objectification with which all actual entities confront one another, and thereby stakes a philosophical claim outside the limited realm of Dasein.'[15] Objectification in this sense thus neutrally designates the ontological structure of 'prehension'.

Harman thus refers to Husserl's insight that every instance of having an object of consciousness is 'either an *objectifying act* or has its basis in such an act' and concludes that human prehenders encounter 'a world already broken up into chunks'.[16] Yet, to understand *Harman's* sense of objectification, it helps to notice that a central claim of his OOO is that there is a complete lack of (metaphysical) contact between objects. They exist, as he puts it, 'in utter isolation from all others, packed into secluded private vacuums',[17] only encountering one another 'despite' their isolation 'as a kind of caricature or objectification – the rock did exist beforehand, but never quite in the way in which the other rock objectifies it'.[18] Given our isolation from other objects, and theirs from us, he argues that an object-oriented ontology requires us to rethink objects, and this without idealism's simultaneous centrality of the subject and the resulting problem of access.

Thus, in *The Quadruple Object*, Harman articulates the distinction his ontology posits between 'real objects' and 'sensual objects'. Real objects both are and exceed the ways they manifest to others; they are in each case the non-reducible being itself, which 'enact[s] the reality in the cosmos of which that object alone is capable'.[19] Sensual qualities and objects are partial expressions (my word) of real objects and qualities; they are the phenomena that arise from objects themselves. As such, they exist only if they do so 'for me, or for some other agent that expends its energy in taking them seriously'.[20] Put another way, 'the sensual is what exists only in relation to the perceiver [a real object] . . . the real is whatever withdraws from that relation'.[21] The thing itself always 'recedes behind any possible objectification of it'.[22] This is not only inevitable, but inescapable; real objects cannot touch one another and indeed withdraw from one another, from their respective objectifications of one another. Thus, prehension of one object by another substitutes the sensual for the real, producing the inevitable 'distort[ion], caricature, and transformation of the hidden reality of things' with which I began.[23] Real objects are objectified, inescapably, in and by their sensual manifestations for other (real) objects.

As I hope is clear, Harman's consideration of objectification is not coextensive with the phenomenon of objectification to which I am calling attention. Still, Harman's position regarding objectification is difficult to pin down – perhaps rightly so. On the one hand, he argues that Husserlian objectification strips objects of their 'objectivity': objects become chunks of being about which *human perception and intellect* give and find meaning, and thus for Harman, 'the "objects" toward which [objectifying acts] point are not very objective at all'.[24] On the other hand, Harman takes seriously the idea that all objects are caught up in relations of mutual objectification, so that to prehend another is to *caricature or objectify it* in this other, non-neutral, object-of-consciousness sense. Thus, I am not justified in appealing to my perception – prehension, caricature, objectification – of the thing to say what the thing is. Instead, I am obliged to 'respect' the object as withdrawing from my and any other partial sensual objectification: the object's *reality* is unknown and unknowable to me and to its other prehenders.

To take up OOO as Harman envisions it is to accept and be awed by the world's capacity to elude, escape, exceed us, and to allow that to command our respect as a way of grounding philosophical practice. Harman's work thus constitutes an important challenge to the still-pervasive 'epistemologies of mastery'[25] – human epistemic mastery over the 'external' world – and thus to orthodox realist metaphysics. Still, it is difficult to calculate what status the objectification of human beings has in Harman's picture of things given that on this description, as in many other places in his work, there is a sense in which the objectifying actor's role in articulating objects does so in ways that *condition* their (sensual) manifestations, but in a way that does not 'touch' the real thing itself. As I will suggest, objectification is not only a way of being perceived by others, it seems to present us with a way of being perceived that inevitably 'touches' and shapes the real thing, if sometimes in unrecognised ways.[26] What does OOO look like when it takes the accounts of objectified – that is, touched – human beings seriously, and what does this suggest about the risks we take – indeed, are already taking – in our dealings with objects?

Objectification

Alongside a deep respect for philosophy and its history, I read in Harman's work a commitment that I, and many others, share: a commitment to the knowledge that 'reality is churning'.[27] There are worldly lives and 'things' happening 'out there in the world', things that are importantly varied and rich and palpably laden with possible – if inaccessible – meaning, with their own relationships that do not include the human 'us'; there are worldly things that are, for many of 'us', inseparable from our needs for and practices of philosophy; there is a sense in which the world 'commands' us, in important ways, and not the other way around. In other words, there is, in Harman's work, a real sense in which questions about access can express a troubling way of being, or not being *in*, *of* and *with* the world. But so, too, I will suggest, can an insufficiently critical sense of worldly access, even access to withdrawal and mystery, to the hidden reality of things.

As I will explore, when feminist philosophers analyse objectification, they do so precisely in response to *direct experience* with a worldly phenomenon. But theorists cannot make sense of that phenomenon without saying something about the ways in which women *appear* not only *as* sensual qualities/objects (in tension with their real object existence), but *to* the person prehending them. That is, even in rejecting the philosophy of access as a philosophy of the gap, we need a way to explain why, for example, when presented with another person or consciousness, many human organisms fail both to prehend and to be corrected about that person's status as consciousness or person. And, in those cases, appeals only to the person's sensual qualities, or to her withdrawal as real object, will not suffice.

To find that women – and other Others – are object-like is neither surprising nor incorrect. They are, like all human beings, things in the world, and objects of consciousness for (certain) others. They have sensual qualities associated with material objects. But they also have sensual qualities that we associate with being a subject that are often systematically and routinely made unnoticed/-able. What solicits analyses of objectification, what some human beings know by living as certain sorts of objects for others, are the ways in which human prehensions often *preclude* noticing some sensual qualities while allowing other sensual qualities to be predominant.

Objectification in these terms might also be understood as a way of 'buying in' to human perceptions as not just direct, but as unproblematically direct. To say that our prehensions are direct need not mean that we cannot be corrected when objects themselves push back against our caricatures of them. But anyone who has been objectified knows that what the objectifier *sees*, directly, is *not* a subject he or she *makes* object in his or her mind. What the objectifier *sees* and has been trained to see is object, and object in particular ways. And, as Beauvoir's insight cautions us, objectification and objectivity are often inseparable; a thing's being regarded as mysterious by powerful human beings often comes to mean that the thing *is* mysterious 'in itself'. Perhaps this is an operation of sensual qualities. But an object-oriented theory that cannot account for and correct this (real and sensual) phenomenon – the phenomenon of uncritical objectivity – seems to cry out for amendment. For this reason, I suggest that the OOO impulse towards tentativeness and modest speculation, to the acceptance of mystery and unknowing, is helpfully informed by accounts of being-objectified.

First, if the real withdraws from the sensual, becoming hidden from the real perceiver, we might need to be tentative about the point at which that withdrawal or becoming hidden occurs. If metaphysical realism is or involves the claim that human beings can be wrong about and corrected by what there is, what the world is like, then we might also be tentative and sceptical – or stronger, wary – about any simple appeal to mystery, to claims about the withdrawal of things, both as exceeding the sensual qualities of things and in human prehensions of those things. *That* things are partially inaccessible and inevitably hidden does not mean that our perceptions of them as such answer the question about the point of inaccessibility 'correctly'; we may not always properly identify which parts are inaccessible.

Second, and in keeping both with feminist epistemologies of objectivity and with parts of the phenomenological tradition, we might notice that if real objects admit of different sensual objects in response to particular prehensive objectifiers, the question '*from what* is this object withdrawing, and *how*?' seems to be an important one to ask. Who (or what, if that is preferable) prehends/caricatures/objectifies and how does she/he/they/it prehend/caricature/objectify? What withdrawals does this seem to produce?

Finally, the asymmetry of consciousness between self and other in traditional phenomenology, namely, that I am never conscious of you (here, my sensual object) the way I am of myself (myself as real object), is extended in Harman's work so that it holds not only for consciousness, but for all sentient and non-sentient things. But, in either case, we need a way of acknowledging that some objects *qua* sensual cannot always correct the perceptions of their real observers; that even if all objects withdraw from their prehensions by others, sometimes what is perceived as withdrawal is nothing of the sort. Sometimes, the prehender is unwilling or unable to prehend in particular ways, and those are incorrectly identified as features produced by the real object.

All of these, as I will suggest, we can accommodate without returning to a philosophical practice that assumes the problems of access while nevertheless attending to the formations and roles of prehensile skills, experiences, and cultural assumptions. Indeed, this approach has been used for decades by feminist and other critically-oriented phenomenologists. In this vein, Simone de Beauvoir provides an important case study in the context of OOO because she is a phenomenologist with strong realist commitments who rejects a philosophy of access. Moreover, her work is taken as foundational for many analyses of human objectification.

My metaphysics, my self

To be objectified is sometimes to 'speak' (sometimes to scream) and be unheard, to be made intelligible only insofar as one is for-others; sometimes, it is to be revered as sacred or untouchable. But to be objectified is often also to know that and how consciousness can get things wrong, can fail in direct experience with the world to know it; it is to know the myriad ways consciousness can resist correction. Analyses of objectification are borne of direct contact with worldly things, from an insistence that, even as we raise questions and argue about access, we are not entitled to retreat from the reality that is 'churning'. There is a world human beings are called to try to understand with accuracy, and this is not just a philosophical exercise, but is often a matter of life and death. But in non-negotiable ways, part of 'what there is' is – and is sometimes shaped by – what human beings think there is. For this reason, Beauvoir, a phenomenologist Harman does not consider, is instructive. She shares Harman's realism without sidestepping being-objectified as part of the 'carnival of the world'.[28] And, importantly, she insists that our basic metaphysics – our basic ways of attending to concrete things – constitute our ways of being a thing in the world. Yet, she does not assume that our metaphysics arise from ourselves alone; indeed, as I will suggest, her attunement to human ways of being a particular kind of thing, touching and thus provoking particular kinds of responses among other things, is inseparable from the touches and responses of others/other things.

Like Harman, Beauvoir takes Merleau-Ponty's phenomenology seriously. Merleau-Ponty attends to the ways in which one's body is one's 'grasp on the world and the outline of [one's] projects',[29] an essentially important feature of Beauvoir's work. But, unlike Merleau-Ponty (and in keeping with Harman's critique of him[30]), Beauvoir does not refuse the embodied subject the role of object. Rather, her phenomenological method locates consciousness as *already* situated as object, as thing, by being embodied. A human being is an ambiguous subject–object in time and space; consciousness is thereby situated in the world as, with and by other *things* of which it can be and is called to be conscious. At the same time, it is also an object of which others are conscious, and to which other objects are (sometimes and particularly) responsive.

Given this grounding, Beauvoir's approach consistently emphasises not only the presence of the body as an immanence (and of its status as object-of-consciousness for others), but also that *doing* metaphysics requires us to attend to our particular metaphysical *experiences* of and as immanence(s). Doing metaphysics, one 'posit[s] oneself in one's totality before the totality of the world';[31] anyone's philosophical attempts to express or to systematise a metaphysics is bound up with one's being as particular subject–object, a particular embodied consciousness in space and time – one's own. Such an attempt reveals, through its particularity of intra-actions with other objects, one's very being, *oneself*. As she puts the point: 'Spinozism defines Spinoza, and Hegelianism defines Hegel'.[32] One's metaphysics, one's prehensive tendencies and capacities, thus constitute, in important respects, one's way of being (a thing) in and with the world.

Experience of those things with which I am situated is a swirling together of directly accessed facticity (through the facticity of embodied consciousness) and the meanings things have been given before, with and by me.[33] For Beauvoir, to be so situated is in part to be *directly* affected by 'the dark weight of other things';[34] I prehend them and am, moreover, *prehended by them* because I, too, am one of those things. Beauvoir's insistence on the human being as ambiguously subject and object, an ambiguity only surpassed as a matter of bad faith, comes from her phenomenological attentiveness to what it is like to be an object of consciousness for others, and *a thing in the world* that provokes others' consciousness to make of it an object.

It is no accident, I suggest, that more than the work of many other phenomenologists, being-object is centrally a part of Beauvoir's ontological picture. It is, moreover, no accident that her own clear realist attention to worldly things (for example, my self and life have facticities that I *cannot* correctly interpret in just any way I choose) is accompanied by an early articulation of objectified human being. Beauvoir cannot forget, overcome or fail to take seriously that she is an object for others; her metaphysics necessarily expresses this feature of her experience, her being manifests this form of 'touch' by others.

Being object

For Beauvoir, no human being is improperly or mistakenly identified as object. With Husserl, she finds that we are each, at the very least, objects of consciousness for others. But she additionally holds that human beings have object-facticity in the world. Like OOO theorists, then, Beauvoir holds robust realist commitments: in particular, when we are dealing with other human beings, we make a mistake – we *objectify* and oppress others – if our perception of them as object is not amended to recognise them as *also* having consciousness, that is, as being subject-object.[35] We can be mistaken about the world and corrected by it. In Beauvoir's work, as in Harman's (for different reasons), objectification is additional to our ontological status as object; but objectification is an epistemic, ontological and ethical failure or mistake for Beauvoir. Objectification in this sense names a way of attending to objects, which not only conditions their manifestation(s), but which also fails to be 'open' to worldly things, foreclosing other objects' capacities to correct us.

This seems to explain why, despite insisting that I attend to the ways in which my experiences and articulations of the general features of reality are situated and mine, Beauvoir also enjoins us to employ a sceptical method. This is not a radical scepticism; one does not proceed primarily by doubting what there is, or what one perceives there to be, but by orienting oneself towards things so that the questions in the back of one's mind are always 'How *is* this thing such that it can appear to me as it does?' and 'How *am I* such that it appears to me as it does?' Her ontology requires a distinction between, and an ambiguity of, facticity and the meanings human beings find in and give to facticity, neither being reducible to the other and both being necessary to any accurate articulation of what there is.

By raising this distinction, Beauvoir effects a loosening of objects of consciousness (or, perhaps, 'objectifying acts') from the things that provoke the response of consciousness. Things command human attention, yet consciousness is never innocent in its effects on the world. We can see this clearly in *The Second Sex*, particularly in the section called 'Biological data'. There, Beauvoir argues that the brute existence and rich facticity of human bodily differences that *can* become sexed and take on gendered meanings give us very few directions about what those differences mean. Not only are we wise to be agnostic about the connection between biological 'imperatives' (using Lingis's and Harman's word) and gendered meanings, we are also wise to be agnostic about the purported connection between biological facticity (for instance, different sorts of bodies with different roles in reproduction) and 'sex difference'. Considering what concrete facticity entitles us to think or claim to know about human bodies, we find it is very much less than the purportedly 'factual' sexed meanings we are trained to *see* as part of brute facticity. The fact of sexual reproduction among human beings (for example, the necessity of two distinct gametes for procreation) not only fails to give us particular gender roles, it also fails to give us the strict demarcations between two sexes in ways we are conditioned to assume.[36] Bodies withdraw, perhaps, from human meanings; their imperatives are their own and do not fully circumscribe the meanings we find and give to them.

We might ask what leads Beauvoir – and many of us – to *know*, to *experience*, that there is, to greater and lesser degrees, a space between a thing's 'imperatives' and human consciousness of the thing and its meaning. I suspect that an answer can be found in Beauvoir's articulation of the situation of woman, in the Introduction to Volume I of *The Second Sex*:

> what singularly defines the situation of woman is that ... an attempt is made to freeze her as an object and doom her to immanence, since her transcendence will be forever transcended by another essential and sovereign consciousness. Woman's drama lies in this conflict between the fundamental claim of every subject, which always posits itself as essential, and the demands of a situation that constitutes her as inessential.[37]

For those who are situated as women – and other Others – in the way Beauvoir describes, positing oneself before the totality of the world (one's ontological experience and capacities for articulating it) might be inescapably overlaid, at the same time, by knowing oneself to be an object for others, by one's experience of being objectified, of being non-essential. Some of us live (parts of) ourselves as comprising the 'churning' reality that is distorted, caricatured and transformed not only by philosophers but through the everyday functioning of cultural ontologies.

For instance, in Iris Marion Young's work on modes of traditional feminine motility (that is, *not* women's motility[38]), she theorises how feminine bodily comportment is characterised by self-reference, self-objectification, taking up the body as an object of motion rather than 'its originator'.[39] To move in culturally feminine ways – for instance, 'throwing like a girl' – involves not only moving with an immanent, concrete body, but being rooted in that body (one part of the body moves, while the rest remains immobile);[40] it involves the underuse of a body's real capacity so that the physical aim is severed from the enactment (a physically manifest 'I can' throw the ball overlaid with a self-imposed 'I cannot';[41] these combine to produce movements which do not form a unity with bodily surroundings (a failure to work 'with' the ball, to move it through the air effectively[42]). As Young puts it, 'the feminine subject posits her motion as the motion that is looked at', an implication of 'the basic fact of the woman's social existence as the object of the gaze of another, which is a major source of her bodily self-reference'.[43] The effect of that gaze might appear as a kind of withdrawal, a 'hiding', but is in fact the overlay of knowledge of the gaze itself, taken up by a real object as 'sensual' manifestation. It is active, not passive. Yet, so long as we accept that feminine motility, for example, is acquired and not real in the essential or teleological sense, the question arises again: '*From what* is this object withdrawing, and *how*?'

On the one hand, that gaze operates with impressive subtlety, as a specialised extension of the basic fact of all human sociality: we are visible to others and we like, perhaps need, to present 'well'. As Foucault reminds us, we are products of a virtual panopticon. Yet, as Sandra Bartky shows, that panopticon is differentially present in the lives of women (and differentially affects women depending on income, racialisation, sexual orientation, (dis)ability). The result is an existence that is psychologically oppressed: the product of being told that one is a person, a subject, and then resolutely being treated as an object. And if one forgets, one is reminded:

> It is a fine spring day, and with an utter lack of self-consciousness, I am bouncing down the street. Suddenly I hear men's voices. Catcalls and whistles fill the air. These noises are clearly sexual in intent and they are meant for me. . . . I freeze . . . my body becomes stiff and self-conscious. The body which only a moment before I inhabited with such ease now floods my consciousness. . . . They could, after all, have enjoyed me in silence. . . . But I must be made to know that I am a 'nice piece of ass': I must be made to see myself as they see me.[44]

These experiences, which are not only common but highly various (being told in a public place by a passing acquaintance that you are the object of his sexual fantasies; being catcalled in the street as *being* some various form of ass – 'hot', 'fat', 'nice piece of' and the like; being critiqued for one's fashion sense on student evaluations[45]), are, as the passage by Beauvoir I cited earlier suggests, also seamlessly and importantly part of the phenomenal field that makes women 'mysterious', inscrutable. The solidity, impenetrability, of objects appears wherever we insist on a certain form of objectification, or wherever it is ontologically intelligible (as it often is for Others) to do so.

For subjects trained not to notice their own status as objects in the world, those who are taken to be objects often seem to have mysterious qualities. This produces important epistemological effects: it can lead to a justification for refusing to know better, for refusing to be corrected by the world – that is, as is prevalent in the cultural talk of women (among others) as mysterious, 'we' are confident in claiming their mystery whenever we do not understand them.[46] And being unable to understand them becomes justifiable on the grounds of their inherent mystery. Failure to understand is thus not mine; it is the result of a stubbornness of my object, preventing the move of building the skills of more subtle, attentive directive-taking from the objects with which we are here, now, in the world.[47] Easy and innocent resort to the inscrutability of objects can also hide the ways in which they have *become* withdrawn; the ways their distortions, caricatures and transportations have made it easier and sometimes safer, in the non-trivial sense,[48] to withdraw than to correct. The objects they may be for others may already be a product of self-consciousness, and, by extension, of the gaze.[49] Ways in which objects are hidden from us does not equate to their ways of being hidden in themselves.

Unknown unknowns

Because he follows Husserl in thinking that basic perception is or involves an 'objectifying act', Harman rejects naive realism, holding that '[h]uman awareness is riddled with objectifying acts that have already sliced up the world into separate pieces' such that 'the same object can manifest itself in countless different ways' and 'the same sensory material can give rise to the most diverse articulations of objects'.[50] Yet, because we are enjoined to focus on things, and not *also* on our particular and peculiar forms of access to them, understanding those different ways of provoking response and articulating themselves go unarticulated, their conditioning effects on manifestation – *from whom/from what* prehensive ontology is this object withdrawing? – are largely passed over.[51] The point is not that we can 'get at' the real object, make it 'surrender to us' in the traditional sense, nor that we should want to. But eschewing sustained attention to the effects of the particular forms of objectification that constitute our individual and collective metaphysics allows us to eschew robustly *responsible*, non-innocent object-orientation. Responsible, non-innocent ontology can be difficult to square with key parts of Harman's theory.

The flesh and blood creatures with whom Barbery's Venus notices her owner cannot 'establish contact', having a presence he 'cannot grasp', might simply be real objects withdrawn from their sensual existence for others, or objects that 'naturally' withdraw in that way in response to contact with other particular objects; but it is also clear that their 'hidden reality', their mysteriousness,[52] can as easily be effected by a failure of others to 'expend [their] energy on taking them seriously'.[53] Yet the underlying real thing is not, I suggest, untouched by that failure. The objectifying ontologies that operate in many women's lives, for instance, often create lived tensions between ill-fitting sensual qualities external to women's own bodies and selves that nonetheless condition those bodies and selves, the 'I' absorbed in relations with other objects (including, perhaps, its own). But there are other ontologies – like the expectation of mysteriousness – that can, as Beauvoir notes, make challenging any lack of understanding a monumental task. Moreover, without an account of conditioning prehensions, it does, indeed, become mysterious why any hidden object would, for example, manifest itself in 'throwing like a girl'. Except that it is not mysterious at all, and that is not an instance of withdrawal.

Even if human interactions with worldly things are simply prehensions among worldly things, ontologically equivalent with prehensions among non-human objects, we would still need to take seriously *how* those interactions reveal their particular form and character, the particular possibilities for human things and the things with which they are mutually prehended, the particular ways they can 'withdraw' from other things (and be withdrawn from by those other things), if we are to be sufficiently precise about what we are talking about. As experiences of objectification attest, for the realist there arise both epistemological risks and openings when human beings are dealing with objects; they cannot always correct us. As objects ourselves, human beings may sometimes have to try to prehend their own prehending – not as a question about access, but as a question about responsibility (and response-ability) to a world in which we are directly engaged. OOO can, I think, shift the central epistemological questions in radical and necessary ways, but it cannot sidestep them entirely; ontology and epistemology simply are not distinguishable in ways that allow eschewing one in favour of the other.

I began with what I take to be a central feature of Harman's thinking, the need for a new *respect* for objects, which involves noticing how objects 'withdraw' from their engagements with other objects, exceeding the other's 'distort[ions], caricature[s], and transformation[s] of the hidden reality of things'.[54] Ian Bogost expresses the point this way: 'When we ask what it is to be something, we pose a question that exceeds our own grasp of the being of the world. These unknown unknowns characterize things about an object that may or may not be obvious – or even knowable.'[55] Read alongside analyses of being-objectified, which describes a pattern of prehensions of others prehending oneself, OOO's way of describing a respect for objects reveals what I take to be an important reason to consider who is making ontological claims. Again, this is not intended as a challenge to the importance of assuming 'unknown unknowns'. Rather, as attentive human objects, a central question of ours needs to be 'unknowable *to whom?*'

Taking objects as ontologically basic, as Harman does, and rethinking both what objects are and the status of subjects as philosophically primary, is highly promising. It suggests, at the very least, a return to rethinking the human being as organism and the importance of the variety of ways such organisms directly access the world. Analyses of objectification, however, highlight both the concrete, ethical hazards of taking things to be what philosophers call objects as well as the need for a way to deal with the epistemological risks of prehensive objectification. The injunction to respect objects on their own terms, instead of also attending to how we already attend to them, does not sufficiently challenge the individualism and disconnectedness of real things that is already dominant in orthodox Western metaphysics, cultural attitudes, preferences and practices. Analyses of being-objectified thus bring to the fore questions of metaphysical responsibility and objectivity such that – as feminist and other marginalised philosophers have long held – it matters who is making claims about an object and which object is having claims made about it.

Moreover, respecting objects as our 'autonomous colleagues' may give us a sense of the 'carnival of the world', but what many of us know from having autonomous colleagues is that respect for autonomy does not generally produce allies or active bystanders. And it does not speak to the ecological need, which is becoming desperate in the Anthropocene, for responsibility to and for other things. For this reason, I have highlighted the ways feminist philosophies recognise and make spaces for human objects that experience sympathetic resonances with the ways in which non-human objects can 'withdraw' from others, as well as the ways in which the 'hidden realities' of objects are distorted, caricatured and transformed by others. The cautions that emerge from analyses of human objectification might give us pause about the operations of withdrawal among non-human objects, as well, and about their need for allies.

Notes

1. Perhaps this is to be expected; the phenomenological work Harman considers is, as I suggest below, unnecessarily constrained.
2. Levi R. Bryant, *The Democracy of Objects* (Ann Arbor: Open Humanities Press, 2011), p. 20.
3. Ibid. p. 19.
4. Graham Harman, 'Objects, matter, sleep, and death', in *Towards Speculative Realism* (Winchester: Zero Books, 2010), pp. 199–207, here p. 202.
5. Here, I consider feminist phenomenologies of objectification, which I take to be, at their most useful, deeply informed by, and inseparable from, articulations of objectification from non-white, colonised, poor/working class, LGBTQI, disabled, and 'foreign' bodies and persons. The theorists I consider here – particularly Simone de Beauvoir – offer phenomenologies that are nonetheless partially tangled up, in difficult and harmful ways, with the category 'woman', from which many people are (still) actively excluded by being non-white, colonised, poor/working class, LGBTQI, disabled, 'foreign'. I hope to see more work on OOO and 'naturalised' social categories.
6. Graham Harman, 'Object oriented philosophy', in *Towards Speculative Realism*, pp. 93–104, here p. 94.
7. Harman does consider objectification in *Tool-Being*, but generally in the mode of what it is like to objectify, as opposed to what it is like to be objectified. See Graham Harman, *Tool-Being: Heidegger and the Metaphysics of Objects* (Chicago: Open Court, 2002).
8. I focus here on respect and withdrawal for reasons of space, but a fuller exploration of this topic would fruitfully include Harman's work on metaphor, allure and charm. See

Graham Harman, *Guerrilla Metaphysics: Phenomenology and the Carpentry of Things* (Chicago: Open Court, 2005), pp. 101–41.
9. Noting with irony Harman's use of the term 'guerrilla', and allowing for differences of language, please see work by, for example, Donna Haraway, Chela Sandoval, María Lugones, Rosi Braidotti, Sara Ahmed, Simone de Beauvoir (whom I consider here), Trinh T. Minh-ha, the 'New Materialist' movement, post-colonial theorists, and work in feminist philosophies of science. The latter, in particular, have long challenged the philosophy of access.
10. See Harman, *Guerrilla Metaphysics*, Part I.
11. Simone de Beauvoir, *The Second Sex*, trans. Constance Borde and Sheila Malovany-Chevallier (New York: Vintage Books, 2011), pp. 268–9. Here, Beauvoir genders the perceiver of woman's mystery as masculine, but I take her observation to be of something that operates more broadly than her language suggests.
12. The closest discussion to this is Harman's analysis of being embarrassed. See Harman, *Guerrilla Metaphysics*, pp. 212–13.
13. Graham Harman, 'Alphonso Lingis on the imperatives in things', in *Towards Speculative Realism*, pp. 14–21, here p. 21.
14. Graham Harman, 'The theory of objects in Heidegger and Whitehead', in *Towards Speculative Realism*, pp. 22–43, here p. 38; *The Quadruple Object* (Winchester: Zero Books, 2011), p. 46.
15. Harman, *Tool-Being*, p. 232.
16. Harman, *Guerrilla Metaphysics*, p. 24.
17. Ibid. p. 1.
18. Harman, *Tool-Being*, p. 208.
19. Harman, *Quadruple Object*, p. 74.
20. Ibid. p. 74.
21. Ibid. p. 110.
22. Harman, *Tool-Being*, p. 85.
23. Harman, 'Objects, matter, sleep', p. 202.
24. Harman, *Guerrilla Metaphysics*, pp. 24–5.
25. See, for example, Lorraine Code, *Ecological Thinking: The Politics of Epistemic Location* (New York: Oxford University Press, 2006); Val Plumwood, *Feminism and the Mastery of Nature* (New York: Routledge, 1993).
26. Perhaps Harman is correct in claiming we cannot rightfully say that objects are *really* (and not just sensually) touched by their prehenders. Causation is indirect and vicarious for Harman (on vicarious causation, see Harman, *Guerrilla Metaphysics*, chs 10 and 11 for a more nuanced account than I can give here). But part of what I am identifying as instructive is that many experiences of objectification seem to ask us for more complex consideration of that assertion, and I am willing to extend that consideration to non-human things. Given that Harman does not want to appeal to real objects as substrata, I am wary of agreeing that there are genuinely untouchable, infinitely receding real things for fear that it opens spaces of thought and action in which the form or shape of sensual prehension makes no *real* difference. To exceed the objectification of other things is a far cry from being genuinely untouched by them. And, if one cannot prehend the real object, it seems as likely as not that the real object is touched or affected, at least indirectly, by at least some prehension – how would we know, one way or another?
27. Harman, 'Object oriented philosophy', p. 94.
28. Harman, *Guerrilla Metaphysics*, p. 2.
29. Beauvoir, *Second Sex*, p. 46.
30. Harman, *Guerrilla Metaphysics*, pp. 45–58.
31. Simone de Beauvoir, 'Literature and metaphysics' [1946], trans. Veronique Zaytzeff and Frederick M. Morrison, in Margaret A. Simons (ed.), *Simone de Beauvoir: Philosophical Writings* (Chicago: University of Illinois Press, 2004), pp. 261–77, here p. 273.

32. Simone de Beauvoir, 'Pyrrhus and Cineas' [1944], trans. Marybeth Timmerman, in Simons (ed.), *Simone de Beauvoir*, pp. 89–149, here p. 102.
33. Whitehead notes that one of the direst mistakes of modern Western thought is 'the bifurcation of nature': the strict distinction in thought between things in the world and our sensory experiences of them. Alfred North Whitehead, *The Concept of Nature* (Cambridge: Cambridge University Press, 1920), p. 30. It seems to me that Beauvoir, at least, does not make this mistake, and yet is still clearly engaged as phenomenologist.
34. Simone de Beauvoir, *The Ethics of Ambiguity*, trans. Bernard Frechtman (New York: Citadel Press, 1976), p. 7.
35. See, for example, *Ethics of Ambiguity*, p. 81.
36. The claim she makes is not that there are not bodies that can bear children and bodies that cannot, but only that the ways those bodies, their 'natures', and their possibilities tend to be uncritically aligned with sexed and gendered ways of being is unnecessarily limiting. For an accessible introduction to contemporary genomic considerations of sex distinctions, see Sarah Richardson, *Sex Itself: The Search for Male and Female in the Human Genome* (Chicago: University of Chicago Press, 2013).
37. Beauvoir, *Second Sex*, p. 17.
38. Women's bodies, men's bodies and bodies that exceed and challenge those categories can and do move in feminine, non-feminine, towards-feminine and away-from-feminine ways. Femininity is distinguishable from female bodies and from women's bodies.
39. Iris Marion Young, 'Throwing like a girl: a phenomenology of feminine bodily comportment, motility, and spatiality', in *On Female Body Experience: 'Throwing Like a Girl' and Other Essays* (New York: Oxford University Press, 2005), p. 39.
40. Ibid. p. 36.
41. Ibid. pp. 36–7.
42. Ibid. p. 38.
43. Ibid. p. 39.
44. Sandra Lee Bartky, 'On psychological oppression', in *Femininity and Domination: Studies in the Phenomenology of Oppression* (New York: Routledge, 1990), p. 27.
45. These examples come from, in no particular order, my colleagues, my friends, my students and my own experiences.
46. Beauvoir's discussion of the myth of woman's mystery (see above, under 'Prehension') is classic, but many contemporary feminist theorists also analyse it in relation to objectification and to exclusion – for instance, from medical research. See, for example, Rae Langton's analysis of objectification, which emphasises this feature of women's 'mysteriousness', as well as the relationship between objectification and objectivity. Rae Langton, 'Feminism in epistemology: exclusion and objectification', in Miranda Fricker and Jennifer Hornsby (eds), *Cambridge Companion to Feminism in Philosophy* (Cambridge: Cambridge University Press, 2000), pp. 127–45.
47. See work on testimonial and hermeneutical injustice by, for example, Miranda Fricker.
48. The risks of not conforming to human expectations often involve violence, up to and including the risks of death, and, for non-living things, being otherwise destroyed.
49. In situations of oppression, this also creates spaces for protecting oneself and developing, with others, ways of keeping and knowing a self away from its objectification, as well as 'secret' knowledge about points of weakness in oppressive systems.
50. Harman, *Guerrilla Metaphysics*, p. 26; see also ibid. p. 17.
51. More's the pity: the colloquial question 'Who knows what women are thinking?!' is helpfully leveraged by shifting it from the rhetorical register to a serious one. *Someone*, we assume, *doesn't* know – and we can ask who and why that is. A similar move is possible with objects: 'Who knows what that object really is?!' My claim is not that they can and should be known, but rather that the prehender matters concretely to and for the object in question, even if it is not the only thing that matters.
52. In philosophical orthodoxy, this mysteriousness often produces frustration – things that 'should' be intelligible to us somehow are not. Despite my specific misgivings,

it is important that Harman is advancing a position that challenges this orthodoxy, wherein things that won't give up their secrets, won't make themselves intelligible to human beings are stubborn, unyielding and metaphysically wrong.
53. Harman, *Quadruple Object*, p. 74.
54. Harman, 'Objects, matter, sleep', p. 202.
55. Ian Bogost, *Alien Phenomenology, or What it is Like to be a Thing* (Minneapolis: University of Minnesota Press, 2012), p. 30.

Part III
Challenges and Prospects

Chapter 7

Merleau-Ponty and the Challenge of Realism, or How (Not) to Go beyond Phenomenology

Marie-Eve Morin

The call back to realism in continental philosophy has been accompanied both by a staunch criticism and an attempt to radicalise certain basic presuppositions of phenomenology, especially in its Heideggerian form. Both the 'speculative materialism' of Quentin Meillassoux and the 'object-oriented ontology' of Graham Harman seek to overcome what they see as phenomenology's restrictive adherence to the description of acts of consciousness (Husserl) or forms of human existence (Heidegger) – that is, to the description of the world as it is experienced by us – in order to develop a truly realist metaphysics that would provide an account of what is in itself independently of us. Though their approach differs radically, both Meillassoux and Harman share a common enemy, which it has now become fashionable to call, following Meillassoux, 'correlationism'.[1]

The phenomenologist who reads these new realist attacks on phenomenology is bound to be puzzled. Not only is it difficult to find a thorough engagement with key writers of the phenomenological tradition in the new realists' texts, it is also difficult to reconcile what the phenomenologist takes phenomenology to be doing with the new realists' accounts of it.[2] This might explain why few phenomenologists have engaged directly and offered responses to the new realists' criticisms. One exception is a recent article by Dan Zahavi, the title of which is a direct response to Tom Sparrow's provocative book *The End of Phenomenology*.[3] Even though I find Zahavi's response convincing, I would like to take a slightly different approach in this chapter: rather than defending phenomenology against its critics, and rather than engaging directly with the positive arguments developed by each of the new realists in developing their various metaphysical approaches, I want to look at how phenomenology can take up the new realist challenge.[4] That is, I want to ask how phenomenology can heed the call to realism, which is also a call to decentre our philosophical point of view by overcoming the anthropocentrism and anthropomorphism that continue to plague much of contemporary philosophy. Whether or not what we will be left with still deserves the name 'phenomenology', it becomes clear that by going through phenomenology, rather than sidestepping it, we can ultimately develop an understanding of 'the outside' that is demanded both by the new realist movements and by our times.

I emphasise the need for a philosophy for our time because this is how the necessity of a move beyond phenomenology and a turn to realism is presented in the first major collection of essays by members of the 'speculative turn':

> In the face of the looming ecological catastrophe, and the increasing infiltration of technology into the everyday world (including our own bodies), it is not clear that the anti-realist position is equipped to face up to these developments. The danger is that the dominant anti-realist strain of continental philosophy has not only reached a point of decreasing returns, but that it now actively limits the capacities of philosophy in our time.[5]

Thus, the ultimate question is one of investment and return. To turn the tables around: is it worth investing in speculative realism or object-oriented ontology if we want to think through the most pressing issues of our day? To answer that, I start with a short discussion of the stake of the phenomenological method and contrast it with the speculative method of the new realists. This allows me to clarify the role played by evidence and motivation within phenomenology, which I link to the question of realism and modesty in an attempt to highlight the equivocation in the use of the terms 'real' and 'outside'. Turning to Merleau-Ponty, I then sketch a different way of seeking an 'outside' of experience and phenomenology. In particular, I retrace the trajectory of his thought out of (a certain kind of) phenomenology, starting from his critique of any phenomenology that would assert the absolute nature of the intentional relation, what Meillassoux has called *strong* correlationism.[6] This critique helps us pinpoint the problems with the new realists' attempt to undermine the correlationist circle in favour of a thought of the 'great outdoors'. I then show how Merleau-Ponty's later philosophy offers us a kind of radical outside akin to Meillassoux's 'hyperchaos' or Graham Harman's 'inner life of objects'. However, unlike these two thinkers, who can maintain the integrity and exteriority of their outside only by completely severing it from the world of experience, Merleau-Ponty recasts the relation between inside and outside through the dimension of depth or latency. I conclude by asking whether Merleau-Ponty has effected a decentring of the human that would be radical enough for out times.

Modest realism and the 'outside'

Crispin Wright famously defined realism as a mixture of modesty and presumption.[7] Its modesty comes from the admission that the world is not constituted by our thought or language: the world's independence leads to the confession that we are not the measure of things and that our thoughts are answerable to an outside. In other words, we are not 'Active Minds'[8] imposing our conceptual schemes on to an inert, meaningless outside. This modesty is coupled with the presumption that we can, if not represent and know, at least aspire to grasp and capture in thought or discourse a 'reality' that remains beyond such thought or discourse. Following Wright, a slide towards the pole of modesty always leads to scepticism, whereas too much emphasis on presumption ultimately leads to idealism.

The modesty of the 'realist experience', which comes from the experience of being answerable to an 'outside', seems to be what is needed in our dire times. In *The End of Phenomenology*, Tom Sparrow claims that 'in addition to correlationism and the linguistic turn, public enemy number one for SR and OOO, as well as new materialism, is human hubris'.[9] In what sense is the phenomenologist plagued by hubris? Indeed, it would seem that the common enemy of the new realists is not hubris but rather the *modesty* of the philosophies of finitude who limit what can be thought or said to what can be attested by human experience. By curbing the ability of thought to reach the Absolute, by asserting the finitude of our thinking, which remains always bound to its own limits, correlationism leads us to affirm not only that we cannot gain any positive knowledge of what things are in themselves (whether and how they are structured for examples) but that we cannot even affirm their existence (since all evidence we have of their existence is evidence for us). The new realists' point, it seems, is that this critical modesty – how do you know that? where's your evidence? – turns into a false modesty once we become strong correlationists: since the outside never appears, *and since we have decided that only what is given can be said to be*, we completely forget the outside, the uncorrelated absolute, and start navel-gazing.

Modesty, then – call it realism if you wish – would require the acknowledgement that we can be wrong, that what we found meaningful (or meaningless) might turn out not to be so *not because we have changed from within* but because something happened to us from without. If we look for a realism that remains modest, we might fare better with what Lee Braver has identifies as 'transgressive realism'.[10] Sparrow objects to transgressive realism in the following way. Although he admits that Levinas provides an account of what it is like to be 'unsettled'[11] from within, he argues that Levinas does not and cannot 'provide us with the *necessary metaphysical evidence* to establish the existence of an absolutely transcendent Other'. Absolute transcendence is not 'verifiable through phenomenological means'. As he explains:

> Just because something surprises us does not necessarily indicate an ontological rupture in immanence. It could just as well indicate a failure of our imagination about what will arrive in the future. This does not provide us with evidence of the existence of the infinite, but it does provide us with evidence of our finitude.[12]

The problem of phenomenology is that it cannot think – or, in Sparrow's terms, prove the existence of – an uncorrelated outside because it has made the choice to be modest, to restrict itself to what is 'immanently' given as it is given (the principle of principles), that is to say, to what shows up in the domain opened by the reduction.

In their presentation of phenomenology, there is a key point the new realists almost always miss. What they forget about the reduction is that its goal is not merely to neutralise questions of the existence of the external world and limit ourselves to describing what is immanently given, but to find within what is immanently given what motivates or justifies, for example, an act of perception to go beyond what is given in person (*leiblich gegeben*) in order to 'intend' – or to use a less active expression, to 'let appear' – a transcendent object. This is the same procedure Husserl employs in the fifth *Cartesian Mediation* when he reduces the transcendental field to the sphere of ownness and tries to find within it a motivation or justification for the experience of the *alter ego*, an *alter ego* whose way of appearing, that is of being intended and fulfilled, is different than that of a number or a house, and who is *alter* precisely *because* of his transgressive way of appearing.

If the reduction recovers the dimension of intentionality and sees transcendence – hitting the object itself, being in touch with what is independently of my intentional act – as an achievement of the act, transcendence does not lose its 'transgressive' character because it is now seen as an achievement (*Leistung*). We should never forget that Husserl's first enemy was the psychologism that assumed that because all truths are achieved by a conscious subject, then all truths are necessarily dependent on factual conditions of thought. But for Husserl, when I say that 2 + 2 = 4, I say nothing about counting even though the truth of the result 4 can only be achieved through the act of counting. The puzzle of phenomenology is how spatiotemporally individuated (factual) acts of consciousness can give rise to Objectivity, that is, to something that is true, and is experienced as being so independently from consciousness. Objectivity is for Husserl a *Leistung* of consciousness, but, as achievement, it brings us outside of the subjective conditions of its genesis. For example, the 'real' is defined as the 'correlate of acts of perception in the narrow sense' by opposition to the 'imaginary', the 'ideal' and so forth.[13] To be real is to be a correlate – there is no denying that Husserl is a kind of correlationist – but a correlate of a specific kind, one that is given in a specific way. It is this givenness that provides the 'motivation' or 'reason' for experiencing what is given as real, that is, as independent from the act in which it is currently given. If the perceived was not given in this way, then it would be experienced as 'imaginary', as a figment of my imagination, and would lose its reality.[14]

To Sparrow's request for 'metaphysical evidence' for the absolutely uncorrelated outside, the phenomenologist would probably reply that she does not understand what such evidence might be, or how it is supposed to lead us to an outside if it consists merely in rational deductions from principles (Meillassoux) or well-crafted metaphors (Harman) that do not find their motivation in phenomenological evidence. Sparrow would reply that all phenomenological evidence lacks the ability to guarantee or prove the 'existence of an absolute outside', but this is because it was never a question of 'proving' anything; rather, the phenomenologist starts from the experience of transcendence and seeks to uncover the motivations for this experience. At this point, it would be a question of describing this experience of the outside, this rupture of 'immanence' and of showing how it distinguishes itself from 'failures of the imagination' in the same way that the givenness of an imaginary unicorn is different than that of a perceived horse.

If we want to claim that such an experience of the 'outside' transgresses the bounds of phenomenology because it goes beyond evidence, then we have a mistaken understanding of what evidence does. Evidence justifies transgression, and 'reality' is, phenomenologically, such a justified transgression, whereas pure thought or imagination do not transgress, at least not in the same way. Understood in this way, phenomenology is far more transgressive than what the reading of the reduction and the principle of principles in the new realists lead us to believe. Of course, one could always be mistaken: what I take to be an 'experience of the infinite' or an 'experience of the uncorrelated' may turn out to be in fact merely a 'failure of the imagination'. But the question is: how will I discover that mistake if not through a better description of the act – givenness is not as easy to describe as it seems – or through a new act that will force me to re-evaluate my previous description, as I do when I realise that what I took to be my friend is in fact a tree, or, more radically, when I wake up from the Matrix and reassess the meaning of my previous experiences of 'the real' in the now larger circle of my experience?

It seems, at this point, that the new realist and the phenomenologist are bound to talk past each other because they do not agree on what it is we are looking for when we speak of an 'outside'. The speculative realists are looking for

> that outside which [is] not relative to us, and which [is] given as indifferent to its own givenness to be what it is, existing in itself regardless of whether we are thinking of it or not; that outside which thought [can] explore with the legitimate feeling of being on foreign territory – of being entirely elsewhere.[15]

This explains their turn to a speculative method, which gives us the means to think what there is when there is no thought, that is, to access the Absolute, by liberating thinking from the categories of thought or from its own conditions of possibilities.[16] This is, at least superficially, similar to phenomenological methods, which require that we put out of play our own prejudices and presuppositions. The outcome, however, is not a description of our experience and of the way in which things are given to, or rendered meaningful for, these experiences. For phenomenology, anything that is transcendent needs to be given in such a way that its transcendence can be attested by experience. For the new realists, on the other hand, such a transcendence, because it is meaningful for us, would never be transcendent enough. Only speculation allows us 'to create a new image of thought: one that is no longer modelled on, or limited to, anthropocentric parameters'.[17] For the phenomenologist, an absolute outside that is uncorrelated to our power to experience, even if it could be thought (with the help of set theory) or imagined (with the help of science fiction or well-crafted metaphors), could never be real because its mere intention could never be fulfilled in any kind of intuition. It would remain just a thought. The question is: are we stuck with this stalemate? Can phenomenology somehow account for an outside that is not merely the transcendence in immanence of a given object? The question is crucial because such an outside is what the turn to realism was supposed to reconnect us with: the world as it is in all its indifference, independence and strangeness. Indeed, how else could it pretend to put us in a better position to take up climate change? It is here that I believe it is useful to turn more closely to Merleau-Ponty.

The limit of Merleau-Ponty's phenomenology

We could say that in *The Phenomenology of Perception*, Merleau-Ponty is a radical or strong correlationist.[18] Yet, even as correlationist, Merleau-Ponty is well aware of the danger of intellectualism that lurks in transcendental phenomenology, which, after having traced the world that is supposed to contain consciousness as an object of psychological study back to the perceived world and then realised that consciousness is coextensive to the world, reduces perceptual consciousness to intellection and turns perception into the active constitution of the meaning of the perceived. Transcendental philosophy discovers in reflection a transcendental ego, which it posits as having always already been there, doing its constitutive work behind the back of empirical consciousness.[19] But if meaning is constituted within consciousness and is imposed on a meaningless, in-itself world, why is it that the perceived does not flatten before my look, is not fully integrated within my consciousness? Where does the depth or latency of the perceived, which marks its difference from a thought or an idea, come from? While perception is correlation between perceiving and perceived, body and thing, it is imperative not to understand this relation as happening either between two positive beings (as empiricism does) or between a positive being (a being in-itself) and a negative being (a for-itself that is no-thing) as Sartre does. The problem of perception, as Merleau-Ponty understands it, is that of a genuine in-itself for us:

> One cannot, as we have said, conceive of a perceived thing without someone who perceives it [hence correlationism is true]. But moreover, the thing is presented as a thing in itself even to the person who perceives it [hence the new realists' interpretation of correlationism is false], and thereby poses the problem of a genuine in-itself-for-us. We do not ordinarily catch sight of this because our perception, in the context of our everyday dealings, bears upon the things just enough to find in them their familiar presence, and not enough to rediscover what of the non-human [or the inhuman] is hidden within them. But the thing is unaware of us; it remains in itself [*la chose nous ignore, elle repose en soi*].[20]

It is important to recall that Merleau-Ponty does not understand intentionality as a one-way relation, where the mind imposes a meaning on to an otherwise unstructured in-itself. Rather, the relation between body and world is one of solicitation and response. The sensible world solicits or motivates my movement (it does not cause anything), and a certain tacit decision with regard to that solicitation then opens up a visual field:

> Thus, a sensible that is about to be sensed poses to my body a sort of confused problem. I must find the attitude that will provide it with the means to become determined and to become blue; I must find the response to a poorly formulated question. And yet, I only do this in response to its solicitation. My attitude is never sufficient to make me truly see blue or truly touch a hard surface. The sensible gives back to me what I had lent it, but I received it from the sensible in the first place.[21]

Perception presents things that have a certain value or meaning in relation to my capacity to interact with them. It is not the direct contact between a subject present to itself and a fully determined object; in other words, it is not direct access to an in-itself but organisation of an area of visibility from which something will show itself as what it is. Hence, the perceived is a relatively positive being, and not an objective, substantial, completed being (not an in-itself). This is why the study of perception leads to a criticism not only of objective thought but also of a transcendental phenomenology of constitution: though the latter returns to the world of experience (and hence to all the obscurities it contains), it still conceives of the world ('the outside') as determinate and as finished somewhere, and hence as objectively present for an unsituated spectator, a *kosmotheoros*.

What must be noted in the context of the recent 'realist turn' in continental philosophy is that, for Merleau-Ponty, even if the kind of in-itself sought by the new realist movements could be thought, that is, even if an uncorrelated outside absolutely independent from our engagement with it could be thought, such a thought would never lead us to anything *real*:

> if my experience formed a closed system, if the thing and world could be defined once and for all, if spatio-temporal horizons could (even ideally) be made explicit and if the world could be conceived from nowhere, then nothing would exist. I would survey the world from above, and far from all places and times suddenly becoming real, they would in fact cease to be real because I would not inhabit any of them and I would be nowhere engaged.[22]

A perceived triangle, for example, what we called 'a real triangle', profiles itself right at the sensible itself: it is not a natural property of the thing spread out in space since it is there only for a certain kind of situated spectator with certain motor skills. It is also not a clear and distinct idea since it always includes an essential latency and opacity, which should not be understood as a flaw, but is rather the mark of its real existence.[23]

Rather than criticising transcendental reflection and the phenomenological reduction for remaining within the intentional relation and attempting to reclaim the possibility of unsituated thought, Merleau-Ponty radicalises transcendental reflection into what he will call 'radical reflection'. Such a reflection is not radical in the sense that it would be complete, that it would succeed in dissolving the unreflected into reflection. On the contrary, that kind of 'absolute' reflection never achieves the kind of completion it claims to because it necessarily ignores its own beginning – or, better, it ignores the facticity of its own beginning – in the unreflected. Transcendental reflection thinks that it can reduce fact to essence, that it can incorporate without remainder its own beginning within itself and thus reach a transcendental sphere purified of the mundane. But in doing so, reflection forgets *itself* as fact. It forgets that there is always a delay between unreflected (already-there) and reflection, or between being and meaning, between the facticity of silent experience and the philosophical speech that articulates its latent meaning. By seeking to ground itself only in itself and be the condition of its own possibility, reflection thinks of its possibility as always given in advance and forgets its real origin (or dismisses it as irrelevant). What a radical reflection uncovers is the dependency of reflection on the unreflected: 'Reflection is only truly reflection if it does not carry itself outside of itself, if it knows itself as *reflection-upon-an-unreflected*, and consequently as a change in the structure of our existence.'[24] The origin is doubled; it is the retroactive illumination of what was already there (but the 'being-there' of which only shows itself as such through the retroactive illumination). In truly Derridian fashion, the origin is the double movement between reflection and unreflected. This is why the last discovery of transcendental phenomenology is time, the time that makes it impossible to complete the reduction (of the empirical to the transcendental, of fact to essence).

This is also the reason why the last word of the *Phenomenology of Perception* is contingency. Radical reflection does not give me access to a 'metaphysical entity', to an unchanging, self-identical world 'in-itself', nor does it lead to the discovery of an absolute in the way that Husserl (a certain Husserl) thinks that the reduction leads to a transcendental ego that cannot have an outside. As Gary Madison puts it:

> If then the ground of reflection, as it itself discovers it, is our bodily being in the world which appears to reflection as a contingent and unmotivated fact, reflection is forced to recognize that it itself exists and that consequently truth exists only on the basis of a radical contingency, that the absolute is unthinkable, and that all meaning maintains itself on the ground of non-meaning.[25]

At this point, Merleau-Ponty has dialecticised the notion of subject and object into one single system of which they are correlates. But phenomenology cannot account for the being of the dialectical relation. It illuminates everything but the origin of the intentional relation itself, which sinks into the darkness of pure contingency. Beyond this correlation, as Merleau-Ponty says, 'there is nothing more to understand'.[26] Because the correlate is posited as the ultimate fact out of which all intelligibility arises, and hence as that which itself cannot be questioned intelligibly, there can be no investigation of the natural world or natural being, of the underside of the phenomenological world, of a kind of pre-world upon which the perceived world rests qua correlate of existence.

From phenomenology to ontology

The move from phenomenology to ontology happens when Merleau-Ponty seeks to understand the belonging-together of consciousness and world, their being applied to one another. It happens when he seeks to understand neither the subject nor the world, but their in-between, that is, how the subject's being in the world and the world's existence for the subject are upheld by something that encompasses them, what he will call 'wild being', or 'vertical being'.[27] The problem with phenomenology and its ultimate assertion of the contingency of the correlation, beyond which we cannot go, is that it remains unable to explain the thingliness of the thing, that is, the thing in so far as it always resists the sense that it gives to me, in any other way than by reference to my finitude. Resistance is a function of the finitude of my access, which means that the thing (thought as Idea in the Kantian sense: infinite synthesis of profile) would be in principle accessible to an infinite access.

If there is no limit, no resistance to the meaningful donation of the thing, even if only in principle, then the thingliness of the thing dissolves into a mere correlate. This is the case with Husserlian phenomenology, which reduces being to meaning (to be x is to be given as x), but it is also a danger facing Merleau-Ponty's early phenomenology. So the problem is neither that the intentional relation is a one-way relation from consciousness to world, nor is it that what is given is always an essence (an idea, Cubeness). Merleau-Ponty's phenomenology overcomes these two prejudices of traditional phenomenology through the dialectical relation body–world. Instead, the problem lies in the fact that the intentional relation (even when dialecticised and incarnate) is still conceived as absolute: as having no limits (or better as having a limit it cannot think). A sign of this is, for example, the way in which Husserl thinks of non-sense: non-sense (what is beyond the limit of sense) is not nothing only in so far as it is given, that is, in so far as it makes sense as non-sense. As Ted Toadvine puts it, phenomenology 'cannot express resistance or contingency', the 'wildness' of things,[28] or it can do so only in Husserl's convoluted way (which is similar to the convolution Meillassoux finds in relation to the fossils: the in-itself is for us, non-sense is a sense). Such convolution points to phenomenology's inability to think an outside, a non-sense, that is not already a kind of inside, a kind of sense. This is the crux of the new realist criticism.

The move from phenomenology to ontology happens when phenomenology undertakes an examination of the logic of the outside, when it questions its own mode of access to that which lies in principle external to it: 'the back side of things that we have not constituted'.[29] In this radical questioning, phenomenology 'overcomes' its own limits. But, unlike new realism, it does not do so by positing a pure exteriority, but rather by meditating its own shadow. As Merleau-Ponty writes:

> the ultimate task of phenomenology as philosophy of consciousness is to understand its relationship to non-phenomenology. What resists phenomenology within us ... cannot remain outside phenomenology and should have its place within it. The philosopher must bear [her] shadow, which is not simply the factual absence of a future light.[30]

Or in the words of Madison again:

> As the shadow of consciousness and its own latency, Being is the absence of light and what consciousness can never illuminate, since it is the very sources of its own light. Consciousness cannot think Being except by thinking its own blindness, what it cannot see because it is that which makes it see.[31]

Phenomenology is not limited to the description of what is given in experience, but becomes the thought of that which is always hidden, of that which cannot be given: the latency which gives to figures all their depth and dimensionality, their visibility – their shadows – and which phenomenology cannot grasp because it 'obliges whatever is not nothing to present itself to consciousness' and forces it to appear in an act, in one *Erlebnis*.[32] Of course, Husserlian phenomenology did think latency but always as internal and external horizon, that is, in relation to other possible objectivating acts, possible constitutions. If the thing is not exhausted by any of our experiences of it, it is not because of our essential finitude (not because it is a Great Object and our access to it is limited, finite), but because it includes negativity, possibility within itself.

Now, if this description of Merleau-Ponty's turn to ontology is somewhat adequate, then this turn should not be understood as a turn to realism. Merleau-Ponty rejects the notion of a Being in-itself of which one could have an intuition and of which one could deduce or describe the essential traits and attributes (for instance, by means of set theory or speculative fictions). There is no access to Being as it would be in itself because, for Merleau-Ponty, there is no such Being.[33]

Hence the rejection of the Husserlian, idealist path does not lead to the affirmation of a transcendent, wholly external *Ding an sich*, something that would exist prior to or outside of the subject–object correlation. Such an affirmation would lead us back to a substantialist philosophy, and hence to objective thought. The debate is not between realism on the one side and an anthropocentric and anthropomorphic correlationism (or idealism) on the other, but between a *pensée de survol*, what Merleau-Ponty also calls objective thought, and a thought that is embedded in and exposed to what it is trying to grasp. Being or 'Nature' is not elsewhere, it is an internal possibility of this world, it is the latency, depth and dimensionality of this world. It is the element, the milieu of things that cannot be reduced to any one thing or another but only transpires in them. Hence we should be careful not to turn Being into a Big Object: a positivity, a congealed infinity, a hidden in itself. Being is openness, but not the openness of the system of adumbrations, which always remains tamed infinity (infinity of profiles that obey a law, Idea in the Kantian sense, and the like). Rather, Being is a 'wild' infinity. If Being is not a positivity, then the phenomenal world / the phenomenon cannot be a mask covering it over; it is its crystallisation, its realisation, its solidification around a dimension.

Another way of describing the openness of Being is to say that it is polymorphous – this is the similarity with Meillassoux hyperchaos, I would argue – and, as such, it *'requires creation of us'* in order to manifest itself.[34] In other words: Being is not organised around any metrics or dimensions; it has no inherent measure, no principle of unity of its own. Perception institutes a level, a background from which an object can emerge; it organises an area of visibility around a dimension. This order of the perceived world (this creation) does not mirror any more than it distorts Vertical Being, because Vertical Being is the pure depth, the dimension of encroachment, of the union of incompossibles; it is the 'world where everything is simultaneous',[35] the *totum simul* of every thing, of every profile.[36]

Conclusion: a philosophy for our times?

I began by saying that the understanding of 'the outside' offered by Merleau-Ponty's later philosophy is demanded both by the new realist movements and by our times. Our times demand a radical decentring of human privilege. If we take this challenge seriously, then part of our assessment of the phenomenology/new realism debate should turn upon the question of which one puts us in a better position to understand and respect the alterity of the world, as well as the alterity within us. I would thus like to ask whether the move I have sketched from the early to the late Merleau-Ponty offers us a decentring of the human being capable of fostering such respect. Is Merleau-Ponty guilty of anthropomorphism, of 'making the world in man's image' by overlaying what is with human predicates? By taking our own self-sensing body as the model of Being, is he not committed to saying that all bodies are like the human bodies, and that matter is self-sensing like the human?

There is a kind of ontological homogeneity or continuity in Merleau-Ponty's philosophy, but Merleau-Ponty explicitly rejects the accusation of anthropologism or hylozoism. His ontology is not the projection of our way of being on to the things of the world, is not the extension of the reversibility I experience in my lived body to every other sensible. It is not the imparting of the corporeity proper to the human being to the entirety of materiality. Things do not have a soul and the world is not an animal. Rather, our way of being is a prototype, a variant, a witness or a cipher (all Merleau-Ponty's words) of Being. It attunes us to the fact that the visible is already a paradoxical being like my body. Let me quote at length:

> When we speak of the flesh of the visible, we do not mean to do anthropology, to describe a world covered over with all our own projections, leaving aside what it can be under the human mask. Rather, we mean that carnal being, as a being of depths, of several leaves or several faces, a being in latency, and a presentation of a certain absence, is a prototype of Being, of which our body, the sensible sentient, is a very remarkable variant, but whose constitutive paradox already lies in every visible. For already the cube assembles within itself incompossible *visibilia* [like my body is at the same time sentient and sensible] . . . Since the total visible is always behind, or after, or between the aspects we see of it, there is access to it only through an experience which, like it, is wholly outside of itself. . . . it is indeed a paradox of Being, not a paradox of man, that we are dealing with here.[37]

In fact, if we did not also partake of the paradox of Being, if we were not one of its variants or prototypes, we would be unable to recognise this paradox that lies in every visible (which is not a visible *for* the human being, but a visible 'in itself'). At the same time, as one who partakes of this paradox, the human being is not a pure consciousness, a pure thinking being, but a being of depth and of many leaves. Some might see in this ontological continuity a form of anthropomorphism: all visibles are not so different from the human being. But we must note that such a continuity also guards us against human exceptionalism. It does not 'make the world in the image of man' by attributing human predicates (here human sensibility) to all other beings. It does not claim that 'all things sense *like us*'.

But then do we not still find in Merleau-Ponty's ontology a certain anthropocentrism in the form of a teleology carried out by the human being? The perceived gives rise to expression, to language, to truth. Thought is seen as a latent possibility and as the highest realisation of the flesh. The return of reflection to its unreflected constitution is at the same time a promotion of sensible existence to its meaning/truth. Intellectual consciousness transcends sensible consciousness, gathers it to express what it is, bringing by the same token the configuration of Being into a cultural logos. Each institution of a new level of meaning opens up a new dimension in relation to which a series of experiences will be able to make sense. Yet, Merleau-Ponty in his later works tries to understand the ways in which these human institutions are not mere creations but arise out of a latency that already contains (in what sense of 'contain' would be the difficult question!) the open totality of all its possible *Wiederholungen*, its possible *reprises*. In a sense, teleology is undeniable here, and the human being remains the privileged site of the revelation of Being. As Merleau-Ponty wrote in the last published note in *The Visible and the Invisible*: 'The visible has to be described as something that is realized through man, but which is nowise anthropology. . . . Logos also as what is realized in man, but nowise as his *property*.' Whether the difference between realisation and property is enough to undo any pernicious form of human exceptionalism is a question I leave open here.[38]

What I hope has become clear is that the meditations that led Merleau-Ponty from *The Phenomenology of Perception* to his later thought allows him to experience and think an outside that is wild, strange, inhuman. He does so not by thinking 'what there is when there is no thought',[39] as if thought could survey Being from above without touching it or being touched by it, but rather by rejecting the separation of thought and Being, by digging deeper into the 'correlation' to find not the fullness of an in-itself, but a being of which I am a part, and which is older than my operations and my acts.[40]

Notes

1. Quentin Meillassoux, *After Finitude: An Essay on the Necessity of Contingency* (London: Bloomsbury, 2009), p. 5, among others. Though Meillassoux is often credited for coining the term 'correlationism', a similar German term, *Korrelativismus*, was used as early as 1928 by Maximilian Beck to describe Husserl's and Dilthey's philosophy, which seeks a third way between objectivism and subjectivism, one where 'Bewußtsein und Welt, Subjekt und Objekt, Ich und Welt stehen selbst in einem derartigen korrelativen, d. i. sich gegenseitig bedingenden Seinszusammenhang, daß obige Disjunktionen überhaupt keinen Sinn haben.' See Maximilian Beck, 'Die neue Problemlage der Erkenntnistheorie', *Deutsche Vierteljahrsschrift für Literaturwissenschaft und Geistesgeschichte*, vol. 6 (1928): pp. 611–39. Cited in Dan Zahavi, 'The end of what? Phenomenology vs. speculative realism', *International Journal of Philosophical Studies*, vol. 24, no. 3 (2016): pp. 289–309, here pp. 305–6 n. 3.
2. Of course, Graham Harman does 'engage' with Husserl, Heidegger and Merleau-Ponty at various points in his corpus. He takes some of these phenomenologists' ideas as a jumping board for his object-oriented ontology. But I think it is fair to claim that his reading of these figures is at best creative and at worst selective and misguided. One flagrant example: In *Guerrilla Metaphysics*, Harman writes, citing from Merleau-Ponty's *Phenomenology of Perception*: 'As was baldly stated in his [Merleau-Ponty's] first major book: "There are two modes of being, and two only: being in itself, which is that of objects arrayed in space, and being for itself, which is that of

consciousness."' See Graham Harman, *Guerrilla Metaphysics: Phenomenology and the Carpentry of Things* (Chicago and La Salle: Open Court, 2005). To anyone familiar with the *Phenomenology*, this passage sounds rather strange. Indeed, the quotation is taken from the section on 'Others and the human world' where Merleau-Ponty is arguing that the existence of others is 'difficult for objective thought', for which there are only two modes of being 'in-itself' and 'for-itself', but also points out that 'we have in fact learned to call objective thought into doubt and we have made contact with an experience of the body and the world' that is irreducible to either mode of being. Similarly, in his small book *Continental Realism*, Paul Ennis states that 'Husserl explicitly precludes knowing the "in-itself" from phenomenological investigation' and then quotes the following passage from *The Idea of Phenomenology*: 'Cognition is . . . only *human cognition*, bound up with *human intellectual forms*, and unfit to reach the very nature of things, to reach the things themselves.' See Edmund Husserl, *The Idea of Phenomenology* (The Hague: Martinus Nijhoff, 1973), p. 17. The phrasing should already alert us to the fact that Husserl is not speaking in his own voice, but, in case it is not clear enough, the passage is followed by these words: 'These examples should suffice. The possibility of cognition has become enigmatic throughout', which means that the goal of the previous statements was to render puzzling the ability of thought to reach the in-itself, or the subjective constitution of objectivity, before moving on to an explication of how phenomenology dissipates that puzzlement. Examples of misquotations and misreadings could be multiplied. Even in a book such as Tom Sparrow's *The End of Phenomenology: Metaphysics and the New Realism* (Edinburgh: Edinburgh University Press, 2014), we find very little engagement with the texts of phenomenology that is not mediated by Meillassoux, Harman or Braver, and we find no attempt at a charitable understanding of the phenomenological method, or of key concepts such as intuition, immanence and noema, as they have been debated within the phenomenological tradition.
3. Dan Zahavi, 'The end of what?', esp. p. 303. Zahavi shows that the new realists' criticisms miss the mark because they are either too superficial (they do not engage with the texts or misinterpret them), too simplistic (they miss key differences internal to the phenomenological method) or lack novelty (they have already been levelled against phenomenology, sometimes from the beginning of the movement, and have given rise to debates and responses within the phenomenological movement). See also L. Ralon, 'Interview with Steven Galt Crowell', *Figure/Ground*, 22 June 2011, http://figureground.org/interview-with-steven-galt-crowell/ (last accessed 13 December 2016).
4. I agree with Peter Gratton that 'what is crucial, however, is not to let this [chapter] serve as a rear-guard defense for the [phenomenologists] in the wake of newer currents in contemporary thought'. See Peter Gratton, *Speculative Realism: Problems and Prospects* (London: Bloomsbury, 2014), p. 116.
5. See Levi Bryant, Nick Srnicek and Graham Harman, *The Speculative Turn: Continental Realism and Materialism* (Melbourne: re.press, 2011), p. 3.
6. See Meillassoux, *After Finitude*, pp. 35–44.
7. See Crispin Wright, *Realism, Meaning and Truth* (Oxford: Blackwell, 1993), pp. 1–2.
8. The term is used by Lee Braver in 'A brief history of continental realism', *Continental Philosophy Review*, vol. 45, no. 2 (2012): pp. 261–89.
9. Sparrow, *End of Phenomenology*, p. 177. By 'new materialism', Sparrow is referring to Jane Bennett. See Jane Bennett, 'Systems and things: a response to Graham Harman and Timothy Morton', *New Literary History*, vol. 43, no. 2 (Spring 2012): pp. 225–33, here pp. 230–1.
10. See Braver, 'A brief history', p. 271.
11. This is Braver's word. See Lee Braver, 'On not settling the issue of realism', *Speculations* IV (2013): pp. 9–14, here p. 13.
12. Sparrow, *End of Phenomenology*, p. 50; my emphasis.

13. See Edmund Husserl, *The Shorter Logical Investigations*, ed. Dermot Moran, trans. J. N. Findlay (London: Routledge, 2001), LI VI, ch. 6, esp. §46.
14. Hence, it is strange to claim that the phenomenologist always reduces the object in-itself to a thought. This is, for example, what Descartes does with vision, but this is certainly not what phenomenology does because, if it did, the phenomenologist would lose the ability to differentiate between ideal, imaginary and real beings, differences that are attested phenomenologically within the 'sphere of givenness'.
15. Meillassoux, *After Finitude*, p. 7.
16. See Shaviro, *Universe of Things*, p. 111: 'The paradoxical task of speculative realism is to undo the conditions that are imposed on thought by the very nature of thought itself. We must disengage ourselves from our own frame of reference, which is to say from the very grids of intelligibility – the Kantian "pure concepts of the understanding" – that we take for granted and that we have always already applied to things in the very act of perceiving them.' See also Sparrow, *End of Phenomenology*, p. 62: 'Speculation is theoretically capable of disengaging objects from subjects in nonarbitrary ways, some of which approximate science fiction but none of which are, in the last analysis, fictitious. . . . Consciousness may indeed be empty without content, but there is little reason to outlaw the claim that content can get along in the world just fine without humans tending it. And once this content is released from the bondage of perception, almost anything (within reason) is possible.' Hence, metaphors are '*precise metaphysical devices*', and 'poetry might have something important to tell us about ontology' (ibid. p. 136).
17. Sparrow, *End of Phenomenology*, p. 111.
18. Here, I leave aside the question of whether it would not be a better strategy to contest this term altogether. While phenomenologists do use the term 'correlation' to describe the relation between subject and object, and speak of noematic correlate (Husserl) or of the thing as correlated to my body (Merleau-Ponty), the way in which correlationism is characterised by Meillassoux seems to distort phenomenology's focus on intentionality as the 'place' where any givenness (or any sense) can take place. Indeed, if we look at Heidegger, we can see that he is critical of the subject–object correlation, which he attributes to Rickert and Natorp, because it 'obstructs access to the real ontological question regarding the mode of being of the subject as well as the mode of being of the entity that may possibly but does not necessarily have to become an object'. See Martin Heidegger, *Basic Problems of Phenomenology* (Bloomington and Indianapolis: University of Indiana Press, 1988), §15. As is well known, Heidegger's starting point is not the subject–object correlation but the unitary phenomenon of Being-in-the-world. As for Merleau-Ponty, though he will say that the thing is correlative to my body, and though the adverb correlatively suffuses the pages of *The Phenomenology of Perception*, he is also critical of the subject–object correlation as it is understood by transcendental phenomenology, or what he calls 'intellectualism' in the *Phenomenology* and 'reflection' in *The Visible and the Invisible*.
19. See, among others, chapter 6, 'Sensation', in *The Phenomenology of Perception*, trans. Donald Landes (London: Routledge, 2012). See also chapter 1, 'Reflection and interrogation' of *The Visible and the Invisible*, ed. Claude Lefort, trans. Alphonso Lingis (Evanston: Northwestern University Press, 1968), p. 44.
20. Merleau-Ponty, *Phenomenology of Perception*, p. 336; also p. 69: 'We must attempt to understand how vision can come about from somewhere without thereby being locked within its perspective.'
21. Ibid. p. 222.
22. Ibid. p. 347.
23. See *The Structure of Behavior*, pp. 211–13. See also the discussion of the demonstration of the Pythagorian theorem in chapter 11, 'The cogito', in *The Phenomenology of Perception*, where Merleau-Ponty shows that the mathematician's demonstration is made possible by modulations of my corporeal presence to the world and

its movements (and hence is only meaningful because I am embodied and spatially oriented). Of course, at this point I could be accused of equivocating on the meaning of 'real'.
24. Merleau-Ponty, *Phenomenology*, p. 63; see also ibid. pp. lxxiii–lxxiv.
25. See Gary Madison, *The Phenomenology of Merleau-Ponty: A Search for the Limits of Consciousness* (Athens: Ohio University Press, 1981), p. 162.
26. Merleau-Ponty, *Phenomenology of Perception*, p. 383.
27. See, again, Madison, *The Phenomenology of Merleau-Ponty*, p. 170. This move should not be understood as a rejection of phenomenology, but rather, as Renaud Barbaras argues, as its fulfilment. See Renaud Barbaras, *The Being of the Phenomenon: Merleau-Ponty's Ontology* (Bloomington and Indianapolis: Indiana University Press, 2004), p. 77. Barbaras is clear that he is not interested in the *Phenomenology* on its own terms, but only in so far as it leads to Merleau-Ponty's later ontology. In this context, the problems with the *Phenomenology*, according to Barbaras, is that it couches the discovery of the perceptual field in a dualism of reflection and the unreflected, and, in doing so, opposes reason to a pre-reflective irrational, the cogito to the natural world, and essence to fact. As a result, the unreflected cannot be grasped as the birth of reason (a reason that is *of* the world in both senses). What is needed is a genuine understanding of the unreflected or the pre-reflective as 'zero of ...' (Merleau-Ponty, *Visible and the Invisible*, p. 257), 'which exists only as the beginning (on the side of the unreflective) or as the conservation (on the side of reflection) of what it negates. . . . Consciousness will have to be grasped as a moment of the world rather than as its opposite' (Barbaras, *The Being of the Phenomenon*, p. 17). This will also lead to a transformation of the understanding of the teleology of consciousness. We will come back to this point in the concluding section.
28. Ted Toadvine, 'Chiasm and chiaroscuro', *Chiasmi International*, vol. 3 (2001): pp. 225–40, here pp. 228, 230.
29. Merleau-Ponty, *Signs* (Evanston: Northwestern University Press, 1964), p. 180.
30. Ibid. p. 178. Barbaras explains this passage by saying that here sense is not opposed to fact and phenomenology is not opposed to ontology. Rather than a phenomenology that would give us the sense of facts or an ontology that would give us brute facts foreign to sense, we are seeking the fact of sense, 'catch sense in the act, at its very Birthplace' (Barbaras, *The Being of the Phenomenon*, p. 78). Here the influence of Derrida's *Introduction to Husserl's Original of Geometry* on Barbaras is undeniable.
31. Madison, *The Phenomenology of Merleau-Ponty*, p. 196.
32. Merleau-Ponty, *Visible and the Invisible*, p. 244.
33. In his reply to Geraets, Madison explains: 'It is this "Being" which is not reducible to being-in-the-world – that is, to the subject–world relation, to "experience" – which allows Merleau-Ponty to overcome *contingency*. But this overcoming of contingency is not a return to *necessity*, for "Being" is here neither a supreme and necessary being (*ens causa sui, ens realissimum*) nor a transcendental logical principle (a "that without which" nothing is thinkable). It has neither logical nor ontic reality; it is therefore not so much a *ground* as an abyss, an unfanthomable and inexhaustible source of *transcendence*' (Madison, *The Phenomenology of Merleau-Ponty*, p. 288).
34. Merleau-Ponty, *Visible and the Invisible*, p. 197. On polymorphism, see Emmanuel de Saint Aubert, *Etre et chair. Du corps au désir: l'habilitation ontologique de la chair* (Paris: Vrin, 2013), ch. V.
35. Merleau-Ponty, *Signs*, p. 179.
36. See Merleau-Ponty, *Visible and the Invisible*, p. 219: 'It is hence because of depth that the things have a flesh: that is, oppose to my inspection obstacles, a resistance which is precisely their reality, their "openness," their *totum simul*.' On encroachment, see Emmanuel de Saint Aubert, *Du lien des êtres aux éléments de l'être. Merleau-Ponty au tournant des années 1945–1951* (Paris: Vrin, 2004). Saint Aubert shows the important of the figure of *empiètement*, developed after the Second World War, for understanding

the ontology of the flesh. *Empiètement* is not only a description of our interpersonal relationship, but also describes the encroaching of objects that are seen in depth, by opposition to the flattened, geometrical perspective of classical paintings. As such, it is related to the concept of 'implication' in the *Phenomenology* and is opposed to the bird's-eye view (*survol*) and to the *partes extra partes*. See *Du lien des êtres*, ch. I. See also Saint Aubert, *Etre et chair*, ch. VII, esp. §§2, 4. As a result, and contra Michel Haar and Bernard Sichère as well as Barbaras (see *The Being of the Phenomenon*, pp. 135–6), Saint Aubert shows how the figure of the flesh as a general *Ineinander* is not absent of conflict and desire, and that the conflictual nature of encroaching and promiscuity that was emphasised after the war remains prominent as Merleau-Ponty's discourse becomes more ontological.
37. Merleau-Ponty, *Visible and the Invisible*, p. 136; see also ibid. pp. 250, 164.
38. Barbaras certainly thinks so. In fact, part of his argument is that in the early works the teleological dimension of objectivity and truth is subordinated to consciousness. In the later works, Merleau-Ponty reconceives consciousness on the basis of a more primordial expressive teleology: 'subjectivity no longer bears teleology; subjectivity is born in teleology' (Barbaras, *The Being of the Phenomenon*, p. 63; see also ibid. pp. 12–14). In his 'Merleau-Ponty, metaphysical realism and the natural world', *International Journal of Philosophical Studies*, vol. 15, no. 4 (2007): pp. 501–19, Simon P. James takes on the charge of anthropocentrism in the context not of speculative realism but of environmental realism and shows that, even in the *Phenomenology*, Merleau-Ponty's account of perception is not anthropocentric because perception is anonymous rather than subject-centred (p. 514). Merleau-Ponty provides us with a transhuman account of experience that challenges the 'broadly subject-centred conception of the world presupposed by realists and anti-realists alike' (p. 516).
39. Alain Badiou, 'Preface', in Meillassoux, *After Finitude*, p. vii.
40. See Merleau-Ponty, *Visible and the Invisible*, p. 123.

Chapter 8

The Radical Contingency of Temporality, Correlation and Philosophy: Merleau-Ponty's Indirect Ontology contra Meillassoux's Hyper-Anthropocentric Idealism

David Morris

> . . . how can a being manifest being's anteriority to manifestation?
> Meillassoux, *After Finitude*

> Nature thus interests us . . . as an index of what, within things, resists the operations of free subjectivity, and as concrete access to the ontological problem. If we refused to grant any philosophical meaning to the idea of Nature, and if we reflected directly on being, we would risk placing ourselves immediately at the level of the subject–object relationship, which is an elaboration and secondary, and we would risk missing an essential component of being: brute or wild being which has not yet been converted into an object of vision or choice. It is this that we would like to rediscover.
> Merleau-Ponty, 'La nature ou le monde du silence'

After Finitude's project of returning philosophy to the 'great outdoors' hinges on a critique of subject–object correlation as central to phenomenology (what Meillassoux terms 'correlationism').[1] A philosophy that pursues being from within the terms of correlation, Meillassoux argues, can never reach being itself and remains anthropocentric. His provocative diagnosis of this problem, via the related problem of ancestrality, presses key questions about philosophy and its beginnings. However, the critique of phenomenology presented in *After Finitude* is all too schematic,[2] missing important phenomenological resources that suggest critical responses and alternatives. For example, Merleau-Ponty's continual struggle with phenomenology's beginnings,[3] via his concepts of radical reflection and passivity, lead him to grasp correlation as rooted in the non-human, and eventually in 'wild being' as a radically contingent pre-phenomenological beginning. Wild being paradoxically appears precisely in non-appearing, as a resistance to manifestation intrinsic to correlation: an invisible of the visible that challenges inside/outside divisions; an opening to being at once anterior to manifestation, yet indicated in its depths. Merleau-Ponty thus exposes methodological and ontological presumptions of Meillassoux,[4] while Meillassoux provokes a deepening of Merleau-Ponty's ontology.

The first section of this chapter lays out Meillassoux's argument in *After Finitude*. This section also serves to frame the second section, which traces Merleau-Ponty's route to passivity and his methods of radical reflection and indirect ontology. In turn, this leads to a critique of Meillassoux as taking the activity of thinking for granted, without attending to its passivity, or the ontological implications thereof. One such implication is that we should not confuse being with determinate being – a confusion crucial to Meillassoux's ancestrality problem. Together, these results show how Meillassoux overlooks indications of radically contingent being within correlation itself. The third section clarifies and supports this claim via physics. Although Meillassoux invokes mathematics and science to advance his position, his treatment of science is schematic and neglects the problem of how mathematics and being connect in the first place. I take up this problem by turning to contemporary cosmology and the difficulties associated with measurement in quantum mechanics, showing how these echo Merleau-Ponty's concept of an invisible of the visible – of there being something less than determinate being within manifestation.

The chapter suggests perhaps surprising convergences between Meillassoux and Merleau-Ponty around the necessity of contingency, since Merleau-Ponty's ontology implies that phenomenology, temporality and being can never have been guaranteed in advance, since being is not determinate. But they sharply diverge on the ontological location of the necessity of contingency: whereas Meillassoux leaps to mathematisable hyper-Chaos, Merleau-Ponty detects it in the invisible depths of being's contingent manifestation. I call the latter contingency 'radical contingency': radical contingency is necessitated, but its necessity is indicated as itself contingent on being, in which it is rooted, and in which it is manifest, indirectly, as anterior to manifestation. This contrasts with a contingency whose necessity we can deduce and only think about. The concluding section suggests that Meillassoux's deduction of the necessity of contingency invokes a hyper-anthropocentric idealism that in effect turns Descartes's god into a hyper-Chaotic evil genius, whereas Merleau-Ponty discovers that perceptual faith is rooted in a radically contingent being that had to (in effect) contingently manifest doubt, non-coincidence, for philosophy or science to have ever been possible. Whereas Meillassoux thinks his way to being, by presupposing philosophy, Merleau-Ponty detects something older than thinking in being, in finding that philosophy itself is radically contingent.

Meillassoux's transcendental argument for the necessity of contingency

After Finitude is a fine-grained and complex work. On its largest scale, though, it proceeds as a philosophical critique, by way of a transcendental argument. Here, I outline this argument to show how its beginning and method lead to the necessity of contingency.

The first chapter identifies correlationism as a key principle of philosophy after Kant and argues that no philosophy operating within the terms of correlationism could ever encounter being in itself – 'the *great outdoors* [Grand Dehors]'.[5] Meillassoux bolsters this claim by showing how correlationism leads philosophy to a principled limit and dialectic (in the Kantian sense), captured in the 'ancestrality' problem. On the one hand, scientists and thence philosophers encounter and need to think about things and events, for instance, galaxy formation, which are far older than any subjectivity to which they could have been given; on the other hand, correlationism would seemingly entail that we access such events and things only via what is now given to subjectivity. Ancestrality is thus a mug's game: we pretend to talk about things extant prior to their givenness to someone, but we are really talking about an intersubjectively warranted claim that rests on givenness. Hence the problem in the first epigraph, which concerns the paradox of the archefossil, of 'a being' that could 'manifest being's anteriority to manifestation'.[6] A correlationist can only access this or that being as given, and so can never arrive at being as having a reality anterior to manifestation. To anticipate, Merleau-Ponty agrees that no determinate being can itself directly manifest being; yet the being of determinate manifestation, precisely in never being able to be fully determinate, indirectly indexes being as anterior.

Meillassoux's second chapter, via a marvellously multiplex analysis of possible philosophical responses, delimits (as I shall put it) the narrow eye of the needle through which philosophy must pass if it is to reach the 'great outdoors', thereby refining the problem Meillassoux must solve (Meillassoux here disqualifies dogmatic solutions). Interestingly and crucially, he acknowledges that philosophy in fact begins within the 'correlationist circle'. As Peter Gratton notes (citing Meillassoux), Meillassoux argues that 'I can access a speculative realism which *clearly refutes*, but *no longer disqualifies*, correlationism'.[7] Meillassoux uses 'disqualify' in cases where one philosophical project rules out the terms of another as illegitimate and having no standing. Remarkably, speculative realism does not disqualify correlationism, but begins from it: the eye of the needle just is the correlationist circle. Speculative realism seeks to leapfrog this circle without succumbing to its conceptual terms that entrap being indoors. This leapfrog after finitude would refute correlationism's claims about being and correlation, without disqualifying correlationism as beginning point.

Indeed, Meillassoux's ontological leapfrog begins from a key datum revealed in the correlationist circle, namely facticity: there being facts, including the fact of correlation. But, as a fact manifest to us, facticity remains 'indoors'. To leapfrog to being, chapter three pursues a 'principle of facticity' – a principle of being in virtue of which facts and facticity are in the first place. If we are to escape the circle, the principle of facticity must be absolute, without limit, proviso or dependence on anything else, including our subjectivity – an absolute that itself is, as opposed to being posited via an absolutism on our part.

Meillassoux's ingenious solution is *hyper-Chaos*.[8] To wit: the principle of facticity must indicate being as necessary being, as absolute in and of itself; but if we could indicate the reasons for the necessity of being in advance (in virtue of our thinking, or dogma, or appeal to divine thinking and so on), we would in effect have trumped being's own absolute necessity with other reasons for it. So we cannot posit any reason why being is necessary. Yet we need to think of being as in itself necessary. Hence the principle of facticity is the *necessity of contingency*. What is necessary is sheer contingency: anything, even time, matter, natural laws, could be or not be – it could be this or that, in any moment, for no reason. This necessity of contingency would thus entail the operation of a being beyond any reason, beyond anything we posit, and beyond anything correlative to us – being as being in ways utterly indifferent to us or anything else.

Note that this argument in effect inverts ontological proofs for the existence of god: by *removing* all reasons for something being, we are left with facticity – being without reason. Also note that it proceeds as a transcendental deduction that specifies the conditions through which alone something we are analysing could be. In this case, though, the something is being itself, and not something manifest to us. This is an audacious and unusual transcendental argument since it leapfrogs transcendental deduction beyond noumenal conditions.

Radical reflection and indirect ontology

This brief rehearsal of *After Finitude*'s central argument lets me frame my strategy of response, which draws on Merleau-Ponty's phenomenology, by noting presuppositions in, and alternatives to, the beginning and end point of this argument.[9]

Phenomenology is dedicated to the critique of philosophical and conceptual errors. Methodologically, it pursues this critique by deriving our conceptual frameworks by means of description of the phenomena. The aim is finding warrant for philosophical concepts in the way things show themselves to be, instead of in our own heads, since our thinking could be prejudiced. Rigorous pursuit of this method thus entails describing how we access phenomena in the first place, such that we are really going 'back to the things themselves' as opposed to shadow-boxing with our own projections. Phenomenological method, then, broaches the problems Meillassoux poses with regard to the correlationist circle.

On this methodological level, Merleau-Ponty's important contribution – which is key to my response to Meillassoux – lies in noticing that phenomenology's project would undermine itself if philosophical reflection on the latter problems were a thinking that actively muscles into the correlationist circle from above, if it were what Merleau-Ponty calls 'analytic reflection'. If we want to temper or rule out our (intellectualist) tendency to project our own solutions on to things (in contrast to getting to things themselves), we need to grasp reflection as an operation itself arising within the circle on which it reflects.[10] This is what is at stake in Merleau-Ponty's method of 'radical reflection', which becomes increasingly important in his philosophy.

Radical reflection involves noticing the correlationist circle as the starting point and the condition of philosophical reflection. But it requires more than that: noticing how our reflection on this starting point is *not* a power granted to philosophy in advance, but one rooted and instituted in the operations of what we reflect on. Ultimately, if we tried to secure our power of thinking as guaranteed a priori, as autonomously constituting itself in advance of what we reflect on, we would not have secured phenomenological warrant for our claims about reflection and philosophy since our claims could be projections of our thinking. Notice how this parallels Meillassoux's argument that we arrive at being only by *not* being able to give a reason for it: for Merleau-Ponty, we arrive at a phenomenologically rigorous account of thinking only by *not* being able to give a reasoned, reflective account of reflection in advance. In both cases, philosophy reaches its goal only via something that undermines the principle of sufficient reason. The difference is where and how this undermining erupts. For Meillassoux, it erupts in being, as thinkable only via mathematisable hyper-Chaos – and thinking *actively* arrives at this thought. For Merleau-Ponty, it erupts in phenomena, as manifesting what I have elsewhere called a 'principle of insufficient reason' – and thinking is *passive* to this eruption. I am claiming, contra Meillassoux, that this latter erupting is an encounter with being. This claim hinges on the philosophical and ontological ramifications of the passivity just mentioned, which I will trace by turning back to Meillassoux's critique and drawing out several strands of Merleau-Ponty's thought in response.

For Meillassoux, approaching being via an eruption *within* radical reflection would look like a doubling or tripling down on his problem with phenomenology: (1) radical reflection begins within the correlationist circle (as does Meillassoux); but then (2) it seeks to derive the terms of encounter with being from within that circle (which entraps being indoors); and, if that were not enough, according to the above, (3) radical reflection conceptualises its own thinking as granted by an operation of the very circle that is the problem! My strategy is to show how the passivity flagged in this third step in fact offers a resource for addressing Meillassoux's problem since the terms of encounter with being do not turn out to be terms we are projecting on to things, or even terms arising within correlation. The third step can then lead, via an indirect ontology, to an ontological hollow of radical contingency that echoes Meillassouxian hyper-Chaos, but *within* phenomena.[11] The key is understanding how our *inability* to claim thinking in advance leads, via passivity, to encountering a radical contingency of being and philosophy within manifestation.

Passivity is the topic of a lecture course that Merleau-Ponty gives in 1954–5 (and is a remarkably pervasive undercurrent of the *Phenomenology*).[12] The central problem of the passivity course is that we encounter a world that makes sense to us, but, precisely in doing so, we do not (prior to reflection) thematically encounter obstacles to our sense making. Yet there must be obstacles, otherwise there would not be error, doubt, illusion, facts, reality, truth or philosophy. How is it that within experience we do not encounter obstacles that must nonetheless be there, if there is a reality beyond us? If we did not encounter obstacles because we actively posited them, they would not really be obstacles – and there would not really be error or truth. However, if obstacles were utterly resistant to the subject, then the only way to account for subjectivity and mind would be by hooking the subject into a natural system in which obstacles cause mind. But then mind and sense (meaning) are lost as distinctive phenomena, as are real norms of truth and error – in that case, everything just is what it is in the machine of nature. Or, if we suppose obstacles are inaccessible things in themselves, dogmatically posited, then mind is its own game, and once again we lose truth and error as being beyond us. (Notice how Merleau-Ponty's problem of passivity echoes Meillassoux's problem of correlation getting to the great outdoors.)

In order to escape this problem, Merleau-Ponty argues that we need to conceptualise passivity as a new 'genus of being with regard to which the subject is not sovereign, without the subject being inserted in it [like a cog in a machine]'.[13] In effect, this means understanding that obstacles cannot be actively constituted or determined as obstacles in advance, either by our cognitive capacity, or by an already given nature. Obstacles have to arise obstinately, passively, on the fly and on their own terms; if they could be orchestrated or harmonised in advance, they would not be really blocking us; they would instead be working for us. This is why passivity entails a new genre of being: obstacles entail a kind of being that does not operate by way of an already fully determinate givenness, but precisely by not being that, by working its own way. Indeed, a being that would be actively and fully present, right now, without remainder would, as determinate, be navigable, workable – and there would not be any questions or problems. Passivity thus indicates a being that can never be deduced in advance and is contingent in a deeply inborne way.

A brief excursion back into the *Phenomenology of Perception* can help clarify these points about passivity and the way they lead to an ontology of radical contingency. The *Phenomenology* keeps discovering that the reality of things involves an in-itself-for-us: a resistance in things themselves to manifestation for us, such that we cannot actively constitute this resistance. A classic example is Merleau-Ponty's analysis of a thing's reality, in virtue of which it can stand as true or illusory. This reality hinges on the thing's inexhaustibility: it can never be fully given or present for-us, can never stand as identical to the determinate X we now take it to be. Hence a tension: we encounter the thing as being in-itself . . . only via its inexhaustibility for-us, our inability to encounter the thing as fully coinciding with itself within any given manifestation. Would this not mean, though, that being in-itself is merely a counterpart to a limitation on our side, such that it is kindred to a merely thinkable noumenon – and is not the great outdoors?

In the chapter 'The thing and the natural world', as well as in a peculiar thread of remarks in the 'Cogito' chapter, Merleau-Ponty in fact detects an eruption of something non-human within phenomena. He writes that

> perception, in the context of our everyday dealings, bears upon the things just enough to find in them their familiar presence, and not enough to rediscover what of the non-human is hidden within them. But the thing is unaware of us, it remains in itself.[14]

He goes on to write that the 'real lends itself to an infinite exploration, it is inexhaustible', which is why things such as, for example, stones, which we can decompose without end, 'are rooted in a background of non-human nature', in contrast to human artefacts, which lose their human-bestowed identities as soon as we break them up.[15] For Merleau-Ponty, 'when we place everything into doubt and suspend all of our beliefs, we only succeed in catching sight of the non-human ground'.[16] That is, even doubt does not wrench us out of the world; rather, it reveals that our world has a non-human ground. This means that the world is not purely interior to me, purely human – but also that an exterior, non-human ground already erupts inside me, even before I doubt. Indeed, this unsettling eruption is the requisite ground of doubt as well as of 'perceptual faith'. As he puts it, 'the interior and the exterior are inseparable. The world is entirely on the inside, and I am entirely outside of myself.'[17] *Philosophy is rooted in and internally open to a non-human ground through which alone doubt, questioning and philosophy are possible.*

Still, for Meillassoux, the question would be how this eruption of a non-human ground within the terms of correlation can really open me to a being that cannot be subsumed to merely being for me. To answer this question, let us first turn back to the 'Sensing' chapter, which contains the *Phenomenology*'s closest engagement with Kant (who presides over this Meillassoux–Merleau-Ponty encounter). This chapter analyses sensing as the most basic structure and condition of our access to things. Without going into extensive detail, the key point is that Merleau-Ponty conducts this analysis via a radical reflection that attends to its own rootedness in that which it accesses (indeed the chapter articulates key results regarding radical reflection). As above, this radical reflection exposes a passivity that we do not constitute, as key to even our most basic access to things. This emphasises that our access to things could not be our own accomplishment, otherwise it would not be an access to things.[18] Formally, Merleau-Ponty draws this out by probing, for instance, spatiality, as what would seem to be an a priori condition of sensing. He argues that actual phenomena of sensing, especially the different sorts of spatiality of the different senses, show that spatiality (as a condition of sensing) cannot be constituted wholly actively, a priori: spatiality must also be a posteriori and passive to (shaped out of) what we sense. For example, what we touch, by way of touch as an activity that is passive to what we are touching, engenders the spatial a priori of touch. The a priori of sensing is thus contingent on what we turn out to have sensed. This contingency is not an obstacle to sensing; rather, this sort of contingent obstacle is necessary if sense is really to get at things. If we could posit such obstacles in advance, and thereby deduce sensing or spatiality as what can surmount them, we would never really have the sense of a something given in its own terms, as really being an obstacle.

This argument amplifies the point we have been tracking, namely that Merleau-Ponty keeps detecting something not of our making, and beyond manifestation, as an inborn condition of manifestation and correlation. Indeed, the 'Sensing' chapter pursues this point into its famous conclusion that 'reflection only fully grasps itself [that is, realises the demand of radical reflection] if it refers to the prereflective fund it presupposes, upon which it draws, and that constitutes for it, like an original past, a past that has never been present'.[19] Ultimately, the non-human ground that erupts within manifestation is in fact an eruption of what never could have been manifest, of a being anterior to manifestation.

Nonetheless, Meillassoux could respond that this past that has never been present, which could never be manifest to us, is in fact encountered only in and through manifestation, and so remains within the correlationist circle and falls to the ancestrality problem. To see how this is not so, we need to note a twofold error implied by Merleau-Ponty's philosophy: first, do not presume that all being is visible, manifest; and this is because, second, we should not confuse being and determinate being.[20] That is, do not confuse the determinate beings that we encounter with being itself; do not think that being itself is determinate, or can be modelled in terms of some sort of determinate being (even an open-endedly determinate being like time conceived as an already given framework); do not try to understand being by negating determinate characteristics of determinate beings and construing what remains as being that is not determinate. Instead, we must grant a positive ontological standing to being that is not determinate – and this cannot be determinately given as a manifest thing. (We saw something similar in the argument that passivity cannot be directly manifest as determinately there and already given.)

If it were the case that all we can access in the correlationist circle is determinate being, or that being in-itself is determinate, then Meillassoux's argument could go through since any determinate being, including being in-itself posited as determinate, would be correlative to us, not 'outdoors'; a determinate being, precisely as correlative to us, could never give us anything altogether anterior to manifestation. But we have seen that the phenomena press us to grant positive ontological standing to being that is not determinate. And the line of discussion above, from radical reflection to passivity, shows how the phenomena reveal this via a kind of excess in determinate beings, where this excess is not determinately given, or is rather an excess of what cannot be given: what Merleau-Ponty calls a hollow or negative in being that is not, however, a deficit or lack relative to a determinate something that could be given.

(If it were a lack relative to the given, it would fall to Meillassoux's problems.)

Still, the question would remain: how are we to think such a hollow as the anterior eruption of being within manifestation, without converting it into manifestation? This underlying ontological issue is often at stake in Merleau-Ponty's discussion of fields or temporality. For example, in the *Phenomenology*'s 'Temporality' chapter, these points about passivity and the original past are echoed in the argument that the condition of experience is not an already given framework of time that would order and enable synthesis in advance, but rather 'transition syntheses', roughly, syntheses we could never actively constitute or ground because they require our undergoing temporality as never fully given or determinate, even as transcendental condition of experience. Experience arises in temporality as always internally reconfiguring itself, as a reality that is radically contingent such that the being of temporality could never itself be manifest – and yet the being of this temporality is the 'inapparent', invisible, condition of every visible manifestation.[21]

I want to approach this point about temporality by discussing the methodological prerequisites of the question above, as to how we are to conceive this being that is in excess of determinate being and manifestation. Obviously, we would misconstrue being if we conflated it with a determinate being manifest to us. Yet, on the other hand, for Merleau-Ponty, we would also misconstrue it if we tried to directly grasp it through our language or ideas, precisely because language and ideas (even if these ultimately arise from being itself) are manifest as determinate beings, not being, and for the most part express something determinate – and when our language manages to express something that is not determinate, it can precisely lose touch with being.[22]

Methodologically, this sort of problem leads Merleau-Ponty to what he calls 'indirect ontology'.[23] Basically, Merleau-Ponty argues that if we try to pursue ontology by reflecting directly on being from within our own thoughts and ideas, we are prone to conceptualise it in terms of determinate things or thought patterns, or in terms of abstract and determinate lines of escape from these. Instead, we have to learn how to read determinate beings so as to grasp the endogenous lessons they offer regarding being itself. But obviously we would not be able to do that, or would be deceiving ourselves, if all we found in determinate beings were a reflective correlate of ourselves. This is what is at stake in the second epigraph to this chapter, from Merleau-Ponty's 1957 note on 'Nature or the World of Silence', where he writes that 'if we reflected directly on being, we would risk placing ourselves immediately at the level of the subject-object relationship, which is an elaboration and secondary', we 'would risk missing

... brute or wild being which has not yet been converted into an object of vision or choice'.[24] If we are to 'rediscover' this wild being, there must be something more, or rather less, in being, than determinate being – which was already detected in the *Phenomenology*'s discovery, *right within* the subject–object relationship, of passivity, transition synthesis and so on. This basically articulates the project of *The Visible and the Invisible*, which is to make these ontological issues explicit and rigorous by understanding the tissue of our visible world as a flesh doubled with an invisible in virtue of which alone the visible can be engendered. This invisible, again, can never itself appear, yet we do not detect it via abstract reflection, but by interrogating being from within and encountering the invisible as inherently non-appearing in the visible. We thereby arrive at invisible being indirectly, by way of visible beings.

It is crucial to notice that for Merleau-Ponty the methodological problem of conceptualising being indirectly, via its eruption within manifestation, coincides with and depends upon that very being having erupted as anterior to manifestation. That is, for Merleau-Ponty, we cannot reason our way out of this problem, we need to see that a solution has contingently been granted by being, as having made it be possible for us to indirectly encounter ... that which cannot be encountered in determinate beings. This is why Merleau-Ponty thinks of wild being and nature in terms of silence: silence is what must be prior to and have contingently granted the possibility of determinate language and sense; yet, precisely as such, silence cannot itself be voiced in any determinate way since this would efface silence by introjecting it with a determinate character; but this also means that, as contingently granting determinate language, silence ends up effacing itself, and showing itself only as effaced in the language it contingently engenders.

I contend that for Merleau-Ponty being especially erupts in effacing itself within a temporality that being itself contingently engendered, a temporality that could not have been deduced in advance: being is indicated as an insufficiency of reason, contingently detectable within and endogenous to ... the very temporality this insufficiency engendered. In contrast, for Meillassoux, hyper-Chaos, as mathematisable, indicates a lack of reason for all time. Put otherwise, for Merleau-Ponty, temporality itself indicates that the correlationist circle arises from a radically contingent being that is deeper than all manifestation and yet is nowhere other than (invisible) in manifestation's depths; whereas for Meillassoux the correlationist circle is the eye of the needle that we must leapfrog so as to think the necessity of contingency, but only from beyond the terms of this circle's givenness.

Nonlocality and the reality of time: things and the cosmos as being less than determinate

We have ascended, or plunged, into highly abstract philosophical matters. To clarify this point about temporality, I want to turn to quantum mechanics and cosmology – and deploy contemporary physics to trouble Meillassoux's claim that hyper-Chaos is obviously supported by scientific claims about mathematics and reality.

Quantum mechanics (QM), though, is no easy topic. Precise discussion of it requires comprehensive technical knowledge of physics and mathematics, and it confronts us with claims about reality that challenge our everyday experience. At the same time, precisely because QM challenges our presumptions and everyday experience, it is a great resource for philosophy, especially phenomenology. This is why Merleau-Ponty is interested in it in his lectures on nature: it shows that 'the perceived world is a world where there is discontinuity, where there is probability and generality, where each being is not constrained to a unique and fixed location, to an absolute density of being'[25] – it undermines the view that being is a determinate plenum or follows an already determinate or necessitated trajectory.[26]

I want to draw out this point and its significance with regard to our questions above, but not by following Merleau-Ponty's analysis of QM, which takes up older QM interpretations in physics. Indeed, I want to avoid the typical interpretations altogether, since these keep multiplying and usually import philosophical presuppositions about being and reality. Instead, I pursue an 'operational' approach to QM by trying to specify, in informational terms, what happens with quantum mechanical entanglement in working technologies deployed for encryption and computational purposes. The idea is to suspend details of theoretical physics and, by describing what QM actually *does*, reveal implications for our description and conception of being, space and time.[27]

To do this let us first imagine Alice and Bob playing a game that does not involve QM. They are sequestered far from each other, incommunicado; each randomly pushes either the left or right button of a machine that then displays either a 0 or 1; each then writes down the number 0 or 1. After each trial, their results are compared and scored as follows: if they *both* pressed the right button, and wrote down *different* numbers, they win; or, if *either* pressed the left button, and wrote down the *same* number, they win. They are trying to win this game cooperatively, but neither knows what button the other will press. Analysis of possible outcomes shows they can win up to 75 per cent of the time if their machines are pre-programmed to always output 1, or if, by advance coordination (or by luck, without coordination), each ignores the machine and always writes down 1. There are other ways of pre-rigging the machines or their responses that can win up to 75 per cent of the time, but no strategy that can reliably exceed that if their button presses and the machines operate independently of one another. (You can check this by analysing the four different button combinations, and the winning number combinations within these cases.)

Let us now turn to the QM variant of this game. In this variant, we generate entangled pairs of quantum mechanical particles, sending one particle to Alice, one to Bob; Alice's and Bob's random button presses set different measurement angles for their apparatus (for example, 0° or 45° for Alice, 22.5° or −22.5° for Bob); and the machine measures particle spin, showing a 0 or 1, which is used for scoring.

Remarkably, QM predicts this game can be won more than 75 per cent of the time (up to 85.4 per cent), and experiments confirm this. Why is this remarkable? The win percentage indicates the correlatedness of events in these games, and correlatedness in the QM case is better than the 75 per cent in the non-QM game. But 75 per cent is the best Alice and Bob can do, even when the machines or their responses are rigged in advance; there is no place to build in some other localizable factor that lets them do better. So, what is going on? The key is the interaction between their measuring apparatus and the entangled particles, which specifies the winning 0s and 1s: something that is going on in *that measurement* yields a correlation[28] better than 75 per cent. But, that measurement depends on the measurement angle, which is set by uncorrelated, random button presses. Given this randomness, the best correlation in a non-QM case (as noted above) *should* be 75 per cent, nothing set in advance could yield a better correlation. So it is as if the particles are conspiring at a distance, leveraging information about the random measurement angles at the two locations, so as to turn up better correlated. But this is not so. The experiment and entanglement preclude faster-than-light communication of information: Alice cannot *choose* to have a 0 turn up, so as to instantaneously communicate a 0 to Bob. Rather, Alice's and Bob's measurements yield a purely random sequence – and yet, the sequence is exactly the same[29] in both places (hence the technology's importance for cryptography: it generates a shared random key and allows testing for eavesdroppers). It is as if Alice and Bob have a 'magic coin' that flips exactly the same way in multiple locations – yet this cannot be because its flips were already programmed in. That is what the contrast with the non-QM game shows us: coordination could not be due to any built-in local factor, a 'local hidden variable'. Indeed, John Bell contrived this game to test his theorem that no physical theory involving localised, hidden variables could ever account for all the predictions of QM: the non-QM version at best allows 75-per-cent correlation by rigging local variables to produce correlations. Local variables, even hidden ones, cannot explain how QM exceeds this.

What does this mean? Quantum entanglement exhibits *nonlocality*. This does not refer to a kind of determinate action, within the sphere of determinate beings or events that we have measured, that would instantaneously stretch beyond given locales in violation of the speed of light. Rather it means (whatever else it means in physics) that we cannot conceptualise the determinate characteristic manifest when we eventually measure a being in a given locale (for instance, a particle's determinate spin) as ultimately resting in something already determinately borne within that locale, something that could always-already be located here or there. Entanglement involves something that cannot quite be here in the way that determinate beings, or even determinate space and time, are. We need to understand that the particles in these two locations are coming to manifest a spin that was not yet determinate, yet in ways not merely local to those two locations. The measured correlation arises as a characteristic of a system that is both here and there, yet the measured characteristics were not determinate in advance, but arise in relation to measurement. In ontological terms, our encountering this phenomenon within manifest things, for instance, in quantum-crypto technologies, implies that there is something operative in the being of manifest, determinate things that cannot itself be manifest as determinate.

This is the sort of ontological point that Merleau-Ponty was trying to get at with his thought of an invisible that is of the visible, and of being as itself hollow: it tells us how being, as doing the work of engendering determinate things, can be indicated precisely through a kind of nonlocality in the being of things, a nonlocality that cannot, however, be manifest in determinate beings because determinate manifestations always have a determinate character precisely locatable within their locale. In quantum mechanics, this ontological point is at issue in the very activity of measurement. In Merleau-Pontian terms, in QM, measurement as an activity that localises things as determinately this or that indicates an operative passivity that is less than and anterior to such localisation.

Now measurement is precisely where mathematics actually connects with being in a cosmos. Meillassoux, though, does not attend to the QM measurement problem in physics, and perhaps this is consistent with his project, since measurement is an analogue of correlation: the problem is how being measures up to our denumeration of it. Yet, whenever Meillassoux talks about mathematics as a way to being, I cannot help asking: how is it that mathematics actually gets at being in the first place? And this leads me to QM measurement as echoing Merleau-Ponty's ontology.

But let us turn in a different direction. Physicists themselves have long asked why mathematics in fact works in doing physics.[30] They have also asked why certain cosmological constants that are key to the physics of our universe have the value they have, and not some other value. Physicist/cosmologist Lee Smolin proposes a philosophically insightful approach to the latter question.[31] He argues that claiming that cosmological constants are, as it were, locally set within the cosmos, for all time, begs the question and violates the principle of sufficient reason: we cannot find the reason for the constants fixed within the cosmos as it now is, for any such reason cannot say why the cosmos is fixed this way. This might seem to fit with Meillassoux's move of stripping the manifest of the reasons for things being (since any reason for being that is manifest to us is entrapped indoors). However, although Smolin claims that we should not understand the reasons for constants as fixed in the manifest cosmos for all time, he argues that we should understand these as engendered in the history of the cosmos – in a reality of time that is not the same as that of the time we now encounter. Indeed, we need to understand time and space, as we now encounter them, as arising in this reality of time – but not because what we now encounter was already predicted by that reality (as this would repeat the problem). The reason for the constants hinges on the unpredicted, contingent occurrence of the cosmos as involving something that must be prior to what we can encounter (this is kindred to Merleau-Ponty's world of silence).

This leads me to think of a reality of time – I call it deep temporality – that is invisible in, yet engendering of, the visible time we now encounter in the same way that nonlocality is invisible in, yet engendering of, the determinate, localisable characteristics of particles. It must be emphasised, though, that this deep temporality, as that in/of which cosmoi, constants, time and so on are engendered, could not already contain what it turns out to have engendered – for then the question why it turns out this or that way would once again be begged by trying to localise the answer in an already determinate being. The why, the reason, is in the telling, in the contingent unfolding; the reason is in their being insufficient reason. What is ultimately at the root of everything is the radical contingency inborn of deep temporality, which is also deep place, since temporality is in/of a singular something. This radical contingency is manifest in/as what I call 'templacement', the engendering of what turned out to be determinate time and place together.

With regard to Meillassoux, the crucial point is that radical contingency conceptualised in this way is internally indicated within every manifestation as its ultimate condition of being. Yet the being of this condition cannot itself be manifest, except in its necessarily non-appearing in manifestation. Nonetheless, what is indicated here, deep temporality, is not over and done with, but is still at work in the being of the cosmos: the cosmos and the manifest are still in principle changeable in virtue of this deeper temporality. So, what is indicated here is a being anterior to manifestation, that cannot, as invisible, be conflated with any visible manifestation, yet is indicated as an invisible of the visible.

This deep temporality 'roots' ancestrality. Radically contingent temporality, as anterior to manifestation, is the weight of resistance and passivity inborn in the present, in virtue of which there is a past that cannot be undone, that precedes us. But this temporality is also that in virtue of which there is a future that will turn out this or that way, in virtue of which being is weighted with reality and resistance such that there can be truth or error, questions and answers.

I suggest this indirectly indicates being as what Merleau-Ponty would call an invisible lining within the visible, in response to Meillassoux's challenge.

Hyper-anthropocentric idealism

I just argued that Meillassoux misses the challenge that measurement poses to his own appeals to science and mathematics, and that this challenge shows how manifestation in fact indicates being as anterior to what is now manifest. This is what we find with what I call deep temporality, which I drew out of cosmology and Merleau-Ponty's phenomenological ontology. If this is correct, we do not need to leap to hyper-Chaos to get to being. Prior to this, I argued that once we note the importance of passivity to phenomena and our own thinking, we find phenomenology offering resources and insights that Meillassoux has disregarded. I now want to extend this analysis into more general critical remarks regarding Meillassoux's neglect of passivity as coupling with a sort of overreach I find in Meillassoux's thinking.

These criticisms are appropriate given Meillassoux's efforts to counter the anthropocentric tendencies of philosophies rooted in our finitude. Meillassoux's argument could work, I think, were our thinking an autonomous activity that can think what it likes. Meillassoux's deployment of mathematics indicates he is operating with this view of thinking: hyper-Chaos is unthinkable in terms of determinate, encounterable manifestation since it is devoid of all manifest reason; yet mathematics can formalise hyper-Chaos – mathematics is up to thinking anything.

To my mind, this power of mathematics is precisely the problem with Meillassoux's position. Mathematics so powerfully ranges across all cosmoi that it cannot determine why the cosmos is just this way and not some other way. But perhaps that is just the point: mathematics can thereby get at what it is that would have made the manifest cosmos be this way without already introjecting the reason why it turned out this way and not that way. Mathematics can thus get at being as prior to manifestation and our reasoning. However, at this point, I do not see how we escape the game of projections that Meillassoux has been criticising: have we not just grasped being in a mathematical image we contrived ourselves? As noted above, when I go to the physicists, they ask the question how mathematics in fact links with reality – and, if the question is genuine, the answer is contingent on the cosmos and is not purely mathematical. Indeed, Smolin argues that we need to understand the cosmos as making mathematics possible: cosmoi arise together with what can enable mathematics (difference, identity, relationality) – although we can then, via our thinking and idealisation, extend and elaborate mathematics beyond actual cosmoi.

In the end, I think that Meillassoux is simply repeating the moves and argumentative strategies of classic idealist philosophy, albeit modulated via his striking insight that we lose being as the great outdoors if we subsume it to the terms of any reason given in advance. I have this suspicion about idealism because I find that the warrant for his claims about hyper-Chaos is solely his own reasoning and not anything beyond that. He is, as it were, deducing Descartes's god as the foundation of being through an inverted ontological argument that removes all reasons for this deduction, turning god into an evil genius who abdicates malice in favour of hyper-Chaotic dice throws without reason. It is true that this would solve the problem posed by Meillassoux, but does the fact that it lets us solve a problem that *we* pose make it true? Are we posing the right problem?

Here I detect a kind of 'hyper-anthropocentrism' in Meillassoux's effort to think his way to being. Meillassoux begins by urgently opposing himself to correlationism as anthropocentric and closing off the great outdoors. But this urgency, I contend, is the most anthropocentric move of all because it presumes that philosophy ought to be oriented *by the question of our being as the already given or absent centre of philosophical questioning* – which is quite presumptuous. Instead, we need to grasp the problem of philosophical beginnings as arising from a being that is not already geared to that question – and hyper-Chaos fails to do this in so far as it is already grasped in mathematical terms and, as I argued above, inherently overreaches being with mathematics. At this point we can also see that Meillassoux's hyper-Chaos is correlative to the question that he himself has set, and in this respect too his position is hyper-anthropocentric.

Merleau-Ponty moves in the opposite direction: radical reflection seeks to understand how the terms of our questioning are set by something older than us – and that turns out to be something older than manifestation itself, yet something that is still indicated in it. But this means something even wilder and more radical than we find in Meillassoux. Meillassoux, in setting the terms of the question, is, I think, *presupposing that philosophy is possible in advance*, and from there he deduces his way to being as hyper-Chaos. That move is the deepest signature of idealism. Merleau-Ponty is getting us to notice that *philosophy need not have been possible*, and that this contingency is intrinsic to philosophy's beginning. Meillassoux's mathematical overreach says that being must always be thinkable as being without reason, as necessarily contingent beyond and anterior to what now is. In contrast, phenomenology notices a kind of 'under-reach' within phenomenology and being itself, an indication within being itself that being need not be thinkable although it has now turned out to be so. Being itself indicates a radical contingency within and anterior to what now is. The arche-fossil is then deep temporality as a radical contingency inborn in manifest being and time, and manifest in correlation and philosophy as well, when we do not claim to be able to think being necessarily and in advance. We notice this when we do not claim that philosophy would have to be for all time. Giving up on that claim, I think, does not, as Meillassoux urges, trap us within finitude; it rather opens us to inner depths of being that exceed us yet grant us time and place for philosophy.

In the end, I suspect that Meillassoux would take my results as evidence confirming that phenomenology, as rooting itself in given beginnings, shuts out the great outdoors, so we need to leapfrog after finitude. What I hope to have clarified is that Meillassoux's claim amounts to a choice about what it means to begin doing philosophy. Meillassoux and Merleau-Ponty both begin from what Meillassoux calls the correlationist circle, but do so with different attitudes about what it means to begin philosophy. For Merleau-Ponty, this means taking up problems that are radically contingent offerings within something older than us. For Meillassoux, it means thinking a problem that must be thought for all time. My sense is that nature refutes the latter, yet does not disqualify it.

Notes

1. Quentin Meillassoux, *After Finitude: An Essay on the Necessity of Contingency*, trans. Ray Brassier (London: Bloomsbury, 2009), p. 26.
2. For example, Husserl is mentioned only six times, is never quoted directly, and the only Husserl work cited is the foundational investigations of the spatiality of nature, to advance a critique of an eternalised ego (*After Finitude*, p. 122) that Husserl himself

would elsewhere contest. Merleau-Ponty is not mentioned. Heidegger is more robustly treated, appearing around thirty times, but more in relation to ontology than phenomenology and its method.
3. For an insightful study of phenomenological beginnings, see John Sallis, *Phenomenology and the Return to Beginnings* (Pittsburgh: Duquesne University Press, 1973). See also Ted Toadvine, 'The elemental past', *Research in Phenomenology*, vol. 44 (2014): pp. 262–79. Toadvine has a different, perhaps less radical, way into issues of time and the non-human in Merleau-Ponty, although also convergent with my approach. In particular, Toadvine's deep time is different from my concept of deep temporality.
4. In addition to points discussed below, Merleau-Ponty rejects the very distinction between the transcendental and the empirical that undergirds Meillassoux's analysis, even as the latter challenges this distinction and the transcendental as inadequate to the philosophical task. See, for example, Meillassoux, *After Finitude*, pp. 22–6 in the English translation, which are not in the French.
5. Ibid. p. 7.
6. Ibid. p. 26.
7. Gratton, *Speculative Realism*, p. 41. Gratton cites Ray Brassier, Iain Hamilton Grant, Graham Harman and Quentin Meillassoux, 'Speculative realism', *Collapse*, vol. III (2007): pp. 306–449, here p. 429. In note 12, Gratton also cites Harman's point that the correlationist circle is not an error, 'but the starting point for all rigorous philosophy'. See Graham Harman, *Quentin Meillassoux: Philosophy in the Making* (Edinburgh: Edinburgh University Press, 2011), p. 3.
8. Meillassoux, *After Finitude*, p. 64.
9. On my view, ancestrality forces Meillassoux's leapfrog only if we grant presuppositions that I am contesting here. Indeed, while I am using his language of correlation and manifestation for the sake of discussion, in the end I think such language is inadequate and grants Meillassoux an impoverished version of phenomenology.
10. See Maurice Merleau-Ponty, *Phenomenology of Perception*, trans. Donald A. Landes (Oxford: Routledge, [1945] 2012), p. 62. The crucial point in the *Phenomenology* is that 'we must consider reflection to be a creative operation that itself participates in the facticity of the unreflected'.
11. Barbaras approaches this point via his concept of phenomenality as deepening into desire and distance – but by deducing this as a transcendental condition of correlation. Barbaras, then, does not escape the correlationist circle. See Renauld Barbaras, 'The Phenomenology of Life: Desire as the Being of the Subject', in Dan Zahavi (ed.), *The Oxford Handbook of Contemporary Phenomenology* (Oxford: Oxford University Press, 2012), pp. 94–111. I suspect Meillasoux's critique is (rightly) directed against this sort of phenomenology. My claim is that Merleau-Ponty's method and results are very different.
12. Maurice Merleau-Ponty, *Institution and Passivity: Course Notes from the Collège de France (1954–55)*, trans. Leonard Lawlor and Heath Massey (Evanston: Northwestern University Press, 2010); see the course résumé for the points discussed in this paragraph. Vallier provides insightful background on this course and the companion course on institution. See Robert Vallier, 'Institution: the significance of Merleau-Ponty's 1954 course at the Collège de France', *Chiasmi International*, vol. 7 (2005): pp. 281–302.
13. Merleau-Ponty, *Institution and Passivity*, p. 206.
14. Merleau-Ponty, *Phenomenology*, p. 336.
15. Ibid. p. 338.
16. Ibid. p. 430.
17. Ibid. p. 430.
18. Schelling is a forerunner of this point.
19. Merleau-Ponty, *Phenomenology*, p. 252.

20. I introduce this distinction and formalise this error to help clarify Merleau-Ponty's project, but it is one I learned from his philosophy. The error is flagged in the *Phenomenology*'s discovery of 'the indeterminate as a positive phenomenon' (ibid. p. 7), and is central to his analyses of movement (from the *Phenomenology*, through his 1953 lectures on the world of expression, into his 1956–60 lectures on nature) as not traversing an already determinate trajectory in an already determinate space, but as more fundamentally engendering the space of movement. The error is also flagged, as we shall see, in his concept of time.
21. On these points about temporality, see David Morris and Kym Maclaren (eds), *Time, Memory, Institution: Merleau-Ponty's New Ontology of Self* (Athens: Ohio University Press, 2015).
22. Cf. Edmund Husserl, 'Addendum XXIII of *The Crisis of the European Sciences and Transcendental Phenomenology*', *Journal of the British Society for Phenomenology*, vol. 44 (2013): pp. 6–9. Husserl grants biology deeper ontological insights than mathematics, precisely because mathematics can spiral into abstraction.
23. See Emmanuel de Saint Aubert, *Vers une ontologie indirecte. Sources et enjeux critiques de l'appel à l'ontologie chez Merleau-Ponty* (Paris: Vrin, 2006). See also William S. Hamrick and Jan van der Venken, *Nature and Logos: A Whiteheadian Key to Merleau-Ponty's Fundamental Thought* (Albany: SUNY Press, 2011), pp. 68–71.
24. Maurice Merleau-Ponty, 'La nature ou le monde du silence', in Emmanuel de Saint Aubert (ed.), *Maurice Merleau-Ponty* (Paris: Hermann, 2008), pp. 44–53, here p. 53.
25. Maurice Merleau-Ponty, *In Praise of Philosophy and Other Essays*, trans. John Wild, James Edie and John O'Neill (Evanston: Northwestern University Press, 1970), p. 154.
26. See note 20 above. Note a convergence between the description of measurement here and Merleau-Ponty's description of expression.
27. This approach and my exposition are inspired by Gisin, from whom I take the 'magic coin'. See Nicolas Gisin, *Quantum Chance: Nonlocality, Teleportation and Other Quantum Marvels* (Cham: Springer, 2014). My approach is also inspired by Scott Aaronson, 'Quantum randomness', *American Scientist*, vol. 102, no. 4 (2014): pp. 266–71; as well as tutorials on IBM Research's Quantum Experience site http://www.research.ibm.com/quantum/ for its online quantum computer (accessed May 2016).
28. Note that 'correlation' here means something altogether different than in the discussion of phenomenology.
29. Granted, for instance, checksum protocols for weeding out sequence differences that would arise given noise and uncertainty.
30. For a classic analysis of this problem, see Eugene P. Wigner, 'The unreasonable effectiveness of mathematics in the natural sciences', *Pure and Applied Mathematics*, vol. 13 (1960): pp. 1–14.
31. Roberto Mangabeira Unger and Lee Smolin, *The Singular Universe and the Reality of Time* (Cambridge: Cambridge University Press, 2015).

Chapter 9

The Realist Challenge: Thinking the Reality of Language after Deconstruction

Peter Gratton

> [T]here is *some thing* that defies all appropriation by thought (for example, its appropriation as 'concept,' or as 'idea,' as 'philosophy' or as 'meditation,' or even as 'thought'). This thing is nothing other than the immanent immobility of the fact *that there are* things. . . . There are things, and their 'there are' makes space for still another thing, which is thought, the supplementary memorial of the immemorial thing.
> …
> Nothing can be thought – in truth, one would not think at all – without the pondering or the weighing of this unthinkable thinghood of thought.
>
> Jean-Luc Nancy, *Birth to Presence*

Who says we were not talking about the real? Leaving aside just who this 'we' would be – the targets of recent self-supposed continental realists have included phenomenologists, those writing under the banner of deconstruction, and indeed all manner of post-Kantian philosophy – there is little doubt there have been forces at work to bring about a turn towards 'realism' in recent philosophy. As I prepared the beginnings of what would become my *Speculative Realism: Problems and Prospects* (2014), I took up the task of understanding what Marie-Eve Morin has called realism's 'challenge' to previous modes of thought. In the book, my task was to approach from the inside, as it were, those arguments by the realists that argue for the systematic rejection of the supposed 'correlationism' of an era that Foucault had already dubbed some years ago the *epistemē* of the 'empirico-transcendental doublet', that is, an era of what we used simply to call 'subject–object' dualism. That this dualism had been critiqued by the very figures Quentin Meillassoux includes in this era of correlationism was, in a sense for me, besides the point. Yes, the late Heidegger, the late Merleau-Ponty, and the work of Derrida especially, contested any such dualism in a manner that testified to that which is heterogeneous to phenomenology's noetic–noematic relation, which can fairly be summed up as the correlation of thought and being as critiqued by Meillassoux. Yes, the readings by Graham Harman and others are more often snide than savvy. Hegel, Husserl and Derrida are hard; declaring their obsolescence has apparently been all too easy. Moreover, witnessing those continentalists taking up arguments for realism in continental circles – those trained in Heidegger, Derrida et al., but now rehashing questions about substance and process and so forth – feels like watching an actor take up boxing in midlife: no amount of additional training will give you the fluidity of movement others long debating realism and anti-realism have with these arguments. Proponents of this realism are bound to sound a bit punch-drunk while rehashing forms of naive realism. But let us not be like a Derridean on one of the reader reports for my *Speculative Realism* book who said, 'Derrida would have dismissed this all with a sentence', as if Derrida were ever a sovereign declaring movements to the gallows with a (death) sentence, and as if this were not some repetition of the type of rejection Derrida himself encountered from analytic philosophers of an earlier era who had not bothered to read him. 'Only non-philosophers read them', some say about the speculative realists, just as was said of the post-structuralists before them; 'no one takes them seriously' is another thing oft-heard about the new realists; and so on. Yet, still, is there not a 'challenge'? Perhaps Morin give us the answer about how much these movements are worth given her choice of that word: 'calumny' and 'challenge' have the same root in the late Latin *calumniāre*, 'to accuse *falsely*'.

Nevertheless, there is a fair family resemblance across a number of recent academic and political movements (the new ecologies, philosophies of nature, post-humanism, cyborgology and so on) calling for an end to constructivism and its supposed reliance on all-too-human sign systems blocking us from discussions of the real. There clearly were some so-called postmodernists, just as there were analytic anti-realists concerning conceptual schemes, that treated texts and textuality as a semiotic update of the Kantian categories forever blocking us from the real (or better: 'real', always in quotation marks). Speculative realism may have provided a frivolous lawsuit, challenge or accusation, but it has been a spur to thought, as the real itself always is.

In what follows, rather than approaching the matter through the realism of time, as I have done previously,[1] I want to respond to the 'false' accusation against deconstruction through the topic of semiology and signification. My task will be to charge head-on into a critique not just of naive realism ('matter', 'objects', 'number' and such are simply *there*, forming the *archē* of various supposedly new realisms repeating the onto-theologies of the past), but of what I would just quickly call 'naive linguisticism', a post-twentieth-century update of Kant's critique of dogmatic realisms. This naive linguisticism would be the view that either (1) we cannot speak to an extra-linguistic or extra-logical *real* (that is, a real irreducible to the *logos* in all its meanings) and should not, or (2) that language is led, *à la* a Peircean ideal, by the real, of which it cannot speak but to which it nevertheless refers, like an asymptote growing closer and closer to what it nevertheless never touches. If the first option seals us within a linguistic idealism, the second tends to think language in terms of a medieval semiology: a *representamen* (what is outside of the language itself) always transcends any given sign – and hence the second option merely repeats a given negative (onto-)theology of the real, one shared among the speculative realists. Like what is offered on a budget airline, this is ultimately an unsatisfactory menu of options, though perhaps all arguments over realism and anti-realism founder on privileging one side or the other, on implicitly repeating the truisms of one or the other. Is there a way for us to think the reality of the sign, as not something over and against the real? In short, let me wage a counter-suit concerning the supposed linguistic idealism of Derrida and deconstruction, since the position of SR critics repeats a naive linguististicism that is but another word for idealism.

The accused

Let us turn, then, for a moment to the scene of the crime, as it were, of which Derrida et al. are accused: any defence will have to take up the facts of the case, even if it is an *apologia* without apology. Derrida's *Of Grammatology*, said to give us a linguistic idealism, says, smack literally in the middle of its pages, the following:

> [I]f reading must not be content with doubling the text, it cannot legitimately transgress the text toward *something other than it* [my emphasis], toward a referent (a *reality* that is metaphysical, historical, psychobiographical, etc.) or toward a signified outside the text whose content could take place, could have taken place *outside of language* [my emphasis], that is to say, in the sense that we give here to that word, outside of writing in general. That is why the methodological considerations that we risk applying here to an example are closely dependent on general propositions that we have elaborated above, as regards the absence of the referent or the transcendental signified. *There is nothing outside of the text* [*il n'y a pas de hors-texte*; there is no outside-text]. And that is neither because Jean-Jacques' life, or the existence of Mamma or Thérèse *themselves*, is not of prime interest to us, nor because we have access to their so-called 'real' existence only in the text

and we have neither any means of altering this, nor any right to neglect this limitation [and so forth].[2]

Here we get the deconstruction of so many readers, even perhaps a certain reader named Derrida. All is text and any referent is but another sign; any supposition otherwise would be attempting to make claims for a 'transcendental signified' outside the play of signs. In context, Derrida is reading Rousseau's and Saussure's claims against themselves: their semiologies argue firstly against such signifieds only to make claims for 'nature' and 'consciousness', respectively, as meaningful outside of the semiologies they proclaim.

I could quickly note that context is everything in reading, or that the place of thought is everything in thinking and writing as such, and one should not universalise, as it were, claims that are context-specific, as all readings are; the rush to use language as non-emplaced, as not context-specific – that is behind the invention of the *logos* and the logocentric thinking of the West that remains fifty years after *Of Grammatology* the hidden premise of much of its thinking. That would be my opening statement to this jury of my peers reading this edited volume concerning the trials and challenges of deconstruction. (As in the *Apology*, I will not waste your time with the written accusations of those in SR against the defendant.) But as soon as I offer this opening statement, you will think to yourselves that any con-*text* returns us to the problem of non-textual referents and therefore I am merely playing on words without ever getting outside of them. The sophists were good at the law courts by providing defences against all kinds of 'challenges', but you, my educated peers, know better than to be bewitched by sophistics; there are the facts of reality beyond sensuous signs and you will be judging me (and the poor defendants I speak for) on whether I can give you these extra-textual facts. You will want me to get real already, to abandon obscure rhetoric, and speak to the thing itself. *Hic et nunc.*

Let me then turn to several important pages in *Of Grammatology* almost wholly neglected in its reception, and certainly in the summary judgements of the new realists (they seem too busy to give time for the defence present its case). The pages concern Charles Sanders Peirce, who Derrida takes up before turning to Saussure. As Derrida notes, logic for Peirce is itself a theory of signs, and so is any given ontology. Derrida writes, in passages usually taken as merely bringing in Peirce as a witness to the unmotivated-ness of the sign (that is, unmotivated by anything to which it refers, including a transcending reality), the following:

> Peirce goes very far in the direction that I have called the de-construction of the transcendental signified, which, at one time or another, would place

> a *reassuring end* [my emphasis, we will come back below to witness another writer wanting the salve, the saving, of this reassuring end] to the reference from sign to sign. I have identified logocentrism and the metaphysics of presence as the exigent, powerful, systematic, and irrepressible desire for such a signified. [That is as clear a definition of this term as one will find.] Now Peirce considers the indefiniteness of reference as the criterion that allows us to recognize that we are dealing with a system of signs. *What broaches the movement of signification is what makes its interruption impossible. The thing itself is a sign.* [The emphasis is by Derrida.] ... According to the 'phaneoroscopy' or 'phenomenology' of Peirce, *manifestation* itself does not reveal a presence, it makes a sign. One may read in [Peirce's] *Principles of Phenomenology* that the 'idea of *manifestation* is the idea of the sign.' Thus there is no phenomenality reducing the sign or the representer so that the thing signified may be allowed to glow finally in the luminosity of presence. The so-called 'thing itself' is always already a *representamen* shielded from the simplicity of intuitive evidence. The *representamen* functions only by giving rise to an *interpretant* that itself becomes a sign and so on to infinity.[3]

My apologies for this long quote. When putting on a defence to a challenge, sometimes the witnesses do go on for a bit. As is well known, Peirce argued in his pre-1904 work for an infinite semiology. Each sign, that is, thing, was itself a signifier-object-interpretant in a chain of other signifiers-objects-interpretants, with no final or first *sign*, since any first sign could not be an object for another sign and so forth. For Peirce that passage of sense was not something extrinsic to the movement of the real, but was the real itself. Derrida takes this less in the direction of a debate over reference than towards a consideration of Peirce's view that the traditional notion of intuition (which Peirce thought to be a holdover of Cartesianism) is one not determined by a previous cognition, which is rendered impossible given infinite semiosis. This would of course come to inform Derrida's readings of Husserl and other phenomenological thinkers. In sum, Derrida is another critic of what Sellars dubbed the myth of the given; this is clearly the meaning of the second half of the above.

But let us pause before that point in the paragraph: what does it mean to think that 'the thing itself is a sign'? The point is crucial, since all manner of post-1950s work is dubbed correlationist by Harman and Meillassoux precisely because of the various invocations of the reality of the sign, or, rather, the supposedly shared view that the sign locks us away from the real, justifying the charge of linguistic idealism one often hears about – though one should worry more these days, I would aver, about linguistic naiveté. One reading of the above would be that, as Derrida himself put it, 'there is no thinking outside of language', that is, outside of signs. But it would also mean thinking that there is not something *extrinsic* or transcending linguistic systems or conceptual schemes, since the things are signs *and vice-versa*. Thinking language only in the first way is to posit a transcendental signified and this must be excluded on Derrida's account, since *the whole sign system itself* (which would then itself be a sign) would refer to an unnameable outside as transcendental signified, and thus we would have doubled down on Platonism in a linguistic register (the appearance of signs and the reality of what is irreducible to appearance). That is, the *whole* sign system would refer to an outside, a view of language that Derrida works to deconstruct as it is beholden to a metaphysics of presence, one that is rewritten line by line in the descriptions of language by the new realists. Derrida's insight was to see Platonist dualism as informing a long line of semiological thinking from Plato to Saussure in terms of the difference of the material signifier and a signified whose form transcends this materiality[4] – a view Peirce came the closest to 'deconstructing' according to Derrida.[5]

The question, then, is can we think the thing itself as a sign? This does not mean dodging the real – we will valiantly face our fears, as Short calls them – but facing up to the fact of the sign as real, not just in its materiality, as marked out on our pages and so on, but also not as simply one side in the human/nature divide. As Derrida surmised in the largely speculative opening of *Of Grammatology*, such a thinking is the happening of science in terms of DNA, computing, post-set theory mathematics and so on, to all the so-called information sciences, which rely on another thinking of the sign. Can a post-deconstructive realism be aligned to such a thinking? From here we enter the work of Jean-Luc Nancy, who, like Peirce before him, thinks language as a passage of sense in and among things – and not just a mystical happening beyond them.

The 'community of things'

Nancy's work is most simply described as something of the odd child of Heidegger and Derrida. From the former he takes up the critique of onto-theology, a certain thinking of immanence (his Heidegger is more Spinozistic than Kantian), and an attunement to thinking the meaning of Being as the ultimate philosophical question. Bearing witness to the nudity of existence, Nancy attempts to think a sense of the world that depends on nothing other. But he does so while thinking this sense (he works with all three meanings of the French *sens*: sensation, meaning and directionality) in terms of Derridean *différance*, refusing the gesture of thinking différantial relations as textual in the reduced sense; he thinks *sens* in terms of the ontico-ontological difference, the open space of the arrival of the meaning of being, with semiotic deferral and differentiation. Let me quote from *Sense of the World* in Nancy's admittedly tricky prose:

> [T]he difference between the being and being is not a difference between terms or substances, but the différance of being, or more exactly, *the différance being is*. Différance *extrapolates* the ontico-ontological difference: it makes it exist. . . . It 'is produced' in the remarkable sense of 'taking place,' 'happening.' The entire aporia of the concept of 'creation' is here: insofar as it takes production for its schema and insofar as it presupposes a creating subject that is itself self-engendered, it does not touch on the act/event of existing that nonetheless haunts it. . . . From being to being, all the accents of the 'towards' ['*à*'] [also 'at' or 'to', PG]: distance, direction, intention, attribution, élan, passage, gift, transport, trance, and touch: *sense* in all senses, sense of the eksistent. . . . [S]ense does not add itself to being, does not supervene upon being, but is the opening of its very supervenience, of being-toward-the-world.[6]

At the heart of Nancy's work is a distinction that informs all others: the difference between sense and signification (analogous to his distinctions between mondialisation and globalisation, *désœuvrement* and an *œuvre*, equaliliberty and general equivalence, ipseity and identity, *jouissance* and addiction, giving and the gift, presence and representation, respectively). Sense is not signification, for Nancy, because any signification, as a fixed determination, gives sense *to* the world, for example, the ordered cosmos of the ancient world) rather than thinking the relationality of the *to* or *towards* as the sense of the world. This sense is its indeterminacy of meaning and directionality, its lack of *telos*. Allied to his thinking of sense, Nancy uses 'exscription' to denote a circulation of meaning (*sens*) by which language is not merely referring to or representing a given *x* outside of it, but has its own bodily materiality through which existence ex-poses itself: 'In writing, the real is not represented' since it marks the 'surprise and freedom of being in exscription'. As he puts it more pithily, 'the heart of things: that is what we exscribe'.[7] This exscription, he argues, replaces a thinking of language as related to a negative theology, whereby language can only ever say what it is not.

For this reason, we are not 'drive[n] back to the ineffable'.[8] Nancy writes:

> Certainly there are proper names and there are deictics. . . . But finally what is shown in denomination is the fact *that* the thing is showable (and that it is therefore never ineffable or unpresentable) – whereas what is shown in the thing, *this* that it is, the matter of the reference, shows itself only as the external limit of deixis.[9]

The *this*-ness is precisely what in the overflowing of the sense of the world resists signification, even as language spreads itself, so to speak, *to* or *right at* (*à même*) the thing, touching upon it. When one speaks or writes in the everyday sense, one moves from the closed circuit of signification to the bodily, singular event of speaking or writing, as the genus ('stones' in general) exscribes itself to the particular (*this* stone) – or as the thing exscribes itself to the material performance of writing or speaking, to the naming of itself:

> 'Exscription' means that the thing's name, by inscribing itself, inscribes its property as name *outside* itself, in an outside that it alone displays but where, displaying it, it displays the characteristic self-exteriority that constitutes its property as name. There is no thing without a name, but there is no name that, by naming and through naming, does not exscribe itself 'in' the thing, as 'as' it, while remaining this *other* of the thing that displays it only from afar. . . . In truth language always ends outside of itself.[10]

Neither word nor thing-in-itself, what is *ex*-scribed is the relation (the 'ex-') united in what we call the thing, the thing itself reaching to 'us' in, through and as language. At the limit of language, there is no more obscure thought in Nancy's writing; it weighs it down in terms of difficulty and gives it a particular weight for thinking language other than as nominational or as a tool of the speculative philosopher.

Writing, then, is what matters in Nancy's thought. If we stopped here, some would have in Nancy's thought the suspicion of a refusal to think thought and signification such that we would ever need to move, as in Meillassoux, to the 'great outdoors'.

> The referent does not present itself as such except in signification. But this 'outside' – wholly *exscribed within* the text – is the infinite withdrawal of meaning by which each existence exists. Not the raw, material, concrete datum, supposed to be outside meaning, which meaning represents, but the 'empty freedom' by which existences comes into presence – and absence. This freedom is not empty in the sense of being vain. It is certainly not directed toward a project, a meaning, or a work. But it passes through the work of meaning [this is what he calls signification, so there is no sense without signification and vice versa] to expose . . . the ungroundable *being* of being-in-the-world. The fact that there is being . . . *has* [as in a property] no meaning.

So much for that possible claim. Going further, Nancy argues that what is signified is not a meaning outside of existence and existence is not a signifier of a beyond:

> Existence does not *have* a meaning, in the sense of a property that could be assigned, determined, or stated in the language of significations. But meaning *does exist*, or again: existence is itself meaning, it is the absolute *signifiance* (the *signifiance* of Being) by and *in* the very fact that it exists. . . . In

existing, existence presupposes itself and calls itself infinitely as a meaning – as the entirety of meaning, absolutely.[11]

It is with passages like this in mind that Derrida writes that Nancy puts forth an 'absolute realism, but one irreducible to any of the tradition's realisms'.[12]

But does not Nancy's claim that 'existence' and 'the real' '*is* only when it is exscribed'[13] reproduce a textual correlationism? That is, just as any *noema* requires the activity of *noesis* in Husserl, does this not mean that being requires the activity of exscription? In meeting the 'challenge' Morin has described, have I not talked my way right into proving the very accusation brought in their suit against phenomenology and post-phenomenological thought? This is why one must think exscription not just in terms of the weight of thought and the materiality of writing – no doubt about it, though, they are every bit as real – but in the wider Peircean context in which the 'thing itself is a sign', that is, the relation of a sign-interpretant-object, which means that exscription is at the very heart of things: there where things exist, there is a circulation of sense to, with and among these things, which is to say that they relate and are 'at' and 'towards' one another. This relation, then, is one of exscription among, with and between the things themselves, without which there would be no sense of the world – only monads as worlds. The circulation of sense is irreducible and thus is *signifiance*. This is why Nancy critiques Heidegger's argument in the 1929–30 course that only a human being 'has' a world given its 'access' to the things of the world, and suggests that all existents have touch, that is, a relation of sense to an other that can never fully grasp it in all its alterity. (Even when one grasps a given thing, one only ever senses that thing from this, that or the other side, never all at once; and, as such, it is still an other never wholly within one's grasp.) In this way, Nancy suggestively writes, a '"quantum philosophy of nature" (or an "atomistic" or "discrete" one) remains to be thought' since sense is inscribed '*along the edge of* the "in itself"'.[14] *This* thing exists. Nancy thus moves to deny the two modes of thinking language dominant in realisms and anti-realisms:

> Eventually, we will have to examine the pervasive tendency to distinguish, in language usage, between a banal, informative usage, governed by the signified alone …, and a grander supposedly poetic usage, wherein language would be its own end [thus language either as positing an *outside* or as trapped within its own hall of mirrors]. In truth, language always ends outside itself.

Pausing for a moment, this could seem to repeat a thinking of the transcendental signified. But Nancy continues:

> In all usage ... arises what is absent to all language, a monstrosity that language itself can demonstrate, but exscribing itself therein. No thinking about 'writing' has had anything at stake [*jeu*] but this: the stake of the *thing*. The thing that is named, the thing that is thought, is not the thing named and thought [but this is because any sense, any existent, is irreducible to signification]. But the two do not maintain relationships of simple exteriority and of the sign's reflection of a referent. They are exscribed in each other as the same thing.[15]

Is this, then, all we need to say at this trial in answer to the 'realist challenge' and for the sake of the accused? There is no getting around or beyond signification – this was the chief accusation against those who took the linguistic turn in continental philosophy, though now we can read this in a different, realist light. It is said that Derrida, Nancy et al. could never speak to the thing itself and the 'play of things' became in post-structuralism just playthings in endless games. We are grown up now, more serious and less afraid as philosophers: we have returned to the real, to the simplicity of signifying a beyond in the great outdoors, and thus we can share in various movements across the humanities to get beyond linguisticism and constructivism – idealisms by another name.

Conclusion

By critiquing these idealisms, Derrida and Nancy show that it is not a matter of having social constructivism on one side and reality on the other – something that typically leads to the *Maurizio Ferraris dodge*, as I will call it after the Italian philosopher repeating such commonsensical notions as the following, in a supposedly critical, philosophical register: maleness, identity and other cultural *names* are socially constructed (how could it be otherwise?) whereas the sciences avail us of a non-constructible reality (even if we must recognise each theory's falsifiability). On the one side discursivity, deferral and difference; on the other, an outside availed to us empirically and denoted (but not reducible to that denotation) by the scientist. We all know the consequences said to result by thinking otherwise about the latter, a political moralism that replaces blackmail for thought. To take an appropriate example given the above, here is T. J. Short discussing Derrida in *Peirce's Theory of Signs* (2009):

> [T]he denial of an unambiguous reference is a perfect cover for someone fearful of facing reality [one must always adore the psychologising of philosophical differences; it's a mark of many doing OOO, for example: one doesn't have a philosophical position but is merely *afraid*, like a child, over against the brave realist philosopher fully instantiated in adulthood], and

that the idea that there is only play invites totalitarianism. For if there is no reality, then there is no reason why one should not impose his vision on the rest of us: 'One view is as good as another, so I'm going to make you accept mine!' Truth's denial leaves a vacuum: the will to power fills it.[16]

This, of course, is less an argument than an emotional appeal, though expected in the prosecutorial tone challenging and thus falsely accusing Derrida et al. But it is helpful in delineating a given thinking of the real that any future realism – including a realism of and about the future and the to-come of time never presentable as such[17] – must supersede: the real is unambiguous; knowledge of it saves us from totalitarianism (never mind that never has a philosophical knowledge of the absolute saved anyone from anything); and the real is the referent of language – and even in a book on Peirce would therefore be non-linguistic.

This is also a good place to begin to think the problematic politics of a given *realist* politics. No doubt, it was the fear of 'realising' or naturalising political categories that still marks a hesitancy in some quarters with regard to the new realisms. Of course, one should not work backwards from a given political position to an ontology just as one should not presume an easy movement from the latter to the former. Nevertheless, it is notable just how anodyne speculative realist and new materialist politics have been: we should pay attention to the things around us (garbage dumps in Bennett's *Vibrant Matter*) or recognise a 'democracy of objects' and so forth. Philosophy has no doubt always faced the trial of the real, to explain 'what is', irrespective of parochial, all-too-political concerns. But, given the various crises that are also a trial for thought, there is a 'so what?' quality to much that is going under the banner of the new realisms.

But let's get real and recognise that any future realism must think language otherwise and must pass through a certain thinking of language found differently in Peirce, Derrida and Nancy. The sharing of sense is not on this or that side of a given correlation and as such the accusation comes less from the speculative realists than, as always, the real itself:

> *Ding, thing* (and analogously, *Sache* and *chose*): they first signified the trial, the place where rights were regulated, the assembly of free men. What case is debated in the thing? And who is *chosé* ('accused' in Old French)? In every instance, it is a case of thought brought before the thing itself. Philosophy has never ceased to be this trial – or to be accused there. Thought is accused of not measuring up to the thing . . . and thus to *sense*.[18]

The case, as ever, is not yet closed and in the trials of the real; we all remain accused, challenged and never signifying all on our own. There remains the real: a sense of the world that preceded us.

Notes

1. See chapter 7 of my *Speculative Realism: Problems and Prospects* (London: Bloomsbury Press, 2014).
2. Jacques Derrida, *Of Grammatology*, trans. G. Spivak (Baltimore: The Johns Hopkins University Press, 1977), p. 158.
3. Derrida, *Of Grammatology*, p. 49.
4. We can ask how much Derrida holds to this later when he takes up, more and more, Levinas's invocation of the face and the other, which repeats this structure of a sign (the face) as referring to an ever transcendent signified (the Other). This will be why Nancy himself refuses a Levinasian thinking of the Other or any sense of being anchored in a given beyond, though Derrida has his own long criticisms of Levinas's positions.
5. No doubt there are other important places in the history of philosophy where a counter-history of the sign is possible. Two important moments I have in mind are Heidegger's post-Second World War writings on language, which are often said to be mystical (which is correct inasmuch as it was certain mystical traditions that held open a thinking otherwise of the sign, as performative and inseparable from the real) and Schelling's notion of the tautegorial. On the latter, Tyler Tritten notes: 'Schelling views the history of mythology as the deployment of Being itself, i.e. as an ontogony or as onto-genesis. Mythic saying is the "tautegorical" – as opposed to allegorical – saying of Being, which says nothing but its own configuration, its own propriety. Myths do not represent a prior meaning which would exist in advance of the myth as the condition of its mythic expression; for, that would be a lapse into transcendentalism. . . . Poseidon, for example, would not be an allegorical manner of depicting the sea, but Poseidon rather *is* the sea.' There is thus an irreducible performativity to language, irreducible to any supposed nominalism, a point I cannot take up below.
6. Jean-Luc Nancy, *The Sense of the World*, trans. Jeffrey S. Librett (Minneapolis: University of Minnesota Press, 2003), pp. 27–8, translation slightly modified. Later on, Nancy argues that this *différance* should not be thought as temporising, but as a 'spacing'. I will not get into the intricacies of Nancy's position, though he thinks temporising simply gives us 'areality' as 'a distension of linear time' (Nancy, *Sense of the World*, p. 35). Mark me down as unconvinced, not least since Nancy, time and again, perhaps always in his writing, tends to think time in terms of the 'instant', which he invariable translates as the 'eternal' in time, as the 'always' in time. This repeats, of course, Platonist conceptions of temporality. While for Nancy what is salutary about this is that any moment has no other end in itself and is a-teleological, I think it is past time to think temporalisation otherwise.
7. Jean-Luc Nancy, *The Birth to Presence*, trans. B. Holmes et al. (Stanford: Stanford University Press, 1993), p. 339.
8. Ibid. p. 175.
9. Ibid. p. 175.
10. Ibid. pp. 175–6.
11. Jean-Luc Nancy, *The Gravity of Thought*, trans. François Raffoul and Gregory Recco (New York: Humanities Press, 1998), p. 80.
12. Derrida, *On Touching – Jean-Luc Nancy*, trans. C. Irizarry (Stanford: Stanford University Press, 2005), p. 46.
13. Nancy, *Birth to Presence*, p. 339.
14. Jean-Luc Nancy, *The Sense of the World*, trans. Jeffrey S. Librett (Minneapolis: University of Minnesota Press, 2003), p. 62.
15. Nancy, *Birth to Presence*, p. 176.
16. T. J. Short in *Peirce's Theory of Signs* (Cambridge: Cambridge University Press, 2009), p. 45.

17. See Jacques Derrida, 'As if it were possible, "within such limits"...', in *Negotiations: Interventions and Interviews*, trans. Elizabeth Rottenberg (Stanford: Stanford University Press, 2002), p. 367, where Derrida writes: 'The deconstruction of logocentrism, of linguisticism, of economism (of the proper, of the at-home [*chez-soi*], *oikos*, of the same), etc., as well as the affirmation of the impossible are always put forward *in the name of the real*, of the irreducible reality of the real – not of the real as the attribute of the objective, present, perceptible or intelligible *thing* (*res*), but of the real as the coming or event of the other, where the other resists all reappropriation. . . . The real is this non-negative impossible, this impossible coming or invention of the event the thinking of which is not an onto-phenomenology. It is a thinking of the event (singularity of the other, in its unanticipatable coming, *hic et nunc*) that resists reappropriation by an ontology or a phenomenology of presence as such. . . . Nothing is more "realist," in this sense, than a deconstruction.'
18. Nancy, *Birth to Presence*, p. 187.

Notes on Contributors

Alison Assiter is Professor of Feminist Theory at the University of the West of England, Bristol. She has published a number of books and articles, including, most recently, *Kierkegaard, Eve and Metaphors of Birth*, with Rowman & Littlefield, in 2015. She is the editor of a book series, Reframing the Boundaries: Thinking the Political, and serves on the editorial collective of a new journal, *Feminist Dissent*.

Lee Braver is Professor of Philosophy at the University of South Florida. His main interests are in continental philosophy (especially Heidegger and Foucault), Wittgenstein, realism, and dialogue between continental and analytic philosophy. He is the author of *A Thing of this World: A History of Continental Anti-Realism* (Northwestern University Press, 2007), *Heidegger's Later Writings: A Reader's Guide* (Bloomsbury, 2009), *Groundless Grounds: A Study of Wittgenstein and Heidegger* (MIT Press, 2012) and *Heidegger: Thinking of Being* (Polity, 2014), as well as of a number of articles and book chapters, and editor of *Division III of Being and Time: Heidegger's Unanswered Question of Being* (MIT, 2015). He is also considered by many to be a Master Griller.

G. Anthony Bruno is a SSHRC Postdoctoral Research Fellow at McGill University. Prior to this, he was a Faculty Lecturer at the University of Toronto Scarborough and an Alexander von Humboldt Postdoctoral Research Fellow at the University of Bonn. He earned his PhD from the Department of Philosophy at the University of Toronto. He has published articles in *Dialogue*, *Rethinking Kant Vol. 4*, *Northern European Journal of Philosophy*, *Analecta Hermeneutica*, *Idealistic Studies* and *Comparative and Continental Philosophy*. He will edit and contribute chapters to *Schelling's Philosophy: Freedom, Nature, and Systematicity* (Oxford University Press) and *Skepticism: Historical and Contemporary Inquiries* (Routledge). His current research investigates the role of facticity in the development of transcendental logic from Kant, through German idealism, to Heidegger.

Vladimir Dukić is a PhD student in the Department of Philosophy at the University of Alberta, working on issues in contemporary continental philosophy, metaphysics and environmental philosophy. His current research investigates the possibilities for ecological thought in the writings of Nietzsche, Heidegger, Deleuze and other contemporary figures in the continental tradition.

Rick Elmore is Assistant Professor of Philosophy at Appalachian State University. He researches and teaches in twentieth-century French philosophy, critical theory, ethics, social political philosophy, environmental philosophy and new realisms. His articles and essays have appeared in *Politics & Policy*, *Symplokē*, *The Cormac McCarthy Journal* and *The Aesthetic Ground of Critical Theory* (Rowman & Littlefield), among others. His work is guided primarily by the question how political, ethical and environmental systems and institutions situate themselves in relation to violence, that is, to issues of inclusion, exclusion, power, force, law, policing and normativity.

Peter Gratton is a professor of philosophy at Memorial University of Newfoundland, Canada. He has written extensively in continental and political philosophy, has edited five books in these areas, and has published *The State of Sovereignty: Lessons from the Political Fictions of Modernity* (SUNY, 2012) and *Speculative Realism: Problems and Prospects* (Bloomsbury, 2014).

Sean J. McGrath researches and teaches in the areas of metaphysics, classical German philosophy (Kant to Heidegger), phenomenology and hermeneutics, and psychoanalysis. He is the author of *The Early Heidegger and Medieval Philosophy: Phenomenology for the Godforsaken* (Catholic University of America Press, 2006, reprinted 2013), *Heidegger: A (Very) Critical Introduction* (Eerdmans, 2008) and *Dark Ground of Spirit: Schelling and the Unconscious* (Routledge, 2012). He is the co-editor of *A Companion to Heidegger's Phenomenology of Religious Life* (Rodopi, 2010) and the editor of *Analecta Hermeneutica*. He is also co-founder, with Jason Wirth, of the North American Schelling Society.

Marie-Eve Morin is Associate Professor of Philosophy at the University of Alberta in Edmonton, Canada. She is the author of *Jean-Luc Nancy* (Polity, 2012), co-editor (with Peter Gratton) of *Jean-Luc Nancy and Plural Thinking: Expositions of World, Politics, Art, and Sense* (SUNY Press, 2012) and of *The Nancy Dictionary* (Edinburgh University Press, 2015) and the translator of Jean-Luc Nancy's *Ego Sum: Corpus, Anima, Fabula* (Fordham University Press, 2016). She is currently working on a comparative study of Nancy's and Merleau-Ponty's ontologies in light of the speculative realist challenge.

David Morris is Professor and Chair of Philosophy at Concordia University, Montreal, and Associate General Secretary of the Merleau-Ponty Circle. His main interests are in phenomenology, especially Merleau-Ponty, with a focus on the philosophy of the body, mind and nature in relation to current biology, cognitive science and also cosmology; other interests include Bergson and Hegel. He has recently completed a book project, *Merleau-Ponty's Developmental Ontology*, and is embarking on a new project focusing on the interrelation of time, meaning and nature. He has written numerous articles and chapters, especially on phenomenology and Merleau-Ponty, in relation to issues of philosophical method, ontology, nature, science and biology, as well as a book, *The Sense of Space* (SUNY Press). He is co-editor, with Kym Maclaren, of *Time, Memory, Institution: Merleau-Ponty's New Ontology of Self* (Ohio University Press).

Anna Mudde is Assistant Professor of Philosophy at Campion College at the University of Regina, Canada. She works on self-knowledge and critical subjectivity, epistemology, social ontologies and Simone de Beauvoir. Her current work looks at human engagements with objects and technologies, and explores the ways in which human knowers and communities use ontological categories to make political, ethical and scientific sense of the world.

Index

Absolute, 4–5, 6, 23, 27, 41, 139
  knowledge of the, 5, 8, 9, 22, 30, 43
'Active Minds', 139
alter ego, 140
alterity, 67, 69, 73, 148, 183
ancestrality, 31, 60, 61, 66, 71, 157, 173n
  and ancestral statements, 30, 34n, 35n, 60, 62
anthropocentrism, 6, 16n, 142, 147, 149, 154n
  hyper-, 156, 171
anthropomorphism, 7, 36n, 138, 149
appearance, 22, 24, 27, 32, 33, 34n, 64, 84, 86, 87 180
  and appearing, 140
  and not-appearing, 34n, 64, 156, 165, 170
arche-fossil, 24, 26, 28, 66, 157, 172

Beauvoir, Simone de, 119, 123
being, 16n, 23, 28, 44, 47, 50, 53, 62, 65, 67, 70, 73, 86, 89, 93, 116, 119, 122, 143, 147, 149, 152n, 158, 172
  determinate, 157, 163, 164, 168
  manifest, 156, 157, 164, 172
  vertical, 146, 148
Bhaskar, Roy, 84, 90
body, 124, 127, 143, 148, 149, 152n
  and embodiment, 118, 124, 125
  and objectification, 117, 118, 121, 122
Brassier, Ray, 2, 10, 16n

Cartesianism, 12, 25, 27, 51
causality, 12, 23, 28
causation, principle of, 85, 88, 91
consciousness, 29, 32, 43, 54, 62, 76n, 87, 93, 106–8, 120, 123, 140, 143, 149
constructivism, 3, 176, 184
contingency, 37n, 46, 146
  necessity of, 9, 53, 158
  radical, 14, 22, 28–9, 156, 161, 169, 172
Copernican revolution, 3, 22, 27, 31, 37n
correlationism, 23
  strong, 4, 8, 138, 142
  weak, 4, 23
cosmology, 166–7

deconstruction, 44, 110, 176, 178, 180, 187n
Derrida, Jacques, 59, 75n, 108, 112, 177–8
determination, 28, 45, 48, 51, 181
dialectic, 145–6, 157
différance, 180–1, 186n
discourse, 8, 67, 102, 110, 139
dogmatism, 21, 23, 30, 36n, 177

empiricism, 44, 55, 143
episteme, 175
epistemology, 38, 41, 65, 86, 130
  and epistemic mastery, 121

evidence, 60, 179
  and phenomenology, 138, 140
experience, as *Erlebnis*, 147
exscription, 15, 181–2, 183–4
exteriority, 51, 68, 72–3, 147, 182, 184

face, 13, 63, 64, 67, 70, 73, 186n
factiality, 158; *see also* contingency
facticity, 22, 28, 29–30, 44, 55, 125, 144–5, 158
feminism, 117, 122, 131n
Fichte, Johann Gottlieb, 41–2
fideism, 6, 9, 62, 74
finitude, 5, 21, 70, 93, 139, 140, 149, 158, 172

givenness, 5, 24, 67, 73, 141–2, 152n
God, 21, 40, 44, 50, 63, 68
Grant, Iain Hamilton, 9
grounding, 83, 85, 88

Harman, Graham, 1, 104, 116, 119, 150n
Hegel, G. W. F., 42–3, 98n
Heidegger, Martin, 5, 32, 35n, 65, 68, 71, 108, 137, 150n, 152n, 183, 186n
hiddenness, 123, 129, 143, 147, 161, 168
horizon, 64, 67, 144, 147
Hume, David, 25, 28, 32
Husserl, Edmund, 16n, 62, 64, 120, 125, 140–1, 146, 151, 183
hyper-Chaos, 148, 158, 165

'I', and not-I, 41–2
idealism, 38, 51, 54, 69, 74, 85, 147
  empirical, 27
  German, 39, 40, 43, 85
  linguistic, 177, 179
  transcendental, 84, 86, 92, 95–6
indifference, 73, 101, 102, 105, 110
in-itself, 35n, 41, 55, 74, 85, 143–4, 151n, 161
intentionality, 53, 64, 73, 140, 143, 152n

Jacobi, Friedrich Heinrich, 25, 31, 34n, 43, 54

Kant, Immanuel, 21–2, 24, 46, 65, 72, 83, 85–6, 89, 104

language, 31, 64, 112, 139, 164, 177, 180, 182, 183, 186n
Levinas, Emmanuel, 60, 62–3, 68–9, 72–4
limits, 9, 42–3, 47, 62, 105, 138, 147
linguisticism, naïve, 15, 177

manifestation, 156, 160–1, 163, 170, 179
materialism, 83, 139, 151n
  speculative, 10, 104, 137
mathematics, 156, 166, 168, 171
Meillassoux, Quentin, 1, 4, 22, 28, 31, 60, 104, 157
Merleau-Ponty, Maurice, 60, 124, 142, 144, 156, 159, 165
metaphysics, 2, 22, 179
  and evidence, 140, 141
  guerrilla, 118, 132n
  and realism, 121, 137

Nancy, Jean-Luc, 180–3, 185
nature-philosophy, 40
noetic-noematic relation, 73, 176
nonlocality, 168
noumenal, 85–7; *see also* phenomenon

objectification, 117, 122, 124, 130, 131n
  prehensive, 123, 125, 129, 130
objectivity, 22, 25, 42, 104, 121, 140, 151n
object-oriented ontology *see* ontology
objects, 16n, 25, 27, 29, 32, 34n, 41, 65, 90, 97, 117
  inner life of, 14, 138
  and objectivating acts, 147
ontology, 10, 65, 86, 102, 108
  flat, 16n, 163n
  indirect, 156, 160, 164
  nihilist, 1, 16n
  object-oriented, 15n, 116, 120
onto-theology, 177
  critique of, 180
otherness, 67, 73, 105, 112
outdoors, 31, 67, 70, 84, 157, 171, 182
outside, 4, 25, 51, 61, 67, 69, 138–9, 177–8, 180, 182
  logic of the, 146

passivity, 72, 156, 160, 170
Peirce, Charles Sanders, 178–9, 184

pessimism, 101–2, 104, 106–8
phenomenology, 16n26, 42, 60, 63–4, 123, 138, 140, 142, 143, 146, 152n, 179
  and method, 63, 124, 128, 142, 146, 151n, 159
phenomenon, 24, 64, 122, 148, 152n
  and noumenon, 88, 89
philosophy
  dogmatic, 21, 23, 87, 161, 177
  negative, 43, 45, 48
  positive, 3, 12, 39, 43–4, 48
prehension, 118, 120, 122, 130, 132n; *see also* objectification
principle of factiality *see* factiality
principle of principles, 140–1
principle of sufficient reason *see* reason
principle of unreason *see* unreason
prius, 44, 47, 49

quantum mechanics, 156, 166–7

realism, 1, 10, 22–3, 44, 60, 62, 73, 84, 138, 176
  critical, 83, 84, 90, 96
  empirical, 84, 91–2, 94
  modest, 139
  speculative, 111, 118, 138, 142, 152n, 158, 185
  transcendental, 13, 26, 28, 31, 40, 90
  transgressive, 139
reality, 59
  and the real, 40, 51, 55, 73, 74, 85–6, 106, 113
  see also signs; time
reason, 3, 9, 88, 96, 141, 165, 169
  principle of sufficient, 21, 160
relativism, 3
responsibility, 71, 131
  and response-ability, 130

Saussure, Ferdinand de, 178, 180
Schelling, F. W. J. von, 12–13, 38–55
  and the tautegorical, 155n

schemes, conceptual, 139, 176, 179
science, 5, 16n, 31, 48, 68, 174, 180
  and scienticism, 7–8
  and realism, 10
semiology, 177, 179
sense, 9, 25, 36n, 41, 62, 64, 119, 149
  and non-sense, 28, 146
  and sensing, 148, 162–3
signs, 178–9
  reality of, 180
spatiality, 162, 172n
speculative realism *see* realism
speculative turn, 5, 138
Spinoza, Baruch, 41, 125

temporality, 103, 111, 164
  deep, 169–70, 172, 173n
  and templacement, 169
  and time-consciousness, 103, 109, 111
  see also time
things, community of, 180
time, 28, 30, 44, 60, 71, 185, 186n
  deep, 173n
  reality of, 111, 169
transcendence, 66, 72, 73, 127, 140–1
transcendental, 173n, 175, 177
  argument, 91, 157
  critique, 32
  deduction, 29, 158
  see also empiricism; idealism; realism

unreason, principle of, 9, 22, 29

visible, 128, 149
  and the invisible, 156, 164–5, 168, 170
vitalism, neo-, 3, 104

withdrawal, 117, 119, 122–3, 127, 182
world, 5, 10, 23, 26–7, 31, 33n, 37n, 59, 65, 67, 71–2, 86, 102, 124, 145, 149, 166, 181, 183
Wright, Crispin, 139

Young, Iris Marion, 127

EU representative:
Easy Access System Europe
Mustamäe tee 50, 10621 Tallinn, Estonia
Gpsr.requests@easproject.com

www.ingramcontent.com/pod-product-compliance
Lightning Source LLC
Chambersburg PA
CBHW051117230426
43667CB00014B/2624